The Case fo

Other titles from Anthem Press on Politics & International Relations:

Russia and Europe in the Twenty-First Century: An Uneasy Partnership (eds. Graham Timmins and Jackie Assayag)

Chechnya: From Past to Future (ed. Richard Sakwa)

Rethinking Indian Political Institutions (eds. Crispin Bates and Subho Basu)

Hollywood, the Pentagon and Washington (Jean-Michel Valantin)

Turkey Today: A European Country? (ed. Olivier Roy)

The Case for Kosova

Passage to Independence

Edited by

ANNA DI LELLIO

Anthem Press

Anthem Press
An imprint of Wimbledon Publishing Company
www.anthempress.com

This edition first published in UK and USA 2006
by ANTHEM PRESS
75-76 Blackfriars Road, London SE1 8HA, UK
or PO Box 9779, London SW19 7ZG, UK
and
244 Madison Ave. #116, New York, NY 10016, USA

British Library Cataloguing in Publication Data
A catalogue record for this book is available from the British Library.

Library of Congress Cataloging in Publication Data
A catalog record for this book has been requested.

1 3 5 7 9 10 8 6 4 2

ISBN 1 84331 245 X (Pbk)

Cover photograph: 'Kosovo in Fog',
Hazir Reka, September 19, 2005

Printed in EU

Contents

The Contributors

Ivo Banac is Bradford Durfee Professor of History, Yale University. His many books include *The National Question in Yugoslavia: Origins, History, Politics* (Cornell University Press, 1984) and *With Stalin against Tito: Comimformist Splits in Yugoslav Communism*, (Cornell University Press, 1988).

Isa Blumi is Assistant Professor of History at Georgia State University. He was a member of the Provisional Government of Kosova during the war of 1998–1999. Among his books are *Rethinking the Late Ottoman Empire: A Comparative Social and Political History of Albania and Yemen, 1878–1918* (ISIS, 2003); *The Consequences of Empire: Albania and Yemen in Transition to the Modern World* (Oxford University Press, forthcoming); and *Being Albanian: A History of Identity and Political Marginality in the Modern Balkans* (I.B. Tauris, forthcoming).

Janusz Bugajski is Director of the New European Democracies Project and Senior Fellow, Europe Program, Center for Strategic International Studies (CSIS), Washington, D.C. He is the author of numerous books, most recently, *America's New Allies: Central-Eastern Europe and the Transatlantic Link*, with Ilona Teleki (Rowman & Littlefield, 2006). His *Nations in Turmoil: Conflict and Cooperation in Eastern Europe* (Westview, 1993) was selected by 'Choice' as one of the outstanding academic books for 1993.

Howard Clark is Honorary Research Fellow with the Forgiveness and Reconciliation Center of the University of Coventry, where his main concern since 1991 has been peace in Kosova. A former editor of 'Peace News' and former executive secretary of War Resisters International, he is currently working on liaising peace and human rights activists in Kosova and Croatia. His book *Civil Resistance in Kosovo* (Pluto Press), was published in 2000.

Catherine Croft is a Senior Research Associate for the Public International Law & Policy Group (PILPG). At PILPG, she has been involved in the Kosovo Program, working on a draft constitution, minority rights legislation, and final status negotiations. Prior to joining PILPG, Ms. Croft spent several years working in community development and public health in Latin America.

Anna Di Lellio is a sociologist and a journalist. She obtained her Ph.D. from Columbia University, New York. Dr. Di Lellio has worked in post-war Kosova as the Temporary Media Commissioner and the Political Advisor to the UN Kosovo Protection Corps Coordinator. She has produced a documentary on trafficking of women in Kosova that was broadcast on the Italian Public Television Channel RAI3 and is currently working on a book on the national master-narrative of post-war Kosova.

Alain Ducellier is Professor Emeritus of Medieval History with a focus on Byzantium and the Balkans at the University of Toulouse II, Le Mirail. He is the author of many books, among them are: *L'Albanie entre Byzance et Venise, Xe-XVe siècles* (Variorum Reprints, 1987); *Chretiens d'Orient et Islam au Moyen Age: VIIe-XVe siècle* (Colin, 1996) and *Migrations et Diaspores du Méditerranéennes, Xe-XVe siècle: Actes du Colloque de Conques October 1999* (Sorbonne, 2002, with Michel Balard).

Vjosa Dobruna is President of the Board of Radio Television of Kosova. Dr. Dobruna is also Board Member of the American University of Kosovo, of the Women's Network and other women's groups, and a consultant for the Strategy for Development of Kosova 2007–2013. She was a member of the UN Joint Administrative Structure (2000–2001) to monitor and recommend regulations on human and minority rights, equal opportunity, good governance and independent media. She was 2002–2003 Policy Fellow at the Carr Center for Human Rights, John F. Kennedy School of Government, Harvard University. She also practices pediatrics, which she studied at the University of Zagreb.

Andrew Herscher is Assistant Professor at the University of Michigan with joint appointments to the Taubman College of Architecture and Urban Planning, the Department of Slavic Languages and Literatures, and the International Institute. With Andras Riedlmayer, Dr. Herscher published *The Destruction of Cultural Heritage in Kosovo, 1998–1999: A Post-War Survey* (Cambridge: Kosovo Cultural Heritage Survey, 2001).

He is currently completing a book on architecture, urbanism and political violence in Kosova.

Bernd Fischer is Professor of Balkan History and chair of the Department of History at Indiana University, Fort Wayne. He is the author of numerous books on Albania including *King Zog and the Struggle for Stability in Albania. East European Monograph,* (Columbia University Press, 1984); *Albania at War, 1939–1945* (Purdue University Press, 1999) and (co-editor) *Albanian Identities: Myth and History* (Indiana University Press, 2002). He serves on the board of the Albanian Studies Program, School of Slavonic and East European Studies, University College, London, the Book and Communication House, Tirana, and the Society for Albanian Studies.

Dom Lush Gjergji is a Catholic priest in the parish of Binqa, Kosova, in the Dioceses of Skopje-Prizren. He earned his doctorate in Psychology at the University of Rome La Sapienza. In the 1990s Dr. Dom Lush was one of the leaders of the campaign for the reconciliation of blood feuds and the founder of the Mother Theresa Humanitarian Society, a grass roots welfare network that was active in the Albanian parallel society of Kosova. Among his books, there is a work on Mother Theresa, *Madre della Carità* (Verlar, first edition 1990) and *Kosovo: non violenza per la riconciliazione*, with Giancarlo e Valentino Savoldi (EMI, 1999).

Ismail Kadare, Albania's best known poet and novelist, was the 2005 recipient of the Man Booker International Prize. He has also been a candidate for the Nobel Prize. Kadare has been based in Paris since 1990. His many novels, which concern Albanian history, culture, folklore, and politics, include *The General of the Dead Army* (1963, tr. 1972), *The Castle* (1970, tr. 1974), *Chronicle in Stone* (1971, tr. 1987), *The Three-Arched Bridge* (1978, tr. 1991), *The Palace of Dreams* (1981, tr. 1993), *The Concert* (1988, tr. 1994), *The Pyramid* (1991, tr. 1996), *Spring Flowers, Spring Frost* (2001, tr. 2002); and *The Successor*, 2005.

Machiel Kiel is Director of the Netherlands Historical and Archeological Institute in Istanbul. He currently teaches Islamic Architecture at Istanbul Technical University, which he also taught for some years at the University of Utrecht. Dr. Kiel is Vice-President of the International Organisation for Congresses of Turkish Art and Advisor to UNESCO for Bosnia and Herzegovina. He has traveled extensively in the Balkans since 1959 and published many works on the cultural heritage of the region.

Muhammedin Kullashi is Professor of Philosophy at the Universitè de Paris VIII since 1992. Dr. Kullashi earned his Ph.D. from the University of Zagreb, and taught at the University of Prishtina until his expulsion in 1991. Among his many books are *Humanisme et haine* (L'Harmattan, 1997); *Parler des camps, penser les génocides* (Albin Michel, 2000) and *Effacer l'autre* (2006).

Paulin Kola is a BBC analyst. Dr. Kola earned his Ph.D. at the London School of Economics. His book *The Search for Greater Albania* (Hurst and New York University Press) was published in 2003.

Albin Kurti is one of the founders of the movement 'Self-determination', which started in 2005. He is a political and human rights activist whose career began in 1997 with the students' movement campaigning for the right to education, and continued in 1998 as the secretary of the General Political Representative of the KLA until his arrest in April 1999. Sentenced to 15 years of imprisonment, he was released from Serb prison in December 2001. Since then, he has been involved in the youth movement Kosova Action Network (KAN), a group with the mission of creating an active citizenry in Kosova.

Noel Malcolm has a doctorate in History from Cambridge University; he is a Senior Research Fellow of All Souls College, Oxford, and a Fellow of the British Academy. His *Kosovo: A Short History* (Macmillan), was published in 1998.

Julie Mertus is an Associate Professor and Co-Director of the MA program in Ethics, Peace and Global Affairs at American University. Her book *Kosovo: How Myths and Truths Started a War* (University of California Press, 1999) is essential reading on the region. She is also the author of *Bait and Switch: Human Rights and American Foreign Policy* (Routledge, 2004), named 'Book of the Year' in 2005 by the American Political Science Association, Human Rights Section.

Jennifer Ober is Peace Fellow with the Public International Law & Policy Group. Ms. Ober heads the Public International Law & Policy Group's Kosovo Program and is resident in Prishtina, Kosova where she is advising the Government of Kosovo on the Final Status negotiations.

Owen Pearson taught Latin and Greek for 40 years to senior forms of preparatory schools. In 1947 he began to compile a full and detailed chronicle of modern Albanian history and over decades assembled an impressive library dedicated to Albania. This collection forms the basis of *Albania in the Twentieth Century* (I.B. Tauris and Center for Albanian Studies, 2006).

Henry H. Perritt, Jr. directs Chicago-Kent's Program in Financial Services Law. The author of many law review articles and books on international relations and law, technology and law, and employment law, Professor Perritt has served on President Ford's White House staff and President Clinton's Transition Team. More recently, he made it possible for groups of law and engineering students to work together in using the Internet to develop democratization and development programs such as 'Project Bosnia' and 'Operation Kosovo'.

Besnik Pula is a Ph.D. Candidate at the Department of Sociology of the University of Michigan. He is a Fulbright Scholar, currently working on Albanian state-formation during the interwar era, examining in particular the manner in which the state enlisted "traditionalism" in its institution-building strategies. He is a frequent contributor to the Kosovar daily *Koha Ditore* and an active member of a number of Kosova-based organizations.

Stacy Sullivan is a senior editor at the London-based Institute for War and Peace Reporting and former Balkans correspondent for *Newsweek*. She is the author of *Be Not Afraid, for You Have Sons in America: How a Brooklyn Roofer Helped Lure the US into the Kosovo War* (St. Martins Press, 2004). She also co-produced a documentary based on her book entitled, *The Brooklyn Connection*.

Paul R. Williams is Rebecca Grazier Professor of Law & International Relations, American University. Dr. Williams served as a legal advisor to the Kosovar Delegation to the Rambouillet/Paris peace negotiations, and is advising the Government of Kosova on Final Status negotiations being held in Vienna in 2006. Professor Williams, along with the Public International Law & Policy Group was nominated for the 2005 Nobel Peace Prize by over half a dozen of his *pro bono* government clients.

Editor's Note

Since this book is about the independence of Kosova, we have preferred to use Albanian names for localities throughout, except in those chapters where the authors preferred the international usage of Kosovo and both Albanian and Serbian names for cities.

Preface

Muhammedin Kullashi

The dissolution of Yugoslavia, a fraught process that would end in bloodshed, begun in Kosova in 1981. This crisis defined the political life of the country, its divisions and its political struggles, for an entire decade. The problems Kosova faces, specifically, derive from the crisis that led to the fragmentation of Yugoslavia. In general, one can say that Yugoslavia's political history, at least in the twentieth century, is marked by the confrontation of two nationalisms: the Albanian and the Serb, each with their own conflicting aspirations to dominate Kosova. However, in observing any particular period of political and social history, it is necessary to analyse the motivations and responsibilities of those actively involved.

The rise to power of Milošević (1987) coincides with the calamitous breakdown of the Yugoslav system. In the 1980's, Serb intellectuals and the political elite answered to a dysfunctional and undemocratic system, by supporting a populist nationalist program that did not criticise the democratic deficiency of the Titoist regime. The modest achievement of this system, for better or worse, was to hold together a country for half a century, despite the conflicts caused by the diversity of the economic and political interests of the regions and people of Yugoslavia.

It was from the issues surrounding Kosova that the Serb nationalist movement took form. It was toward Kosova that the program for the 'correction of the injustice suffered by the people' took aim, which in turn animated the public to demand reparation for supposed historical injustices. Mass rallies and the manipulation of a rich nationalist and religious iconography became a powerful, dominant and daily form of political expression. This nationalist activism dismantled federal institutions, by upholding the ideal of 'a state for all Serbs'. The terror of the Milošević regime did not just plan to dominate the Albanians, or merely maintain a strict ethnic discrimination, but rather carry out a radical and fundamental change to the ethnic structure of Kosova. For example, the prohibition of Albanians from accessing the only public swimming pool in Prishtina in 1991 cannot be explained by any concrete Serb 'interests'. The systematic repression by the police and paramilitary units of the regime, their obstructionist policy in health care, right to work, and any activity normal within a democratic society was devised to force the Albanian population from Kosova, while at the same time colonising the region. However, these extreme measures succeeded only partially. This is the reason why, ultimately, Milošević saw war as the only means to realise his project of 'ethnic cleansing', not only within the institutions of political and social influence, but of the entire territory of Kosova.

Facing the systematic terror of the Serb state, the Albanians of Kosova maintained a peaceful resistance for many years. However, toward the end of the 1990's, when non-violent political methods proved ineffective, they turned to armed resistance and the Kosova Liberation Army (KLA) was born, with widespread public support. Rather than being mutually exclusive, these two forms of protest (armed and unarmed resistance) should be seen as complementary: each has contributed, depending on the circumstances, to defending and realising the aspirations of the people of Kosova.

The question over the status of Kosova cannot be viewed in abstract from the political situation surrounding the breaking-up of the Yugoslav federation. The legitimacy of the Albanians' demand for the independence of Kosova rests on the same arguments as those put forward by the ex-Yugoslav states contesting political autonomy. The voices of these states have been taken into consideration by the international community. The juridical-constitutional status and the political will of the majority of Kosova's population must also be noted. Kosova has known only systematic terror at the hands of the Serb state, most distressingly during the last two decades. This terrorisation culminated with the 1999 'ethnic cleansing', the massacres of civilians and the deportation of 900,000 Albanians across the borders of Kosova. The independence of Kosova does not open a Pandora's Box, the situation stems from the dissolution of Yugoslavia and the resolution of the current crisis should follow the pattern of the ex-Yugoslav states.

Those politicians from Serbia or the European Union who claim that the independence of Kosova could destabilise the Balkans forget that the domination of Serbia over Kosova has been one of the most unstable and dangerous situations for Yugoslavia and the Balkans during the entire twentieth century. Supporting the domination of Serbia over Kosova (in the name of vague geopolitical interests or the principle of the state territorial integrity) contributes to a deepening conflict, pushing the region toward a perilous impasse.

In this context, it is helpful to recall the political assessment of the Serb social democratic leadership (Tucović, Popović, Nokanović etc) at the beginning of the twentieth century. In their writings they judged the 1912 advancement of Serb troops into Kosova, against the will of the majority of Albanians, not only an act of aggression but also a serious mistake, with nefarious consequences for the Balkans. They also criticized Russia and France, the two countries that supported this military action. It was not that these intellectuals felt moral indignation for the injustice of the situation, rather they analysed and weighed the political reality. They feared that the ramifications of the Serb domination of Kosova, which they referred to as 'colonial', would be the source of dangers for peace in the Balkans and, in the long run, for Albanian-Serb relations. It was recognised that a Serbia engaged in violent military domination would lose any chance of democratisation and development. These lucid and fearful analyses, at the very beginning of the conflict, were realised in the Serb military-police aggression toward Kosova in 1998.

It is clear that the view of the European Union toward the western Balkans will largely depend on the solution of the question of status for Kosova. In line with this, new Albania-Serb relations, markedly different from those of the twentieth century, can be built on the recognition of Kosova's independence. However, this recognition implies a responsibility for Albanians to build a democratic state and overcome all forms of ethnic discrimination.

Introduction

Anna Di Lellio

This is a decisive time for Kosova. 2006 will be the year when Kosova's final political status is settled and the conflict that culminated with Serbian attempted genocide, interrupted by the NATO air campaign, and subsequent pacification, reaches a formal, juridical conclusion.

Kosova now is governed through a system of overlapping authorities. It is a United Nations-administered protectorate, but also has the apparatus of representative government: a Prime Minister, cabinet, and parliament, known as the Provisional Institutions of Self-Government. These are 'provisional' because Kosova was, until 1999, a province of the Federal Republic of Yugoslavia, and it is still under the formal sovereignty of Belgrade, as stipulated by the UN Security Council Resolution 1244.[1] Neither the war nor the UN-led administration changed that, although the settlement talks revolve around the issue. The current hybrid arrangement was always meant to be temporary, and in 2006 negotiations began in earnest, convened by UN Special Envoy Martti Ahtisaari with the goal of finding compromise among the competing claims over Kosova.

This book is written without prejudice, but not without a point of view. We wish to make the case that an independent Kosova, fully sovereign, with territorial integrity, can be democratic, economically viable, secure, and respectful of the rule of law and minority rights, and that this outcome is not only possible, but legitimate and desirable.

---

[1]Resolution 1244 reaffirms the sovereignty of the Federal Republic of Yugoslavia. However, in 2003 the Federal Republic of Yugoslavia, formed in 1992 by Slobodan Milošević after the disintegration of Yugoslavia, changed its name to Serbia and Montenegro. In May 2006, Montenegro seceded from the union by popular referendum.

Kosova traditionally has had more defenders than advocates in its past. This book advocates.

Independence is the demand of the majority Albanian population of Kosova. It represents the fulfillment of the right of self-determination; and it closes the long chapter of Serbian colonization starting with the 1912 annexation from the Ottoman Empire, then in a condition of accelerating collapse, through the brutal Milošević regime. The Serbian government's present position on final status holds that Kosova should remain under its sovereignty, but be granted self-government in relation to Belgrade, while Serb-majority villages and areas in Kosova enjoy a reciprocal autonomy from Prishtina. Serbia argues that any unilateral change of internationally recognized borders would contravene international law and pose potential threats to security both in the broader Balkan region, and anywhere else separatist movements thrive. Belgrade also requests that any negotiated settlement be internationally guaranteed for an estimated period of twenty years, but eventually renegotiated as part of a process of integration into the European Union. The consensus among international diplomats has been, for some time, that the status quo could not be sustained and that any solution for Kosova must avoid partition, union with any neighbouring state or parts of them, and the return to the pre-war situation. Some western governments have made it understood from the start that they favor 'conditional independence', meaning dissolution of legal ties between Kosova and Serbia, without granting Kosova full state status. In this scheme, Kosova remains an international ward for a time yet to be determined, with a significant presence of international troops in charge of security. Similar to post-Dayton Bosnia, a High Representative Office under the auspices of the European Union would retain some executive and monitoring powers over some state functions (the police, the courts), and guarantee the peaceful coexistence of substantially autonomous Serb territorial entities inside the territory.

Given these three starting positions, we aim to spell out arguments in favour of full sovereignty and unconditional independence, while addressing the concerns and counter-arguments advanced to the contrary. We hope to meet the need of a wider audience for clarification and information as non-specialists, including even the casual reader, seek to come to terms with both the current political debate, and future discussions.

In discussions about Kosova and its Albanian population, tired stereotypes, clichés, and bad history compete for adherents. Here we hope to correct the ignorance that makes fertile ground for misconception, and pollutes the understanding of a society with a rich and embattled past. Our premise is that much misinformation comes not just from ignorance, but from outright historical distortion, when the reality of Kosova is seen through an ideological lens that allows only a particular angle of vision.

One crucial angle, long upheld in Serb intellectual, religious and political circles, is the image of Kosova as an ethnically pure medieval Serb state, lost to the Turks in the fourteenth century, setting the stage for a clash of civilizations between Christianity and Islam. Caricatured as an 'Albanian Muslim camp', Kosova then becomes fair game for all sorts of allegations. Albanians are depicted as demographically aggressive interlopers in a space that belongs to others by ancestral heritage. They are portrayed repeatedly as primitive and hostile to the 'western community of values' and judged collectively guilty by association with a few criminal groups. The influence of this reservoir of stereotypes over the intellectual and political debate about sovereignty is noticeable and pernicious.

Other rich veins of distortion exist. A leftist revisionist school in the West, active in universities and on mainstream editorial pages, has typified Kosova through the prism of a critical attitude taken towards the NATO intervention. Often, two motives inspire this commentary: opposition to perceived US imperialism, and sympathy for Serbia as the last bastion of socialism. This view often colors the Yugoslav conflict with an emotional attachment to the myth of the Yugoslav resistance against Nazism; the current situation becomes just another turn in a cycle of violence between rival nationalisms, in play since World War II. Thus it becomes easy to make light of recent losses experienced in Kosova and elsewhere and then to attribute responsibility for the Yugoslav break-up and later sufferings to western intervention as well as reactionary, putatively pro-Nazi groups, such as the Croatians and the Albanians.[2]

---

[2]For more detailed and broader discussion of this phenomenon, but with a focus mostly on the English literature, see Marko Attila Hoare, 'Genocide in the former Yugoslavia: A critique of left revisionism's denial', *Journal of Genocide Research*, vol. 5, no. 4, December 2003. Notable names among the NATO intervention critics are, among others, Toni Negri and Regis Debray. The latter travelled to Kosova in May 1999 and publicly denied the mass expulsion of Albanians, having experienced normal life in the capital of Kosova, albeit under the escort of Belgrade government's minders: see 'Lettre d'un voyager au président de la République', *Le Monde*, 13 May 1999.

This book engages the political and intellectual sources of a distorted understanding of Kosova, but also aspires to go beyond them. Its purpose is to make the case for independence and sovereignty, by debunking the construction of Albanians and others in essentialist terms. One opponent may argue that an independent Kosova potentially threatens regional peace. Another contends that Kosova, unsupervised, eventually will tend to *Jihadist* Muslim extremism. Still others may object to its mono-ethnicity, or its lack of an economic future. These arguments all tend in the same direction: Kosova is represented as dangerous, immature, and incapable of running its own affairs. This image is not an innocent reflection on the current poor conditions of a post-Communist and post-conflict society. Its roots are older and are not confined to rival nationalist circles. They reach back to nineteenth century western stereotypical constructions of the Balkan region under Ottoman rule as alien to the European community, an antagonistic and backward civilization, of which Albanians often serve as a perfect type. The main elements of these stereotypes, however diluted in the apparently neutral collective perception about Kosova, continue to be reproduced uncritically, often unwittingly, by media pundits, journalists, politicians, and diplomats. They become the commonplaces of private conversations, even among an educated public. This merits critical attention. It is significant for example, that a comment made by an authoritative and independent group of experts immediately after the Dayton Conference repeats a classic biased cliché about Kosova: 'Kosovo is claimed on historical grounds by the Serbs as the cradle of the medieval Serbian kingdom, and by the Albanians on demographic grounds (90 percent of the population is Albanian). The Serbs claim it in the name of the past, the Albanians in the name of the present and the future.'[3] Even the seeming neutrality of descriptive language in daily newspapers—for example, 'ethnic Albanians' or 'Muslim' to signify the majority of Kosova—belies an acceptance of categories that entrap a diverse society into a position of subordination, as an object of control and reform.

In the past decade there have been serious criticisms of this phenomenon, which have met with relatively more success in the academic

---

[3]*Unfinished Peace: Report of the International Commission of the Balkans,* Berlin: Aspen Institute/Washington D.C.: Carnegie Endowment for International Peace, 1996, p. 29.

world than outside.[4] In reality, as a small community with a relatively limited institutional experience, the Albanians of Kosova have been unsuccessful in questioning and correcting their stereotypical image, a failure particularly damaging at this critical time when they are hosts to an ambitious international efforts toward of state-building.

The 18 contributors to this book have been set carefully chosen tasks: to address representative questions that arise from common arguments or allegations made over the years. Each essay is prefaced with one or more brief declaratory sentences drawn from official sources, political analyses or mainstream media reports that serve to capture the essence of each question. Taken together these arguments contribute to an overall image of Kosova that is invoked, in part or in whole, by those who would deny its right to become a sovereign state. Some of the questions might appear provocative, but only because they are based on provocative arguments; others take up genuine issues which have been debated widely, but usually in a superficial manner, with little creative reflection. The writers are all well prepared in their respective areas of either academic expertise, or of personal experience, and each has been selected to answer questions that draw on their area of greatest particular competence. The reader may choose to disagree, but these are not views that can be disregarded or discarded lightly. Contributors include historians of the region such as Ivo Banac, Isa Blumi, Alain Ducellier, Bernd Fischer, Noel Malcolm, and Owen Pearson. Paulin Kola and Stacy Sullivan are journalists and analysts. Howard Clark, Julie Mertus and Besnik Pula are both human rights activists and social scientists. Paul Williams, Jennifer Ober and Catherine Croft contribute to the book with their legal expertise and Janusz Bugajski with his knowledge of security issues. Andrew Herscher is an architectural historian and Machiel Kiel an art historian, both deeply schooled in the region's cultural heritage. As protagonists

---

[4] On the Balkans, see Maria Todorova, 'The Ottoman Legacy in the Balkans' in Carl L. Brown (ed.) *Imperial Legacy: The Ottoman Imprint on the Balkans and the Middle East* (New York: Columbia University Press, 1996, pp. 45–77) later expanded in the book *Imagining the Balkans* (New York: Oxford University Press, 1997). For a focus on Albanians but also more in general the connection between globalized academia and media, see Isa Blumi, 'The Commodification of Otherness and the Ethnic Unit in the Balkans: How to Think About Albanians', *East European Politics and Societies*, vol. 12, no. 3, Fall 1998, pp. 527–69.

of Kosova's political and social life before and after the NATO war, Vjosa Dobruna, Dom Lush Gjergji and Albin Kurti offer their insight on important issues of the present. The book has a clear, general point of view. However, each contributor has only been asked to comment on specific questions, and the answers are informed and rigorous, embodying the particular expertise of the writer.

It would be agreeable if there were a statute of limitations for national grievances based on nostalgia: the memory of distant empires, imagined wrongs and demonizing ideologies. Unfortunately, they continue to be presented and accepted as salient to contemporary political decisions on the life of Kosova. This book means to be an antidote to the use—and abuse—of historical narratives for advancing political agendas during the negotiation over Kosova's statehood. Much that is wrong has been written and said about Kosova in recent years. Join us now in an effort to redress some of that.

1. Is Kosova a late creation of the Yugoslav state and should it be considered the cradle of the Serb nation?

Isa Blumi

THE ALLEGATION

Mr. Drašković, what is your attitude to Kosovo's past, present and future? For me, a Serb, Kosovo is and will go on being what it was in the past: the cradle of the Serb state, spirituality, culture, ethos.

(Vuk Drašković, Serbia and Montenegro Foreign Minister, SPO President and writer).[1]

There are historical and religious reasons, as one argument goes, that justify Serbia's claim to sovereignty over Kosova: it was the cradle of Serbia. The world-wide media uncritically repeats this argument as fact, never failing to mention that Serbia sees Kosova as 'the cradle of Serbia's statehood', 'of Serbian culture and civilization', 'of the Serb nation' and 'of Serb culture and history'.

Serbia's historical rights would disprove that Kosova ever existed as such, outside the particular arrangements established by Communist Yugoslavia, as in the following statements:

After World War II Communist power transformed Kosova into the unique administrative entity it had never been. Why did they do that?

---

[1]Fahri Musliu and Dragan Banjac, *Untying the Kosovo Knot: A Two-Sided View* (Belgrade: Helsinki Committee for Human Rights in Serbia, Helsinki Files no. 20, 2005), p. 13.

> *The answer is very simple: after World War II the Yugoslav Communist Party was subordinated to its pre-war Comintern-style politics intent in pushing back the claims of 'Greater Serbia's hegemonism'... This explains also the fact that a regime of territorial and political autonomy for the Albanian minority was established only in Serbia and not in Montenegro and especially in Macedonia, both with a large Albanian minority.*
> (Vojislav Koštunica, Prime Minister of Serbia and Montenegro).[2]
>
> *Kosovo and Metohija is an ancient crime of the Yugoslav Communist Party, perpetrated by the IV Congress of the Party in Dresden in 1928, when they decided to split Yugoslavia into Soviet Republics and independent states and to 'reattach' Kosovo and Metohija to Albania.*
> (Dobrica Ćosić, Serb writer and politician, President of the Federal Republic of Yugoslavia in 1992).[3]

The Answer

Belgrade's claims to Kosova based on the state's link to a medieval empire that retained an ethnically 'pure' character have circulated since the mid-nineteenth century. Belgrade intellectuals and politicians have consistently argued that the remarkable collection of medieval buildings in Kosova somehow demonstrates a distinctive Serb national character to the region, excluding any place for non-Serb peoples in making an historical claim of their own. Key to this calculation is the assertion that religious affiliation immediately determines a community's ethno-national heritage. Since most of these historical sights are associated with the Patriarchate of the Southern Slav Orthodox Church (most commonly identified as Serbian today), their very physical presence in Kosova has therefore been used to prove that Kosova is an integral part of Serbia.

This complicated and ambiguous institutional history infuses much of the story of Kosova's past with patterns of association that assume cultural and political uniformity. What this reasoning fails to acknowledge is those social interactions that, if properly read, directly contradict

---

[2]'How everything started' (15 May 1995), in *Entre la Force et le Droit, Chroniques du Kosovo* (Paris: L'Age de l'Homme, 2002), pp. 15–21, p. 17.
[3]*L'Effondrement de la Yugoslavie* (Paris: L'Age de l'Homme, 1994), p. 65.

any possible claim made in the context of a twenty-first century state on ethno-national grounds. If, on the other hand, we can accept that throughout the Lazar and Ottoman periods, well until the end of the nineteenth century, a form of cohabitation created recognizable spaces for Serbs, Albanians, Turks and others to live together and see their interests as common, the significance of Kosova itself no longer contains a specific ethno-national one, but rather a compilation of shared spaces that may in fact suggest Kosova is an entirely different historical entity, with people living in it that are unique.

For one, claims made in Belgrade today about Kosova's distinctive Serbian character are predicated on a number of misrepresentations of medieval political power. It has already been successfully argued that the empire referred to as founded in Kosova was originally based in Rascia, to Kosova's north. Indeed, most of the historical structures related to that period of 'Serbian glory' remain well outside the widely accepted boundaries of Kosova. That Kosova as a region eventually becomes incorporated into Lazar's Empire in itself cannot be a worthy argument because similar territorial claims are not made on areas to the south in present-day Greece, which the empire at its height actually comprised as well. Moreover, these nationalist claims and assumptions about the nature of the population in Kosova obscure an important fact: that a variety of peoples lived in the region, suggesting Kosova itself has retained for much of its history a distinctive cultural, political and economic identity/place in Balkan history that is multi-ethnic at its base.

Kosova needs to be studied outside the confines of nationalist territorial claims, in order that we address current claims. An important first step is to adopt a non-ideological assessment of the long history of institutions such as the Southern Slav Orthodox Church. Such a history would recognize that contributing factors to the Church's history are construed along political lines, contradicting any assertion that such organizations functioned as an incubator for particular ethno-national interests. The Slav Orthodox Patriarchate, for example, has often been brought under the direct control of outside powers/states, including the Ottoman Empire, which for a period beginning in 1557 used the reconstituted Southern Slav Church to counterbalance the power of the Ecumenical Patriarchate based in Constantinople.

Equally, the assumption that the Serbian Orthodox Church was alone in serving the spiritual needs of ethnic Slavs actually misrepresents the importance of faith to other peoples living in the region. Throughout an extended period of Kosova's administrative existence—both during the reign of the Lazar kingdom and later under the Ottomans—the confluence of the Balkans' social, cultural and economic dynamism enlivened key towns such as Peja/Peć, Prizren and Mitrovica with a multi-sectarian significance which included both Catholicism and Orthodox Christianity. Most importantly, the patterns of sectarian self-identification largely reflected the range of political and cultural possibilities of the time, not the specific ethnic divisions that existed between one group and another. Prior to the advancement of Islam in the region, for instance, everyone living in Kosova was either Catholic or Orthodox Christian. Adherence to the Orthodox or Catholic Church, therefore, does nothing to properly explain the cultural, linguistic and subsequently 'ethnic' composition of the region's population. Rather, they are a reflection of the political realities of the time, one in which assured sectarian identities coincided with the institutional ascendancy of a particular kind of state.

The problem with an anachronistic line of thinking that emphasizes ethnicity lies in the fact that throughout Kosova's history, identity, be it ethnic or religious, was by its very nature fluid and therefore multiple, as people faced new kinds of structural and economic realities.[4] This can be further explored by concentrating on how, during the expansion of the early Ottoman state, the existing religious communities in Kosova (both the Eastern and Western churches) interacted with the Islamic state. The very fact that Orthodox institutions pre-dating Ottoman rule are still functioning highlights a dynamic of cohabitation rather than cultural (and ethnic) hegemony over the entire 1400–1912 period. Religious affiliation in the Ottoman context was a basic reflection of the community within which one lived, not one that, in the eyes of Muslim administrators, required conversion of other 'people of the book' (in other words, Jews and Christians). In fact, widespread conversion to Islam was probably never desired by the new Muslim administrators in Kosova, and many of the peoples that were under the religious tutelage of the Orthodox patriarch or Pope were left to continue to live in the region as Christians. What did emerge culturally

---

[4]For Clifford, understanding these fluid, 'conjunctural' identities is essential to appreciating human culture. See James Clifford, *The Predicament of Culture: Twentieth-Century Ethnography, Literature and Art* (Cambridge: Harvard University Press, 1988), pp. 10–1.

as a result may be best interpreted as a reflection of indigenous social practices that in most cases would be construed as reflective of a distinctive, Kosovar identity.

As has already been amply demonstrated, in the early Muslim Arab conquest of the Middle East, fiscal stability required that the region's Christian populations continue to conduct their economic activities in order to produce taxable surpluses. As in earlier times, the Ottomans also practiced a system of taxation that specifically did not seek to convert large numbers of Christians into Islam. The dividing of administrative districts and more importantly, the appropriation of the proceeds of the region's annual wealth within the established Sancaks of Iskodra (consisting of Peja/Peć/Ipek and Dukagjin that are relative to our interests here), Vushtrii (including Prishtina and Novobrdo) and Prizren, created new economic communities but not necessarily religious ones.[5] In other words, Ottoman administration led to a redirection of regional economies, ones which connected the Adriatic with the centers of global trade at the time, including the oasis cities of Central Asia, the Arab world and beyond, but did so with the intention of assuring that non Muslims (who were not protected from taxation) produced the vast majority of taxable wealth.

At the same time, however, it is clear that there was a considerable amount of conversion to Islam. Practical economic considerations as well as complicated cultural interactions rather than proselytizing may account for much of this conversion. One contributing factor may perhaps be that former subjects of the earlier Christian states recognized the range of new opportunities presented to those who could tap into a world that the Ottomans brought to the Balkans. In the context of an extended Ottoman Empire, being Muslim presented new opportunities as a soldier or merchant. The recruitment of young men to serve the Ottoman state, largely misrepresented in the twentieth century as 'enslavement of Christian boys', actually offered rural communities and local community leaders the opportunity to secure a direct link to the halls of Ottoman power by way of the military. The system worked very much the same way as the US Marine Corps or the elite forces of France and other volunteer armies today. The honor of sending a son to be trained to become the best and brightest of Ottoman society had

---

[5]Halil Inalcik *Hicri 835 Tarihli Suret-i Defter-i Sancak-i Arvanid* (Ankara: Turk Tarih Kurumu, 1954).

its long-term economic rewards.[6] These *Janissaries* (children trained in Istanbul to serve as administrators in the outer regions of the empire) formed tight-knit communities that retained their native languages and helped extend trade networks: for Albanians, this eventually linked the neighborhoods of Tunis, Algiers, Cairo, Baghdad and Damascus with Kosovar towns.

Of course, aside from economic and political opportunities presented by something akin to a *Pax Osmanica*, there is ample evidence to suggest that people also converted to Islam for strictly spiritual reasons. Sufi missionaries from dozens of *tekkes* established a foothold in the region, proselytizing to larger numbers of people whose sensitivity to both the power of the state and the message of a new faith contributed to the massive conversion of the region's Christians. While there were periods of hostility, older Christian traditions and the growing influx of Iberian Jews, most of whom were eventually encouraged to settle in the Balkans, created a fascinating spiritual space that conjoined Sufi *tekkes* from the Helveti, Nakshibandi, or Bektashi orders with local Christian sects. Such a spiritual mix would eventually create an environment of considerable importance as idiosyncratic movements among the region's Christians, Jews (*dhimmi* or 'people of the book') and Muslims interacted in ways that could be read as distinctive from other regions. There are numerous examples of local religious movements emerging to face open threats of persecution as heretics by the guardians of the official institutions that represented Christians, especially the Rum Patriarch in Istanbul and the Slav Orthodox Church in Peja/Peć/Ipek. Among the more interesting examples are the *Donme*, Jewish converts to Islam who followed the teachings of a charismatic Rabbi cum Sufi saint, as well as a long line of Sufi charismatic preachers popular among local audiences, both Christian and Muslim.[7]

---

[6]For details of how this system worked, see Metin Kunt, 'Transformation of Zimmi into Askeri', in Benjamin Braude and Bernard Lewis (eds.) *Christians and Jews in the Ottoman Empire*, 2 vols. (New York: Holmes & Meier Publishers, 1982), vol. 1, pp. 55–68.

[7]Perhaps the most interesting study of the early rise of Sufism in the Balkans in English is H T Norris, *Islam in the Balkans: Religion and Society Between Europe and the Arab World* (Columbia S.C.: University of South Carolina Press, 1993). Another invaluable work which provides a comprehensive summary of the long history of Sufism in Albanian populated areas is Jashar Rexhepagiqi,

As hinted at above, we seem to understand this history in terms of 'ethnic' communities who implicitly retain a distinct cultural identity. Embedded in this logic is the idea that religious affiliation determined the ethnic community, while any possibility that local practices represented a vibrant exchange was treated as impossible. This unfortunate way of reading social historical processes allows many to assume that Muslims, for example, were foreign to the region, therefore most likely to be 'Turks' who were introduced into the region following the military conquest of the Ottoman Empire. Inferred from this line of thinking, at least in some still-influential corners of the academic communities in Serbia, Greece and Turkey is that the non-Slav Muslims of Kosova today are either Turkish by origin or were imported from elsewhere.

Kosovar Osmosis

While migrations are not the reason for a rise in the Muslim population in Kosova, itinerant proselytizers, many from Sufi orders founded in central Anatolia, did make their way to the Balkans and had a profound impact on this process of cultural integration.[8] I would suggest that patterns of integration taking place to absorb Ottoman culture precisely through the preaching of the region's great purveyors of Islamic spirituality are distinctive to the post-conquest period. This process is important since, as we have already noted, there is little demographic evidence of significant numbers of settlers from Anatolia. Rather, what accounts for the growing number of Muslims is the conversion of those already living in Kosova for both economic and spiritual reasons. From the late fourteenth century onwards a process of cultural fusion of already fluid communities occured. This fusion was created, in part, by mystic orders which permitted ordinary people to adopt otherwise dramatically different spiritual traditions, in order to fit in with the contemporary realities in their lives. Much like the impact of Ottoman state policies in the

Dervishet dhe Teqetë në Kosovë, në Sanxhak dhe në Rajonet tjera Përreth (Pejë: Dukagjini, 2003).
[8]See Speros Vryonis, *The Decline of Medieval Hellenism in Asia Minor and the Process of Islamization from the Eleventh through the Fifteenth Century* (Berkeley: University of California Press, 1986), pp. 358–60.

area that sought to maximize state revenues, this early period of spiritual conversion did not represent a dramatic disruption (most inhabitants of the region would retain distinctive and unorthodox methods of worship), but an adaptation.

This may best be demonstrated by the way in which locals adopted the spiritual lifeline that connected the larger Islamic world with Kosova. There are a number of fascinating examples in which Albanian language texts, written in Arabic letters and with a strong influence of Persian, Turkish and Arabic mysticism, circulated in the region from the fifteenth century onwards. Dervish Hasani from Rahovac in central Kosova, for instance, a member of the Halveti *tekke* (founded by Shaykh Süleyman Ejup Dede of Potoçan in the 1680s) is the author of the oldest surviving example of cultural syncretism later to be translated into a vibrant genre of Albanian literature called *Bejtexhinj*.[9] Contrary to a rigid formalism suggested by those focused on high Islamic culture, there is a dramatic expansion of the local production of Ottoman spirituality that speaks of a varied and complex Islamic world operating in regions such as Kosova. This reflected a general Ottoman policy of pursuing continuity rather than oppression in all aspects of life.[10] State and religious forces blurred to the point where 'Turks' and 'locals' could be not readily be distinguished using our modern terminology. This same observation must be applied to Kosova prior to the Ottoman invasion in the late fourteenth century.

Much of the secondary and primary material, therefore, is largely unhelpful in understanding the imperial legacy in Kosova because we today are so fixated on a narrow and unrepresentative way of understanding our world. It would be quite easy, for instance, to conclude after reading census data from the nineteenth century that it is difficult to talk about a specifically Turkish or Serbian legacy in Kosova. As one senses from visiting the region, talking to the people and exploring the documentary past, Kosova, like the rest of the Balkans, was indelibly

---

[9]Other prominent authors using Arabic letters to write in Albanian include Tahir Efendi Gjakova from Yakova (early nineteenth century), Mulla Beqiri from Vushtrri near Prishtina and Mulla Dervish Peja from Ipek.

[10]This process, a 'schism of cultural identity', is replicated in any number of ways. Robert Elsie's wonderful work on Albanian literature demonstrates how Turkish and local literature fuse. See Robert Elsie, *History of Albanian Literature*, 2 vols. (New York: East European Monographs, 1995) vol. I, pp. 85–117.

touched by a variety of cultures, in the plural. Rather, it should be said that the 'ethnicized' narratives coming from Greece, Serbia and elsewhere since the late nineteenth century must be looked at again with a new sense of concern about their inaccurate abuse of ethno-national terms of reference.[11]

[11]For summary research into the region's populations that come to the same conclusion for earlier periods, see for instance, Sulejman Rizaj, *Kosova gjatë shekujve XV, XVI dhe XVII: administrimi, ekonomia, shoqëria dhe lëvizja popullore* (Prishtina: Rilindja, 1982), p. 448, Goran Stojančević, *Srbija u vreme beçkog rata 1683–1699* (Belgrade: 1976), p. 329 and Joseph Müller, *Albanien, Rumelien und die österreichische-montenegrinische Grenze* (Prague, 1844), pp. 23–8.

2. Were Albanians always on the side of the Ottoman Empire against Christian powers?

Isa Blumi

THE ALLEGATION

The series of long-scale Christian national movements in the Balkans, triggered off by the 1804 Serbian revolution, decided more than in the earlier centuries the fate of Serbs, and made ethnic Albanians (about 70 percent of whom were Muslims) the main guardians of Turkish rule in the European provinces of the Ottoman Empire. At a time when the Eastern question was again being raised, particularly in the final quarter of the nineteenth and the first decade of the twentieth century, Islamic Albanians were the chief instrument of Turkey's policy in crushing the liberation movements of other Balkan states.

(Dušan Bataković, Former Ambassador of Serbia and Montenegro to Greece, historian and advisor of President Boris Tadić on Kosova).[1]

From this perspective, the 'Ottoman legacy' in Kosova implies the creation of an Albanian-Muslim camp historically destined to wage war against Christian communities on their way to becoming nations.

---

[1]'The Age of Oppression', in *The Kosovo Chronicles* (Belgrade: Plato, 1992), also http://www.batakovic.com [Consulted on 26 March 2006].

The Answer

As representatives from Kosova and Serbia in Vienna debate the region's long-term status, religion, in particular the assumed 'natural' animosity between Muslims and Christians, has once again emerged as a factor. What is not generally appreciated by outsiders is that the rhetoric of sectarian conflict emphasized by prominent figures in Serb social and political life is based on an inaccurate and distorted history of Kosova's religious diversity—the product of tactics initiated in the late nineteenth century by Russia, Greece and later Serbia and Montenegro. Indeed, Serbia's territorial expansion since the second half of the nineteenth century has consistently been justified along sectarian lines.[2] Today, proponents of Belgrade's position are arguing to the rest of the world that Serbian Orthodox Christians face cultural annihilation by Muslim Albanians, an assertion that exploits the anti-Muslim hysteria currently affecting the West. Religious leaders claiming to be promoters of inter-sectarian understanding, like the Orthodox bishop of Prizren Artemije Radosavljević, warned for instance, that any attempt at 'detaching Kosovo from democratic Serbia would mean a virtual sentence of extinction for my people [Serbs] in the province who continue to face unremitting violence from *jihad terrorists* and criminal elements that dominate the *Albanian Muslim leadership*' [Author's emphasis]. The bishop continued to argue in a recent speech that a 'pure mono-ethnic and mono-religious Kosovo' could result from independence, an event that he claims would 'definitely be used to strengthen what we call the "white al Qaeda"', a clear reference to Kosova's Muslim Albanian population.[3]

By ignoring a long history of communal cohabitation, this understanding distorts the nature of Kosova's political life. Its premise relies

---

[2]Historians in particular have been consistently justifying the expulsion of non-Orthodox Slavs from Kosova by combining historical claims made on the basis of Orthodox Christian monuments found in the region and demands to respect Serbian communal rights which are predicated on Kosovar Serbs living under Serb rule. See for example, Jovan Hadzivasiljevic, *Juzna Stara Srbija*, 2 vols. (Belgrade: Stamp, 1913), vol. I, pp. 23–31.

[3]Sherie Gosset, 'Kosovo Bishop Warns Not to Hand Jihadists a Victory', CNSN News.com, 1 March 2006, http://www.townhall.com/news/ext_wire.html?rowid=46651 [Consulted on 12 March 2006].

on sentiments that mirror a pattern of xenophobia sadly observed by analysts as an insidious lens through which the international community sees events in the Balkans.[4] It is telling that arguments justifying sectarian separation due to historical animosities between Muslims and Christians no longer find much support in academic circles—such arguments have long ago been dismissed by non-partisan historians as fear-mongering—but are still upheld by nationalist groups and ring true for some policy makers, journalists and the larger public. In the end, the myths of provincial thinkers and their distortion of the past still dominate our understanding of Kosovar history, crippling the ability of Kosovars of all faiths and ethnicities to rediscover the pattern of interaction that was in evidence for much of the 1400 years since Slavs migrated to the region.

As in the past, the best way to respond to these arguments is to return to the history of Kosova. Long before the creation of nation states in the Balkans, medieval and early modern societies lived heterogeneous and religiously ambiguous lives. The initial phases of Ottoman military expansion were first and foremost political victories. Far from being a mark of military domination driven by religious zealotry, the Ottomans' conquest used a combination of military strategy and refined skills of negotiation to undermine the rivals of the empire in Southeastern Europe. The ability of Ottoman officials, for instance, to secure alliances with local Christian lords, including George Stracimirovic Balšic, lord of Zeta, guaranteed Sultan Murad's infamous military successes during the second half of the fourteenth century. The Ottoman military campaigns in the Balkans, in other words, entailed the recruitment of thousands of local men, all of them originally Christians, who proved willing to fight against their former Christian overlords. This was especially clear at the fateful battle at Kosovo Polje in 1389, where Prince Lazar's relatives ultimately forged an alliance with the Ottomans through the marriage of Lazar's granddaughter Olivera with Sultan Bayezid, Murad's immediate successor.[5]

---

[4]David Campbell, *National Deconstruction: Violence, Identity, and Justice in Bosnia* (Minneapolis: University of Minnesota Press, 1998).

[5]See Gábor Ágoston, 'A Flexible Empire: Authority and its Limits on the Ottoman Frontiers', in Kemal H. Karpat and Robert W. Zens (eds.), *Ottoman Borderlands: Issues, Personalities and Political Changes*, (Madison: University of Wisconsin Press, 2003), pp. 15–29.

This practice of forging alliances through marriage was to shape the nature of Muslim and Christian dynasties throughout the medieval and early modern period; it reflects a long-held tradition of medieval political life that is no longer disputed. Alliances between Slav Christians and Muslims consummated by marriage, treaty and power-sharing schemes were a common feature of early modern Balkan politics. In this regard, it was never considered an act unbecoming of Christians to forge an alliance with a rival power, even Muslim, a feature of local politics that was to continue for centuries.

Ignoring this aspect of Christian and Muslim cohabitation distorts history for the purpose of advancing a political agenda, building on a supposed sectarian irreconcilability. There are countless examples of alliances forged between early Christian leaders in the regions around Kosova, including an alliance between the Ottoman Sultan and Vuk Lazarević that led to the defeat of Vuk's brother, Stephan, for control over the southern Balkans in the decades following the fall of Prince Lazar's empire. In the course of this alliance with both Vuk Lazarević and George Branković, along with Albanian lords in the region, the Ottomans were able by 1421 to secure absolute control of the Western Balkans. In subsequent attempts to build their armies of volunteers and placate loyal vassals, the Balkans and the landed elite, including the largest Slav grandee families, continued a long tradition of forming marriage alliances with the Ottomans for over three hundred years after the fall of Lazar's kingdom.[6]

Rather than seeing the subsequent five hundred years of Ottoman rule in terms of Christian subjugation, it has been cogently argued by Ottoman historians that state-building demands required that Istanbul continue to forge alliances with local Christians, who remained in the majority in the Balkans throughout Ottoman rule. Perhaps the most suggestive example in the face of the current sectarian hysteria is that it was the Ottoman state that resurrected the Serb Patriarchate in 1557. This must be read as yet another act of political gamesmanship to secure local cooperation and ensure that the collection of taxes went smoothly. For the Ottoman Grand Vizier, Mehmed Sokollu Pasha, it was possible to obtain the loyalty of much of the Balkan Slav Orthodox Christian population at a time when the Ecumenical Patriarchate in

---

[6]Cemal Kafadar, *Between Two Worlds: The Construction of the Ottoman State* (Berkeley: University of California, 1995), pp. 23–65.

Ottoman-controlled Constantinople tried to secure domination in the region. Sokollu Pasha actually appointed his brother Macarios as Patriarch, a decision resulting in the separation of the Serbian Church from Constantinople control that lasted until 1766.

These practices reflected the political and economic realities of the time, which did not emphasize a community's sectarian identity, but a rationale of governance that assured stability and continued economic productivity. It is important to highlight, therefore, that through the very mechanisms of these medieval and early modern governmental practices, locals found ways to capitalize on changes in power. As a result, the structures of local power, often entrenched in earlier state-run associations such as the Church and the communities that gravitated around them, quickly fused with the larger Ottoman state apparatus once it fully conquered the region.[7] The logic behind this method, far more akin to cooperation than subjugation, was the maintenance of Kosova's many religious, cultural and economic traditions, and not, as claimed by recent nationalist historians, their destruction.[8]

This plainly contradicts the claims by nationalist leaders who assert that relations between Albanians and Serbs are predicated on perpetual religious animosity. Indeed, in the late Ottoman period, there is considerable evidence pointing to long periods of collaboration between Muslim Albanians and Serbs, who often shared a common enemy. For instance, the Albanian Muslim from Mitrovica, Isa Boletini, took part in a number of campaigns with both the newly created Serb state and local Christians (Albanian Catholics) in struggling against the Ottoman state after 1908. The region in which Boletini operated was economically devastated by the forced deportation of Albanians from the border regions newly awarded to the Serb state after the Berlin Congress of 1878. That he was nevertheless capable of forging alliances with Serb counterparts is telling. This was made clear to any number of contemporaries of the period. Among others, Serb intellectual Jovan Had i-Vasiljevic

---

[7]Halil Inalcik, 'Ottoman Methods of Conquest', *Studia Islamica* II (1954), pp. 103–29.

[8]Since the sixteenth century the Ottoman state had attempted to control the flow and redirect its significant waves of immigrants and refugees, resorting to forced resettlement (*sürgün*) when possible. Ömer Lutfi Barkan, 'Les déportations comme méthode de peuplement et de colonisation dans l'Empire Ottoman', *Iktisat Fakültesi Mecmuasi*. 11 (1949–1950), pp. 67–131.

(a Muslim) rationalized the massive deportation of upwards of 210,000 Muslims from newly ceded territories in the Toplica and Kosanica regions as the means to assure a 'pure Serb nation state'. That being said, a number of Serb intellectuals and military officials, including General Jovan Belimarković who resigned in protest, believed that the brutal measures taken by Serb settlers were counter-productive. In particular, General Jovan Belimarković recognized that Albanian Muslims shared many interests with their Serb neighbors that required greater cultivation and not destructive manipulation.[9]

Focusing on the districts along the Kosova–Niš frontiers created after 1878, Milan Gj. Milićević lamented the destructive campaign directed by northern Slavs against the local Albanian communities. In the areas around Jabllancia, Pustareka and Toplica, Milićević realized that such devastated areas needed the return of Muslim Albanians in order to secure an otherwise vulnerable border region from potential raids by Bulgarians or even the Ottoman state.[10]

Patterns of territorial cleansing that were practiced in the 1930s, 1950s and 1990s by Serb nationalist forces contradict any assertion that events in the Balkans are determined by Muslim–Christian animosity alone. The single most persecuted community in the region during Serb and Montenegrin territorial conquest happened to be Catholic Albanians. Reviewing witness reports and archival materials reveals a brutal campaign that specifically sought to target Albanian Catholics who posed the biggest long-term problem for a Serb-dominated empire. Catholic clergy reported on forced conversion and the brutal eradication of all evidence of non-Orthodox communities, especially churches.[11]

Local Catholic Albanians, as well as Muslims, were victims of the Serb brutal state expansion also during the wars of 1912–1913. Their

---

[9] See Olivera Milosavljević, *U tradiciji nacionalizma* (Belgrade, 2002), pp. 80–1.

[10] Milan Gj. Milićević, *Kraljevina Srbija: Novi Krajevi*. (Belgrade: Štampa i izdanje Kr.- Srp. dr avne štamparije, 1884), p. 137.

[11] For a contemporary account of the events that transpired in Kosova and Macedonia during and after the fall of the Ottoman army in late 1912, see Zekeria Cana, *Gjenocidi i Malit të Zi mbi Popullin Shqiptar, 1912–1913* (Prishtina: Instituti Albanologjik i Prishtines, 1996). For the perspective of Turks, see Süleyman Kocabas, *Son Haçli Seferi Balkan Harbi, 1912–1913* (Istanbul: Vatan Yayinlarii, 2000).

plight would be highlighted in the Carnegie Endowment's Special Commission reports published in 1913. Here too the Christian–Muslim divide does not explain much. In one particularly gruesome section, the Commission characterized Serb actions in Albanian populated areas as a systemic policy of murder and deportation aimed at instituting 'the entire transformation of the ethnic character of regions inhabited exclusively by Albanians'.[12] The Austrian consul at Prizren also reported extensive abuse of local Muslims and Catholics, characterizing the tactics used by groups in Serb military uniforms as large-scale economic exploitation, corruption and utter disrespect for the cultural rights of the region's non-Slav population. The reports of Austrian consul Kohlruss and most of the memoirs written by locals living through the experience spend considerable time focusing on the cruel policy of forced baptism, conversion and collective humiliation of non-Orthodox Albanian Christians.[13]

The assumption that cultural and political identities are fixtures on a collective body of humanity that transcend time and even place has resulted in a very modern interest in asserting links to the past. This is not a new idea, but its application in order to assert political order in our time is reflective of the very inaccurate logic that one's religion is primordial and ontologically hostile to others. There is no natural justification for religious communities, in Kosova or anywhere else, to be in conflict and to stir the fires of sectarian violence today. It is unfortunate that the rhetoric of religious violence still has weight among Serb leaders and has an audience in much of the world, despite efforts by generations of historians to argue to the contrary.

---

[12]Carnegie Endowment for International Peace, *Report of the International Commission: To Inquire into the Causes and Conduct of the Balkan Wars* (New York, 1913), p. 151.

[13]HHStA PA XXXVIII/405, Kohlruss an Berthold, dated Prizren, 27 January 1914. Another eyewitness captures the fascinating but equally nauseating story of the Montenegrin conquest of Peja in 1912 and 1913 in a newly published memoir. Zef Mark Harapi, *Ditt e Trishtimit n'Pejë e nder Rrethe, 1912–1913* (Peja: Dukajini, 2004), pp. 33–81. For a sense of how similar tactics were used during Belgrade's latest effort to eradicate Peja's Albanian population in 1999, see Matthew McAllester, *Beyond the Mountains of the Dammed: The War Inside Kosovo* (New York: New York University Press, 2002).

3. Is it true that Albanians in Kosova are not Albanians, but descendants from Albanianized Serbs?

Noel Malcolm

THE ALLEGATION

Until the middle of the eighteenth century, Kosovo and Metohija remained a homogenous environment with a Serb majority. However, in the first decades of the eighteenth century the Albanians began to massively descend from the mountains into the cultivated regions of Kosovo and Metohija ... Some of these Albanians came as Roman Catholics and converted to Islam in Kosovo and Metohija. Records exist even today of how and when villages or entire regions of Kosovo and Metohija were usurped by the Albanians, and the Serbian Orthodox population living there forcibly Islamized, and then Albanianized.
(The Memorandum on Kosovo and Metohija of the Holy Synod of Bishops of the Serbian Orthodox Church, September 2003).[1]

Whereas the Albanian Christians who emigrated with the Slavs became Serbs, the majority of Slavs who stayed behind in these areas were Islamized and even Albanianized.
(Stevan Pavlowitch, Emeritus Professor of History at the University of Southampton, England).[2]

The presence of Albanian settlements in pre-modern Kosova has been explained as communities that were previously Serb, but later

---

[1]http://www.spc.yu/Vesti-2003/08/memorandum-e.html [Consulted on 3 April 2006].
[2]*Serbia. The History of an Idea* (New York: New York University Press, 2002).

forcibly Albanianized. This argument, shared by the Serbian Orthodox Church and Serb intellectual and political circles, espouses the idea that Serbs were a stable population of Kosova, while the Albanians were relative newcomers, migratory people.

The Answer

Serbian nationalist historiography has made use of two alternative theories to account for—and, implicitly, to discount or devalue—the presence of an Albanian population in Kosova. One claims that the Albanians of Kosova are all immigrants from Albania, who came after the so-called 'Great Exodus' of the Serbs in 1690 or, in some versions of the theory, during World War II; this claim is used to suggest that they do not really belong there. The other theory suggests that they do belong there, but claims that they are not really Albanians. This is the so-called *arnautaš* thesis, which argues that they are in fact Albanianized Serbs, for which the special term *arnautaš* is used.

Both theories have coexisted since the late nineteenth century, in spite of the apparent conflict between them. Maximal versions of the *arnautaš* thesis do offer a way of solving that conflict: they claim that all Ghegs (northern Albanians) are Albanianized Serbs, which would mean that 'Albanians' who migrated from the Malësi (highlands of northern Albania) into Kosova were just Serbs moving from one place to another. This maximal theory was proposed by two Serb nationalist writers of the 1870s and 1880s, Miloš Milojević and Spiridion Gopćević; but experts, including Serbian ones, were quick to point out that their scholarship was defective, and to dismiss their overall claims as absurd.

The version of the *arnautaš* thesis which holds that all the Albanians of Kosova are Albanianized Kosovar Serbs seems, at first sight, less extreme. But simple logic suggests that it is very unlikely to be true: if, at the outset, the population had been entirely Serb, how and why would the process of Albanianization ever have got under way? To make the thesis plausible, it must be reduced to the claim that some significant percentage of the Albanians in Kosova are Albanianized Serbs, and must be taken to rest on the assumption that the pressure to

Albanianize came, at first, from a major presence of genuine Albanians, whether immigrants or old inhabitants.

It is undoubtedly true that, over time, some Slavs have been Albanianized, just as some Albanians have been Slavicized (and some Vlachs have been Serbianized, and some Roma have been assimilated in both directions). No ethnic or linguistic group in the Balkans has ever lived in a water-tight compartment. In one specific case, that of the Luma villages, just outside Kosova, to the south–west, we know that the Slav villagers first converted to Islam and then, in the eighteenth century, shifted from the Slav language to Albanian. But the question here is whether the Albanianization of Serbs in Kosova has been a general and predominant process.

The historical evidence suggests that it has not. While there are some recorded cases of Islamized Slavs gradually adopting the Albanian language (for example, immigrants from the Sandžak near Mitrovica), there are well-attested cases of Muslim Slav populations keeping their Slav language (for instance, the Gora villages in southern Kosova). In the case of mixed marriages, it was normally—but not always—the bride who had to start speaking the husband's language: Albanian girls were as likely to be Slavicized by such unions as Slav girls were to be Albanianized. But the level of inter-marriage between Muslim Slavs and Muslim Albanians was generally very low.

Some proponents of the *arnautaš* thesis have relied on indirect evidence: they have argued that any trace of folk-religious practices of Orthodox origin among Albanians in Kosova is proof that they were originally Orthodox Slavs. Such an argument, however, misunderstands the whole nature of religious syncretism in the Balkans. It also misrepresents as exclusively Serbian Orthodox some practices (such as the *slava*, the celebration of a family patron saint's day, and the *badnjak* or Yule-log) which have pre-Christian origins and are found far beyond the area of the Serbian Orthodox Church.

What is most problematic about the *arnautaš* thesis, though, is not its historical claims, which can be tested against the evidence, but its political or ideological implications. What its proponents tried to suggest was that an Albanian-speaking person, born of Albanian-speaking parents and identifying himself or herself as an Albanian, was not *really* an Albanian, because an ancestor in the eighteenth century might have been a Serb. The implication was that, deep down, there was a continuing—indeed, unalterable—Serb identity, and that this identity could be recovered by a process of Serbianization—a process which, since it merely undid a previous Albanianization, was somehow natural and right, even if it was forced. It is, one hopes, not necessary to elaborate on the morally repugnant consequences of such a view.

4. Is the Muslim conversion of Albanians the main cause of the estrangement between Slavs and Albanians?

Noel Malcolm

THE ALLEGATION

Mass conversion to Islam by Albanians is believed to have opened an era of prevarication and inter-ethnic conflict, and to have inaugurated a deeper divide between the two groups, a divide configured as a clash of civilizations.

There was no conflict between the Serbs and the Albanians in medieval Serbia. These problems began only at the end of the seventeenth century with the intensified Islamization of Albanian newcomers.
(The Memorandum on Kosovo and Metohija of the Holy Synod of Bishops of the Serbian Orthodox Church, September 2003).[1]

The Ottomans' breakthrough into the heart of Southeast Europe also marked the beginning of the five-centuries-long clash of two civilizations: European (Christian) and Near Eastern (Islamic). The conflict, alive to this day, is visibly evident also in the clash of the two nations: the Serbs, mainly Orthodox Christians, and the ethnic Albanians, mainly Muslims.
(Dušan Bataković, Former Ambassador of Serbia and Montenegro to Greece, historian and advisor of President Boris Tadić on Kosova).[2]

---

[1]http://www.spc.yu/Vesti-2003/08/memorandum-e.html [Consulted on 3 April 2006].
[2]'Kosovo and Metohija: Clash of Nations or Clash of Civilizations', in *The Kosovo Chronicle* (Belgrade: Plato, 1992), also http://www.batakovic.com [Consulted 26 March 2006].

The Answer

On the face of it, the suggestion made by this question is plausible. If 'estrangement' means something more than just a consciousness of difference, if it means some sort of alienation or suspicion that leads to hostility and conflict, then a general estrangement between two populations looks as if it must have some general causes. Religion does constitute a general difference between Serbs and Albanians: almost all Serbs are Orthodox, and the great majority of Albanians in Kosova are Muslim. In both cases, the religious label may imply active participation in religious life, or it may refer only to cultural background; much of the urban population today goes neither to the mosque nor to church. On the other hand, language is an even more general difference: all Albanians, both Muslim and Catholic, speak Albanian. But it would be odd to suggest that hostility between Serbs and Albanians arises simply from their speaking different languages; the fact of difference does not necessarily lead to the fact of conflict. Some other conflict-engendering factors must be involved.

Where the claim about religious difference engendering hostility is concerned, those other factors are, we are told, to be found in the whole nature of life under Ottoman rule. Christians had a legal status in Ottoman society, but that status was a secondary one; they suffered some disabilities, such as their testimony not being accepted against that of a Muslim in court, and paid some extra taxes. The ruling class—above all, the big landowners, who exercised local power—was Muslim. Therefore the Christian Serbs resented the Muslim Albanians.

Although there is some truth in this, there is not enough to justify a 'yes' to the question. Oppression by local pashas was a fact of life, but it bore on Muslim peasants as well as Christian ones. The great majority of Serbs were peasants working the land; the great majority of Muslim Albanians were peasants working the land; for most of the Ottoman period their conditions of life, and their grievances, were virtually the same. In 1689 both Serbs and Muslim Albanians joined with the Austrian army in Kosova to fight against the Ottomans. In 1822 about 3,000 people took part in a great protest march from Kosova to Istanbul to demand the removal of a tyrannical pasha from Prishtina: the protesters included both Serb peasants and the imams of the local mosques. Only in the mid-nineteenth century did the religious divide begin to act as the fault-line of an internal political conflict. The cause lay in the geopolitics of the surrounding region: new states with Christian identities (Serbia and Greece, at first) were eager to extend their territories, and therefore keen to activate 'unredeemed' populations of ethnic brethren outside their borders. And when they did acquire new territory, they expelled or mistreated the Muslim population. The Ottoman Empire went onto the defensive, and its Christian inhabitants began to be regarded, by their own Muslim neighbours, as a potential fifth column. For some Albanians, this furnished a pretext for the mistreatment of local Serbs.

Serb nationalist doctrine emphasized the role of the Orthodox Church as an essential constituent of Serb identity. Albanian nationalist doctrine, on the other hand, emphasized the Albanian language, accepting the religious diversity of the Albanians. There was thus a basic asymmetry between the two positions. But the Serb doctrine was, historically, the more important: it was formed earlier, it was embodied in a Serbian state long before the Albanians had any government of their own, and it was that state which, in 1912, conquered most of Kosova and put it under *de facto* Serbian rule. Religion thus mattered, to a certain extent, in reality, because it mattered in Serbian national ideology.

The main reason for the 'estrangement' of the Serbs and Albanians in Kosova lies, therefore, in modern political history. But the most important part of that history is the period from 1912 to the present. The massacres of Albanians during and following the initial conquest; the systematic maltreatment of Albanians in the inter-war years; the vicious reprisals against Serbs during World War II; the heavy repression of the early Tito period; the quasi-apartheid and mass-expulsions of the Milošević years: these are the most important factors in explaining any contemporary 'estrangement'. Compared with these, religion is just one part of the background.

5. Is it true that Albanians invaded Kosova?

Alain Ducellier

THE ALLEGATION

*Albanians are first mentioned in the eleventh century under the name of
'Arber' by Byzantine chronicles and their uninterrupted link with Illyrians
is highly disputable and cannot be proved by modern historical science.
Arberia was situated in the central area of today's Albania and until the
fourteenth century there are no records of Arber (Arvanite, Albanian)
settlers on the territory of Kosova and Metohija. Therefore, between the
third century AD when Illyrians are last mentioned as a distinct political
factor and the appearance of Albanians/Arberians there are no events which
prove any link between the two, which makes this Illyrian theory more a
romanticized myth than a historical fact ... According to many Serb
medieval chronicles and documents one may conclude that the number of
Albanians in Kosova did not exceed 2 per cent of the population which was
predominantly Serbian. and it is only in the later period that the number of
Albanians increased due to migrations in the Ottoman period.*
(Serbian Orthodox Church Hieromonk Sava, responding to the
comment made by the late President Ibrahim Rugova during a
press conference on 25 August 1995 in Prishtina).[1]

The argument recently spelled out by Hieromonk Sava, although
containing a disclaimer—he states that he does not claim that
'Albanians or their ancestors (whoever they were) never lived in the

---

[1]'Kosova has been inhabited by Albanians since ancient times.' http://
www.Kosova.com/rugova_hist.html [Consulted on 15 March 2006].

territory of today's Kosova and Metohija'—sets out a demographic justification for Serb sovereignty over Kosova.

This is an old claim. By 1913 Serb diplomats had already presented a memorandum at the Conference of London in reply to the Albanian government of Valona, asking to include parts of Kosova and Macedonia in the newly formed Albanian state. The main arguments of the memorandum against this request were: Serb historical and religious rights over Kosova; the moral right of the more civilized Serb nation; and the ethnographic right against 'the recent invasion by the Arnauts'.[2]

The Answer[3]

Historical arguments should never be the justification for a people's claim over territory that they have long lost: the national character of a region is not determined by its early inhabitants, but by the recognized national majority that currently lives in it. While taking note of how persistently the Serbs claim that Kosova is theirs because they are its most ancient inhabitants, it is interesting that we can refute this argument by also showing that for once history and the present agree: not only is Kosova demographically dominated by Albanians today, but Albanians, as direct descendants of Illyrians, are the ancient inhabitants of Kosova. All the 'history' arguments cannot but go against the 'Serb' thesis, because history teaches us that in Kosova Serbs were the invaders who arrived relatively recently.

Nationalism is a modern invention, fortunately unknown to medieval people who were not as sensitive as we are to the 'foreign' character of those who temporarily dominated them. Michael Aubin pointed to the fact that Kosova constituted the 'economic and political center of the medieval Serb kingdom'.[4] According to his argument, it is

---

[2]Marco Dogo, *Kosova. Albanesi e Serbi: le radici del conflitto* (Lungro di Cosenza: Marco Editore, 1992), p. 54.

[3]This chapter is largely based on 'Les Albanais ont-ils envahi le Kosova?', pp. 1–8 in Alain Ducellier, *L'Albanie entre Byzance et Venise, Xe-XVe siècles* (London: Variorum Reprints, 1987).

[4]Michel Aubin, 'Du Mythe Serbe au Nationalisme Albanais,' *Le Monde*, 5–6 Avril, 1981, p. 2.

only the Ottoman conquest that, after having eliminated the Serbs from their better land, finally forced them, especially in 1690 and 1738, to emigrate towards southern Hungary; Islamic elements from Northern Albania replaced them. But the establishment of a political and economic power in a given territory does not guarantee, especially in the Middle Ages, that those who have political authority are also ethnically dominant: the small Serb Despotate of Serres, in northern Greece for example, dominated, from 1355 to 1371, a massively Greek population.[5]

For the sake of the argument, let's agree that Serbs were the majority in Kosova in the thirteenth century. That being said, we cannot avoid asking who inhabited the place before them. Slavs were the last of the Indo-European-speaking peoples who entered Europe, arriving in successive waves of invasions during the sixth and seventh centuries.[6] We also know that, at that time, many centuries of Romanization had not caused the disappearance of the old autochthonous populations living in the Balkans, namely the Dacians in Romania, the Thracians in Bulgaria, and the Illyrians in Dalmatia, Albania and Macedonia. Since the eighteenth century BC many Illyrian political formations were born and developed in Kosova, changing from a tribal state to the status of small kingdoms, among the most important of which were the Dardanians, the Penestes, and the Paeonians.[7]

Linguistic and archeological studies tend to prove that the Illyrians are without any doubt direct descendants of the Albanians.[8] Following

[5]Georges Ostrogorskij, *Serska oblast posle Dusanove smrti* (Beograd, 1965).

[6]On Slavic invasions, see the synthesis of Francis Dvornik, *The Slavs, their early history and civilization* (Boston: American Academy of Arts and Science, 1956); on Serbs in particular, H. Gregoire, *L'origin et le nom des Croates et des Serbes* (Byzantion, 17, 1945) and Stojan Novaković, Srpske Oblasti X, XI veka, Glasnik Srpskog Drustva, 48, 1880.

[7]The bibliography on Illyrians is formidable. Among others, the archeological work *Iliria* (6 volumes, appeared in Tirana in 1971–1976), Muzafer Korkuti, Skënder Anamali, Jorgji Gjinari (ed. Français Kolë Lukaj), *Les Illyriens et la genèse des Albanais: Travaux de la session du 3–4 Mars 1969* (Tirana: Universitè de Tirana, Institut d'histoire et de linguistique,1971) and the *Actes du Congrès des Etudes Illyriennes*, 2 volumes, Tirana, 1974.

[8]Korkuti et al., *Les Illyriens et la genèse des Albanais à la lumière des recherches archeologiques albanaises*, in the book by the same title, pp. 11–39; on linguistic data, Ekrem Çabei, *L'Illyrien et l'Albanais*, Ibid., pp. 41–52.

World War II, when Albanian archeologists were funded to increase their research, there was an abundance of new finds. Archeological studies of ceramics and jewellery (earrings, brooches, rings, and especially pins) show that there is an extraordinary continuity of forms and techniques between objects from the ancient Illyrian necropolis and the discoveries found on medieval sites dating back to the sixth and seventh century of our era (Kalaja and Damalcës near Pukë and especially Kruja). Yugoslav archeologist B. Cović was able to date the material from Kalaja and Damalcës to the sixth and seventh century BC.[9] To be sure, this Illyro–Albanian continuity is not found only in the actual territory of Albania: the discoveries made in the necropolis of Mjele, close to Virpazara, in Montenegro, and the two sites of the region of Ohrid, Macedonia, brought to light objects belonging to the same civilization.[10]

In the absence of documents that could prove the extermination or the mass migration of the local Illyrian population when the Slavs invaded the region, it is natural to think that during the entire High Middle Ages, Kosova, like Albania, retained an essentially Illyrian population, and that means Albanian, even after the migration of Slavs. Obviously, there was a phenomenon of Slavicization, of which toponyms are the best evidence, but toponymy is not of great value when determining the ethnic character of a population. We find a great number of Slavic toponyms in Albania, for instance, but that does not mean that the majority of the population there has ever been Slavic. This argument will never serve the supporters of the 'Serb thesis' because the majority of the Slavic toponyms of Kosova and Albania seem to be Bulgarian rather than Serb (unsurprisingly, since Bulgarians occupied the region from the ninth century and especially the end of the tenth century, at the apogee of the last Bulgarian empire, whose capital was Ohrid).[11] At that time, Serbs were still far from Kosova: in fact, in the ninth and tenth century their first coherent formation coalesced at Rascia, in the valley of the Ibar, west of Morava, and Zeta, an area that corresponds largely to modern Montenegro. It was only when prince Stepan became king in 1217 that the Serb state grew to include

---

[9]B. Covič, *Osnovne karateristike materijalne Ilira na njihovom centralnom producju*, Symposium de Sarajevo, 1964, p. 101, cf. Korkuti et al., *Les Illyriens*, p. 35.
[10]Ibid., p. 185 and p. 192.
[11]A. M. Selichtev, *Slavjanskoe naselenie V Albanii* (Sofia, 1931) has a pro-Bulgarian bias.

the region of Peja/Peć while most of Kosova still remained outside its borders.

Did Serb domination cause the old Illyro–Albanian population to disappear? Serb texts prove exactly the opposite: in 1348, a donation made by the grand Czar Stepan IX Dušan to the Monastery of St. Michael and Gabriel of Prizren shows that there were at least nine villages surrounding the city that qualified as Albanian (*Arbanas*).[12] The following year, the famous code promulgated by this same sovereign confirms that Vlachs and Albanians lived close to the Slav population in many villages in his domain. Their dynamism must have been considerable, because the Czar made an effort to limit their settlements.[13] To be precise, the Vlachs and the Albanians were considered nomads, not because they were 'originally shepherds', but simply because they were directly affected by economic and political pressure of the dominant people. In 1328, the same happened in the regions of Diabolis, Kolônée and Ohrid where Jean Cantacuzènc places the meeting of the Byzantine emperor Andronic II with the 'nomadic Albanians' of central Macedonia.[14] Ostensibly, the newly emerging state tried to disperse the indigenous population economically and politically to better secure control of the region.

Serb domination was hard for Albanians. In 1332 the Crusade propagandist Guillame d'Adam wrote that 'both Latin and Albanian people are oppressed by the unbearable joke and very hard indenture of the Slavs, who are odious and abominable to them because they heavily tax their people, beat and despise their clergy, often enchain their bishops and their abbots, dispossess their nobility ... for these reasons everybody, together and individually, believes that they can make their hands holy if they dip them into the blood of Slavs'.[15]

Let us add that Byzantium's authors were very sensitive to the unity of the population from Albania to Macedonia. The fifteenth century historian Laonikos Chalkokondylis, after having emphasized that the

---

[12]Stojan Novakovic, *Zakonski Spomenici Srpskish Drzava Srednjega Veka* (Beograd, 1912), pp. 682–701.

[13]Chapters 77 and 82 of the Dušan's code, N. Radojcic, *Zakonik Cara Stefana Dusana* (Beograd, 1960), pp. 57–8.

[14]Jean Cantacuzène, *Histoire*, ed. De Bonn, I, 55, Tome I, p. 279.

[15]Brocardus, Directorium ad Passagium Faciendum, 'Historiens de Croisades', Historiens Armeniens, pp. 484–5.

Albanians of his times were very different from Serbs and Bosniaks,[16] concluded that there were no other people that resembled Macedonians more than Albanians.[17] It is in this context that the Ottoman conquest started and it is true that as a consequence Albanians could resettle in Kosova, but certainly not in the way that is commonly described. Far from arriving in the 'enemies' trucks' the Albanian population, from the lake of Shkodra to Kosova, were one with the other Christian populations. At the time of the Ottoman invasion of 1389, Greek authors mention, after the Serbs and the Bulgarians, the Northern Albanians, those of Himara, Epyrus and the coast.[18] The Chronicles of Idrisi Bitlisi mentions the participation of the Albanians from the region of Shkodra, whose prince, Georges Balsha, brought 50,000 men to the battlefield.[19] The same information is also found in other Ottoman chronicles like those of Ali and Hoca Saadeddin.[20]

The defeat of 1389 completely disorganized the Serb state, and left the field open to the most dynamic local lords, among them the Albanian princes of the North and the Northeast. The most remarkable example is Jon Kastriot, the father of Skanderbeg, from the high region of Mati, who at the end of the fourteenth and the start of the fifteenth century succeeded in carving a large principality from the estuary of the Ishmi to Prizren, at the heart of Kosova. In 1429, as a consequence, he bestowed upon the Ragusians (inhabitants of Dubrovnik) commercial privileges that secured access to trade routes that ran from the coast 'to Prizren over his land'. This new Albanian power contributed to the development of a mercantile class within a population that had previously been very poor. The archives of Ragusa prove, for example, that a certain number of Albanian traders of Ragusa willingly lived in Kosova. In March 1428 this was the case of Marcho de Tani, to whom the Republic sent a letter while inhabiting Prishtina.[21] Even after the submission of

---

[16]Laonikos Chalkokondylis, *Histoire* (Budapest: ed. E. Darko, 1922–1926) I, pp. 23–4.

[17]Ibid., pp. 277–8.

[18]Hierax, *Chronique sur l'Empire des Turcs*, Satas, Bibliotheca Graeca, I, p. 247.

[19]Idrisi Bitlisi, *Chronique*, fol. 188 a–190 a, in Selami Pulaha, *Lufta Shqiptaro-Turke ne Shekullin XV; Burime Osmane* (Tirana: Universiteti i Tiranës, Instituti i Historisë dhe Gjuhesisë, 1968), pp. 134–8 and p. 142.

[20]Pulaha, *Lufta*, pp. 251–2 and p. 297.

[21]State Archives of Dubrovnik, *Litterae et Commissiones Levantis*, X, f. 84 v (17 March 1428).

Kastriot to the Ottomans we still find in the same town, in 1448, the Albanian Chymo Mathi de Tani.[22]

We have no reason to think that the Ottomans, in this phase of their conquest, found support among the Albanians who would have opposed the Slavs. Albanians were Christian like the Serbs and had no special inclination to submit to the Ottomans. If it is out of the question to talk about the work of Skanderbeg (also known as Kastrioti, under whose leadership the Albanians waged a long struggle against Ottoman occupation), who operated at the borders of Kosova, we must remember that the Byzantine historian Ducas, in the middle of the fifteenth century, cites the defeat of the Albanians, from Dalmatia to Thracia, as the main reason for the ultimate success of the Ottoman occupation.[23] As for Ottoman chronicles, they always mention Albanians in Kosova, including one written in 1467 that witnesses the 'rebels' pillaging livestock in the region of Tetovo, under the leadership of a 'traitor' identified as Iskender.[24]

It is therefore evident that a sizeable Albanian population was in Kosova before the Ottoman conquest and there is no evidence of a massive immigration to Kosova. The fact that there was no tension between Slavs and Albanians at the time of the Czar Dušan and especially at the time of the formation of the principality of Kastriot, suggests that 'Albanian power' was generally well accepted by the local populations, largely because they already comprised of important Albanian elements. It is almost impossible to determine the relative importance of Albanians in relation to the Slavs in Kosova in the fifteenth century, despite new sources drawn from recently available editions of Ottoman cadastral records (*defterler*).

The best example of these new sources is Selami Pulaha's 1974 study of register of the Sand ak of Shkodra, dated 1485 and covering the regions of Shkodra, Peja, Podgorica, and Bihor.[25]

Pulaha work examines the rich toponymic and anthroponymic data provided by this source. He states that an Albanian could have a Slavic name and a Slavic or Albanian toponym would not prejudge the ethnic

---

[22]Ibid., XIII, f. 248 (5 January 1448).
[23]Ducas, *Istoria Turco-Byzantină* (1341–1462) (Bucarest: ed. Grecu, 1958), p. 179.
[24]Kemalpasazade, 'Chronique', f. 254, in Pulaha, *Lufta*, p. 191.
[25]Selami Pulaha, *Defteri I Regjistrimit te Sanxhakut te Shkodres I vitit 1485*, 2 volumes, (Tirana, 1974).

nature of the population.[26] However, the joined usage of a double toponym and a double anthroponym suggests an ethnic mix whose components can be evaluated according to the region. In the Sandžak of Shkodra (that includes all the Kosovar area of Peja) Pulaha distinguishes three areas where there was an Albanian population: the region of Shkodra, where Albanians were the majority; the regions of Piper, Shestan, Altun-ili, where it seemed there was a certain equilibrium between the two populations; the zone of Peja, where the Albanians constituted a considerable minority[27] and where one could observe, among other things, that a good number of villages that carried a Slavic name were in reality populated by a majority of Albanians.[28]

The conclusion is that a very intimate mix of the two populations would be completely unimaginable if one or the other were recently settled in the region. The Ottoman cadastre of Shkodra shows therefore, especially for the area of Peja, that Albanians constituted a very ancient component of the local population. Because there is no record of any massive migration of Albanians towards Kosova before the sixteenth century, we must conclude that a good part of the Kosova Albanian element has its roots in the ancient Illyro–Albanian population.[29] In central Kosova (Vilkili), the Bosnian historian A. Hanzić draws exactly the same conclusion from an old cadastral register dated 1455: the strong mixing of the two populations implies the continuity of the old Albanian substratum.[30]

This Albanian population was reinforced, at the beginning of the fifteenth century, by 'economic' immigration due to the exploitation of Kosova's rich mineral wealth, especially the silver of Srebrenica and Novo Brdo. These Albanians, always Christian of course, were technicians who came mostly from the Albanian northern coast (Tivari,

---

[26]Ibid., pp. 31–2.
[27]Ibid., pp. 31–2.
[28]Ibid., p. 34, names other 15 villages in this case.
[29]Ibid., pp. 34–5. The same conclusion is drawn by the great Yugoslav historian Milan Sufflay, assassinated by Ustasha, in *Povijest Sjevernih Arbanasa* (Prishtina, 1968), pp. 61–2.
[30]A. Hanzić, *Nekoliko vijesti o Arbanasima na Kosovu I Metohiji v sredinom XV vijeka*, Symposium on Skanderbeg, (Prishtina, 1969), pp. 201–9. Selami Pulaha, 'Elementi Shqiptar sipasnomastike se krahinave te Sanxhakut te Shkodres ne vitet 1485–1582', *Studime Historike*, 1972, I, p. 63 ff.

Shkodra), but also from the mountains (Mati), emigrated towards Ragusa.[31] They settled in Kosova many generations ago, including Petar Gonovich Pritzenaz (from Prishtina),[32] Johannes Progonovich de Novomonte (Novo Brdo), and others.[33] This Albanian Catholic immigration continued well into the seventeenth century and, according to records of visitors sent to the region by the Pope, the migrants settled mainly in Novo Brdo, Gjakova and Prishtina, Trepca.[34] This does not, however, in any way contradict the argument that Kosova was already an integrated, multi-ethnic and multi-sectarian region before the arrival of the Ottoman Empire.

In conclusion, starting from the seventh century, Slavs or Slavicized populations (first Bulgarians and later Serbs) occupied Kosova, whose population had been largely Illyro–Albanian since antiquity. Of course, the Slavic settlements and the inevitable Slavicization of part of the original population allowed the Serbs, at the beginning of the thirteenth century, to make Kosova their main political and economic center. However, nobody can ever know precisely what the respective ratios of the two populations were. We know that they coexisted without any problem. Afterwards, the Ottoman conquest and the progressive weakening of Serbia allowed the Albanian population, both because of internal dynamics and the peaceful migratory flux of the Northern Christian Albanians, to have a greater role in Kosova. Many studies are still necessary to confirm this, but it is likely that even before the Slavic migration of 1690 and 1738 Albanians were, if not the majority, an important minority in Kosova. It would be unfair to forget that Serbs were not the only ones to escape the Islamized areas. At the time of the great migration of 1737–1738, several thousand Christian Albanians left the

---

[31]Documents selected by Mihailo Dinić from the State Archives of Dubrovnik, especially *Iz Dubrovackog Archiva*, I, (Belgrade, 1957), for example p. 65, 'Dom Marin de Antivaro', 'Andria Nicholich Arbanexo de Matia.'

[32]Ibid., p. 68.

[33]Ibid., p. 69, also State Archives of Dubrovnik, *Acta Matrimonialia*, II, f. 103 v (11 December 1459).

[34]Injac Zamputi, *Relacione mbi gjendjen e Shqiperise veriore dhe te mesme ne shekullin XVII*, Tome I (1610–1634), (Tirana, 1963) and in particular the report of the Apostolic visitor Pietro Maserecco (Mazrek) in 1623–1624, 'thirty years ago there was an abundance of gold, silver, and other metals in these places, and for this reason Catholics found themselves among Serbs, because some from Albania, some from Bosnia came to the mines', p. 342.

mountainous region of Shkodra and went to Karlovac. In Croatia, where the Austrian government used them in the framework of the politics of military colonization, these 'Klementiner', as they are called in the Austrian texts, found themselves intimately mixed with the Serb population who had migrated and resettled in the same way. These Albanians would maintain their tradition and their language until 1910, the date of their definite Slavicization.[35]

---

[35]L. von Thalloczy, 'Die Albanische Diaspora, Illyrish-Albanische Forschungen', Vienna 1916, Tome I p. 314 ff. This article is based on the Archives of Karlovac, on 'Archiv des Gemeinsamen Finanzministeriums,' Vienna, in particular, VI, 25, 1739.

6. Is it true that Albanians are responsible for an orchestrated campaign to destroy Kosova's cultural heritage in modern times?

Andrew Herscher

THE ALLEGATION

The rubble of Orthodox churches across Kosovo stands us a monument to Kosovo Albanian vandalism and to Nato's indifference or—at least—incompetence ... This demolition cannot be just 'revenge',—Nato's usual excuse for the destruction under its auspices. You do not just fill with rage and spend days gathering explosives to blow up churches. This is vandalism with a mission.
(Robert Fisk, British Journalist).[1]

The theme of a systematic and orchestrated destruction of Serbian churches and monuments as a protracted campaign of genocide throughout history is very common, especially after the burning of Serbian Orthodox sites in the post-war period.

The Answer

Religious sites have been vandalized, damaged and destroyed at various times throughout the modern history of Kosova. The

---

[1]'Nato Turns a Blind Eye as Scores of Ancient Christian Churches Are Reduced to Rubble', *The Independent*, UK (www.independent.co.uk), 20 November 1999.

buildings and monuments of all religions present in Kosova have been targeted: Islamic mosques, schools and community centers; Serbian Orthodox churches, monasteries and graveyards; and, to a lesser extent, Catholic churches. This violence has been inflicted by the state in times of war and social repression and by individuals, groups, and emissaries of the state in times of social unrest and conflict. While there have been traditions of sharing religious sites across ethnic communities in Kosova, violence against religious sites has served to foreground and strengthen the identification of these sites with particular communities, as well as to sharpen conflicts between these communities.[2]

The above comprises one way of contextualizing violence against religious sites in Kosova: this contextualization suggests that violence has been inflicted both against sites identified with Albanians and sites identified with Serbs. Neither of the primary ethnic communities in Kosova, in other words, maintains a monopoly on violence against the religious sites of the other. A more profound contextualization, however, recognizes that concepts of ethnicity do not stand before and outside violence inflicted in the name and on behalf of an ethnic community. In other words, 'ethnic violence', of which violence against religious sites forms a prime example, is not the product of a static and homogenous ethnic community, but a performance of ethnicity, a performance that gives cultural meaning and social value to ethnic identity. Thus, to point out the persistence and intensity of violence against religious sites in Kosova is not to pass immediately and unproblematically into the realm of 'ethnic violence'—a violence based in some way on the different ethnicities of perpetrators and victims. Rather, as recent studies of violence in anthropology, sociology, and political science have come to recognize, the 'ethnicity' of violence is an abstraction, an interpretation, and a staging; violence comes to be understood as 'ethnic' in narrations undertaken both by perpetrators and victims.[3]

---

[2]In Kosova, ethnicity and religious affiliation are strongly related, with Albanian ethnicity correlated to Islam and Serbian ethnicity correlated to Serbian Orthodox Christianity. On the use of religious sites across ethnic lines, see Frederick W. Hasluck, *Christianity and Islam under the Sultans* (New York: Octagon Books, 1973 [1929]) and Ger Duizings, *Religion and the Politics of Identity in Kosovo* (New York: Columbia University Press, 2000).

[3]See, for example, John Mueller, 'The Banality of "Ethnic War"', *International Security*, 25 (Summer 2000); Rogers Brubaker, *Ethnicity Without Groups*

In what follows, I will briefly pursue both contextualizations of violence against religious sites in post-World War II Kosova—one pointing towards the sharing of violence against religious sites between Albanians and Serbs in Kosova, and the other towards the relation between that violence and the ethnic definition of communities in the first place. These contextualizations suggest that the answer to the question posed in the title of this essay is that representatives of both Albanian and Serb communities have inflicted violence against the other's religious sites and have documented and memorialized violence against their own religious sites, in each case in order to shape particular notions of ethnic identity—what it means to be Albanian or Serb in Kosova.

During the Second World War, when Kosova was divided into occupations zones controlled by German, Italian and Bulgarian forces, many Serbian Orthodox religious sites in Kosova were damaged or destroyed, with much of this violence inflicted by Albanian forces fighting both within and apart from German and Italian forces.[4]

After the war, most damaged Serbian Orthodox religious sites, in Kosova as elsewhere in socialist Yugoslavia, were restored.[5] At the same time, post-war urban modernization targeted other religious sites, along with other examples of pre-modern architectural heritage, for destruction.

In Kosova, urban modernization was more damaging to Islamic religious sites than to Orthodox ones, a result of both the Ottoman-era urban morphology of Kosovar cities and an Orientalist ideology that posed Ottoman-era heritage as a product of a primitive pre-modern culture. To the slogan of 'Destroy the old, build the new!', brigades of 'Popular Front' volunteers in Kosova, as elsewhere in Yugoslavia, destroyed mosques as well as Ottoman-era bazaars and other buildings as part of modernist urban renewal projects in cities such as

---

(Cambridge: Harvard University Press, 2004) and V. P. Gagnon, Jr., *The Myth of Ethnic War: Serbia and Croatia in the 1990s* (Ithaca: Cornell University Press, 2004).

[4]Djoko Slijepcevic *Istorija srpske pravoslavne crkve*, vol. 2 (Munich: Iskra, 1966), p. 687; Sabrina Ramet, Balkan Babel: *The Disintegration of Yugoslavia from the Death of Tito to the War for Kosovo* (Boulder: Westview, 1999), p. 104.

[5]Miloslav Protic 'Izgradnja crkava v poratnom periodu', in *Srpska pravoslavna crkva 1920–1970* (Belgrade: Sveti Arhijereskog Sinod, 1971).

Prishtina/Priština, Peja/Peć and Prizren.[6] The significance of targeted religious sites as ethnic symbols was less explicitly salient to the socialist state than their significance as symbols of the pre-modernity the state was striving to overcome. Nevertheless, the state's endorsement of the targeting of these politically significant buildings created a template for communicating socially significant meanings through destruction; just like the construction of new buildings, the destruction of religious sites was a means to transcribe social meaning onto the very form of built environment.

When Albanians subsequently demonstrated for increased political autonomy and civil rights in cities across Kosova in 1968 and 1981, these demonstrations were accompanied or followed by vandalism targeting Serbian Orthodox religious sites such as churches, monasteries and graveyards.[7] On one hand, this vandalism comprised 'a passive but nevertheless tangible resistance' in the face of heightened security and social control.[8] On the other hand, it re-cast a political conflict over sovereignty in Kosova as an ethnic conflict, a re-casting that was productive for legitimating nationalist projects in both Albanian and Serb contexts. In both contexts, nationalism was a critique of the Yugoslav state's attempt to negotiate between and balance the interests of ethnically-defined nationalities, an attempt that allowed ethnic affiliation no political salience.

As recorded in both state media and Serbian Orthodox publications, vandalism continued to be inflicted against Orthodox religious sites through the 1980s.[9] Assertions of the need to protect the Serb population and Serbian Orthodox religious sites of Kosova were then, in the late 1980s, seized upon by Serbia to revoke Kosova's political autonomy

---

[6]Dragan Cukič, ed., *Kosovo i Metohija, 1943–1963* (Prishtina: Skupstina Autonomne Pokrajine Kosova i Metohija, 1963) and Esad Mekuli and Dragan Cukič, eds, *Pristina* (Belgrade: Beogradski graficki zavod, 1965).

[7]A list of the Serbian Orthodox Church's petitions protesting attacks on vandalized church property between 1982 and 1986 is given in Atanasije Jevtič, et al., eds, *Zaduzbine Kosova: spomenici i znamenja srpskog naroda* (Belgrade: Eparhija Rasko-Prizrenska i Bogoslovski fakultet, 1987), pp. 831–42.

[8]Branka Magaš, 'Wrong Turn in Kosovo' (1982), in Branka Magaš, *The Destruction of Yugoslavia: Tracking the Break-Up 1980–1992* (London: Verso, 1993), p. 6.

[9]Vjekoslav Perica, *Balkan Idols: Religion and Nationalism in Yugoslav States* (Oxford: Oxford University Press, 2002), pp. 123–32.

and impose direct rule. The transformation of Kosovo's political status, the forced removal of Albanians from state employment, increased state surveillance and repression of Albanians, and a series of human rights abuses inflicted by Serb security forces in Kosova all contributed to escalating tensions between Albanians and Serbs through the 1990s. In the late 1990s, an armed movement, the Kosova Liberation Army, initiated an insurgency against Serb government forces in Kosova. This campaign focused its violence not on religious sites but on Serb military, police and civilians.

During the counter-insurgency campaign waged by Serb forces against the Kosova Liberation Army in 1998–1999, however, along with the mass expulsion of Albanians from Kosova, religious sites associated with Islam were targeted for destruction. Approximately 200 of the more than 600 mosques in Kosova were damaged or destroyed during 1998 and 1999, along with Sufi lodges and Islamic schools, archives and libraries.[10] The vast majority of this violence was not the result of collateral damage inflicted in the course of military operations; buildings were ruined by deliberately inflicted violence, including vandalism, arson, shelling or toppling of minarets, and the dynamiting buildings from within. Violence against religious sites in the 1998–1999 Serb counter-insurgency accompanied a range of other forms of violence, ranging from the forced expulsion of Albanian communities from their homes, through robbery and extortion, to rape and murder. Violence against religious sites served to code all this violence as ethnic, as part of a history of ethnic conflict between Albanians and Serbs, and thus, to legitimate and justify this violence in the context of ethno-nationalist ideology.

After the war, during the UN administration of Kosova, Albanians have inflicted a counter-violence on Serbian Orthodox religious sites. Much of this violence comprised so-called 'revenge attacks' in the months immediately following the end of the war, and much of this violence was also inflicted during the riots of March 2004. To date,

---

[10]Andrew Herscher and Andras Rieldmayer, *The Destruction of Cultural Heritage in Kosovo, 1998–1999: A Post-War Survey* (Cambridge: Kosovo Cultural Heritage Survey, 2001). The Islamic Community of Kosova's list of damaged and destroyed Islamic religious sites is given in Bashkësia Islame e Kosovës, *Serbian Barbarities Against Islamic Monuments in Kosova* (Prishtina: Dituria Islame, 2000).

approximately 140 Serbian Orthodox churches and monasteries have been damaged or destroyed since June 1999, mostly through vandalism, arson, or dynamiting.[11] While violence against Islamic religious sites during the 1998–1999 war accompanied a state campaign to expel Albanians from Kosova, post-war violence against Serbian Orthodox sites appear to have been carried out by individuals or groups without explicit affiliations to state institutions. However, the post-war destruction of religious sites occurred in a climate of intimidation and violence that caused the mass migration of tens of thousands of Serbs, dramatically altering the demographic character of the province. As events like the riots of March 2004 revealed, Albanian politicians have consistently shown a remarkable failure of leadership, to the point of helping legitimate violence against Serbs in Kosova.[12]

In both Albanian and Serb contexts, violence against the religious sites of the ethnic other is often endowed with religious, cultural and historical meanings and therefore justified. At the same time, in both Albanian and Serb contexts, violence against an ethnic community's 'own' religious sites is often understood to reflect or embody 'genocide', 'culturcide' or 'cultural genocide'. This understanding emerged in the 1980s and now is among the dominant frames in both contexts for reading Kosova's history as a history of ethnic violence, and for legitimating counter-violence against the ethnic other as historical. Yet, the targeting of religious sites does not represent a history of 'ethnic violence' in Kosova, as much as an ongoing attempt to inextricably enmesh ethnicity, religion, violence and history for contemporary political ends.

---

[11]The Serbian Orthodox Church's list of damaged and destroyed religious sites is given in Eparhija Rasko-Prizrenska, *Crucified Kosovo* (Prizren-Graçanica: Eparhija Rasko-Prizrenska, 2001 [3rd ed.]) and Dragan Kojadinovič, ed., *March Pogrom in Kosovo and Metohija* (Belgrade: Ministry of Culture of the Republic of Serbia and Museum of Prishtina, 2004).

[12]Human Rights Watch, *Failure to Protect: Anti-Minority Violence in Kosovo, March 2004* (July 2004), http://hrw.org/reports/2004/kosovo0704/, 57–61 and International Crisis Group, *Collapse in Kosovo* (April 22, 2004), http://www. crisisgroup.org/home/index.cfm?id=2627&l=1, 25–7 [Last visited 26 April, 2006].

7. Have ethnic and religious animosities caused the destruction of the artistic and cultural heritage of Kosova during the Ottoman period?

Machiel Kiel

THE ALLEGATION

They [Albanians] *formed military bands notorious for crimes, or volunteered as Janissaries in order to gain special privileges with the Turks, and then proceeded to loot and confiscate Serb villages, churches and monasteries, and ultimately began to settle here.*
(The Memorandum on Kosovo and Metohija of the Holy Synod of Bishops of the Serbian Orthodox Church, September 2003).[1]

The looting of churches and other church properties during the Ottoman period, especially after their alleged descent en masse from the mountains to the plains of Kosova, is another complaint raised against Albanians.

The Answer

A very short answer to this question would be, in German, *jain*, which means 'yes and no'. The destruction of the cultural heritage of the 'other' has always been part of the history of mankind. Yet most of the destruction is simply the result of unstable times and wars, when

---

[1]http://www.spc.yu/Vesti-2003/08/memorandum-e.html.

the restraints on the destructive forces of humanity become looser. Kosovo is no exception. Even the most recent violence against religious sites has little to do with Serbian–Albanian or Muslim–Christian antagonism and a great deal instead with the suspension of civil order brought about by war. In the same region, when the law went unchallenged and people did not feel their security threatened, different religious communities and sites have peacefully coexisted. In similar circumstances, the pattern of tolerance that can be found in the past history of Kosovo can be replicated.

In the long Ottoman centuries (for Kosovo from 1456–1912), the conquest of the Balkans developed along two patterns. Some areas were incorporated during military actions that were accompanied by the usual war-time destruction and plundering. However, there was also the peaceful annexation of large territories, after local dynasties died out without producing candidates fit for succession. This happened, for example, in most of Macedonia, where territories that included important towns such as Kastoria, Kratovo, Ohrid, Prilep, Petrić, Štip, Strumitsa, and Velbužd (Kyustendil), were annexed without fighting or great upheavals, and thus little or no destruction. The lower nobility, accustomed to Ottoman rule during the long years in their service, became the 'Christian *Sipahi*' of the early Ottoman army. In the fifteenth century we see these noblemen, clearly identified by their names as patrons of the church, depicted in the donor's scenes of frescoes; the same names appear in the fifteenth century Ottoman registers.[2] In the course of time, the Christian *Sipahis* slowly disappeared, absorbed in the Ottoman ruling class. One of the last was perhaps 'Voin Spahija' who in 1592 erected the monastery of the Holy Trinity of Plevlje, now in Montenegro, where we can see him represented in a painting while offering a model of his church to Christ.

After conquest, the Ottomans behaved in strictly legalistic terms. Christian Churches had their fixed place in the Ottoman legal structure, anchored in the Islamic Holy Law, the *Sheriât*. Non-Muslims paid their taxes, often very moderate ones, and were not harassed. They lived under their own ecclesiastical authorities, elected by the various religious denominations and confirmed by the Sultan. Monasteries that

---

[2]This combination of art history fieldwork and Ottoman administrative records was first applied by Gojko Subotić, *Ohridska µkola XV veka*, (Belgrade, 1980).

are the most important works of the Slavic Middle Ages in the entire Balkans owe their survival in large part to their Muslim guards. The Orthodox monasteries of Dečani, Dević in the Drenica region and the Peć Patriarchate were protected by armed guards selected by local Albanian Muslim communities in whose territory each monastery was situated and confirmed by the ecclesiastic authorities and by written orders of the Sultans.[3] Towns that had surrendered to the Ottomans by treaty kept their churches undisturbed: in Kastoria 70 small medieval churches survived, in Prilep half a dozen, in Serres (taken in 1383), all the churches remained in Christian hands. The Ottomans, who settled in the towns had to build their own mosques outside the towns walls and continued to do so until 1912.

In places taken by force, the situation was different. By right of conquest everything inside the captured city belonged legally to the victor. Yet, for practical reasons, when the number of Muslim settlers in one particular town remained relatively low for example, Christians kept their churches. A case in point is Thessaloniki.[4] Although their city had been taken during a violent siege and the Christians had in theory forfeited their right to keep their old churches, the small Greek Christian community kept more than 30 churches throughout the Ottoman centuries. To witness the confiscation of Christian churches in Thessaloniki one has to go back to 1492, when Grenada, the last Muslim stronghold in Spain, fell to Their Catholic Majesties Ferdinand of Aragon and Isabella of Castilia. The defeated Muslims were baptised by force against the stipulations of the treaty of surrender, while the massive expulsion of Arabs from Spain provoked a wave of anti-Christian riots in North Africa and Ottoman territories.

---

[3]For these monastic guards see especially Mark Krasniqi, 'Manastirske Vojvode u Kosovsko-Metohijskoj Oblast,' in: *Glasnik Muzeja Kosova* I Metohije, III, (Prishtina 1958), pp. 107–28. Olga Žirojević published a number of sixteenth century Ottoman documents preserved in the Monastery of Dećani, giving an inside perspective of the relation between the Muslim state and the Christian monastery and its property.

[4]In the fourteenth century, according to the detailed research of Ovide Tafrali, the city had 53 churches and 19 monasteries. Only two were taken by the victors and transformed into mosques. Some other churches, apparently damaged during the conquest, were demolished and their expensive marble decoration was taken to Adrianople/Edirne, Murad's capital, as is reported in the written sources.

In several Ottoman cities, angry Muslim mobs took over churches and transformed them into mosques. It is not by chance that the Dominicans of Istanbul and their Galata church became the victim of Muslim mob rule, as they were precisely the religious order that was the most fervent persecutor of non-Catholics—the 'Domini Canes' or the 'Dogs of God'—a very well known fact to the Arab refugees flooding Istanbul. A fabricated moral justification for taking away the church maintains that it was originally the mosque of Maslama, the Umayyad Prince who had besieged Constantinople in the seventh century and had received from the Byzantine Emperor the right to build a mosque. The real Mosque of Maslama, however, had been inside the walled city of Constantinople and not in the suburb of Galata on the opposite side of the Golden Horn. In Thessaloniki, the great church of St. Demetrius was taken and converted into the Kasimiyye Mosque. The Sultan, the pious Bayezid II, could do little other than accept the illegal take over and allot State funds to maintain the buildings and pay their staff.

Another aspect of the behaviour of the Islamic state towards Christian churches is illustrated by what happened in Skopje. Skopje was conquered in 1392 by Ottoman forces under Pasa Yiğit Bey, a story very little known except through the work of the early sixteenth century historian Kemalpaşa-zâde. His account, recently published and not yet noticed by local Macedonian historians, describes in some detail the fierce struggle for Skopje, centred on a fortified monastery on a hill outside the walled city. This can only be the Monastery of Sv. Georgi na Serava, the little tributary of the Vardar River that separates the hill from Skopje proper. The monastery was burnt and remained a ruin until 1436–1437 (840 H.), more than 40 years after the conquest, when Sultan Murad II constructed his Great Mosque on the same site. The Ottomans had ruled that places of worship unused by other religious groups for more than forty years could be transformed into mosques, or demolished and replaced by mosques. This happened in Skopje and elsewhere as well, most memorably in the case of the Little Aya Sophia in Constantinople, a work of Emperor Justinian, that was transformed into a mosque in 1506–1507.[5]

---

[5]During his Grand Vizierate (1506–1511) Hadim Ali Pasha transformed the famous church of the Holy Saviour in Chora to the Kahriye Mosque. In the last years of the fifteenth century the great church of St. Andrew in Krisei, was

A different story is offered by the fate of the churches of the Epirotic capital and the old Christian and Islamic cultural centre of Ioánnina, annexed to the Ottoman Empire by treaty in 1430. A deputation of the nobility travelled all the way to Thessalonica to offer their town and province to Sultan Murad II. From 1430 till 1611 the Greeks of Ioánnina and the Ottoman newcomers lived in relative harmony together: the Christians had 25 churches and five monasteries in the walled town, the Ottomans had their mosques outside the walls. In 1611 the ex-Bishop of Trikkala, the magician Dionysus 'the Dog's Philosopher' (*Skylosophos*), who had been deposed by the Church because of his activities as astrologer and his alleged contact with demons (therefore also called "*Demonosophos*"), excited a crowd of illiterate peasants with his magic and staged a revolt.[6] Mobs exterminated the Muslim population of two villages, took Ioánnina in a surprise attack, and slaughtered the Muslim and Jewish inhabitants. The revolt was suppressed by regular troops, but the old treaty had been broken. The news was reported to the Central government in Istanbul and in 1612–1613, after some hesitation, a *ferman* (Imperial Order) was sent to Ioánnina to authorise the deportation of half the Christian inhabitants from the old walled town; two years later, the order came from Istanbul to remove the remaining half and confiscate all churches inside the city walls. Christians were allowed to build new houses and churches in the suburbs and did so; Muslims and Jewish inhabitants moved into town, churches were demolished or given a different function and disappeared in time. On the site of the former Prodromos Monastery on the highest point of the walled town, the Ottoman Governor of Epirus,

---

made into the Mosque of Mustafa Pasha by Sultan Bayezid's Vizier Koca Mustafa Pasha. For these churches, see the solid survey of dates and plans of Marcell Restle, *Reclams Kunstführer Istanbul, Bursa, Edirne, Iznik*, (Stuttgart 1976), pp. 158–74 and pp. 182–92. For a more popular account see: Süleyman Krimtayif, *Converted Byzantine Churches in Istanbul*, their transformation into Mosques and Masdjids, (Istanbul 2001).

[6]For the revolt see the chronicles published by François Pouqueville, *Voyage de la Grèce*, vol. V, in its entirety and as extracts by William Martin Leake, *Travels in Northern Greece*, (London 1835), vol. IV, pp. 562–67, Skylopophos on p. 563–4. For the Sultan's order see: L. Vranousis, *Istorika kai topografika tou mesaionikou kastrou ton Ioanninon*, (Athens 1968), pp. 37–9. Official copies of the original order must be preserved in the Prime Minister's Archives, henceforth B.B.O.A. in Istanbul but have not yet been spotted.

Arslan Pasha, completed in 1617–1618 the construction of a *külliye* (complex), consisting of a mosque, a great theological college, a hot bath and *imaret* (kitchen for the poor and the students). It was the betrayal of the treaty of 1430 that caused these great changes in Ioánnina.

One last aspect of the situation of Christian churches in the Ottoman period has to be mentioned in this context. The *Sheriât* did allow Christians and Jews to repair their old churches and synagogues and even to erect new ones, but only on the site of a decaying old one.[7] Yet, besides the legal reality, there was the reality of the daily practice of running a multi-religious and multi-lingual Empire. New research based on thousands of volumes of the protocol books of the Cadi courts, some dating as far back as the mid-fifteenth century, show that the Cadis were much more concerned with the 'nizâm-i alâm', or 'keeping the World in Balance' rather than with the strict letter of the *Sheriât*. How can we explain the many churches and synagogues in cities that did not exist in the Byzantino–Slavic Middle Ages and were founded by the Ottomans, or emerged out of market places and local administrative centres? In Sarajevo, Mostar or Banja Luka in Bosnia, or in Razgrad, Osman Pazar (Omurtag), Tatar Pazardžik and scores of other places, no one could ever claim that there had been a church or synagogue before the 'Imperial Conquest'. In order to build or repair a church or synagogue written permission of the authorities was needed, some times from the Cadi but more often from Istanbul. In the local Balkan historiography a lot of fuss is made about these permissions. What is simply forgotten is that permission from Istanbul was needed also for every new mosque, or for the simple upgrading of a *mesdjid* to a mosque for the Friday service.

---

[7] See the article 'Dhimma' in *Encyclopaedia of Islam*, 2, vol. II, 1965, pp. 227–31, or H A R Gibb—J H Kramers, *Concise Encycl. of Islam*, fourth impression, (Boston–Leiden 2001), p. 75–6. With more detail (but still incomplete) Antoine Fattal, *Le statut legál des non-musulmans en pays d'Islam*, (Beirut 1958). For the Ottoman context, see F W Hasluck, *Christianity and Islam under the Sultans*, 2 vols, (Oxford 1929), still unsurpassed. On the problems of church building, a different perspective is offered by Rossitsa Gradeva, 'Ottoman Policy towards Christian Church Buildings', best accessible in *Rumeli under the Ottomans, 15th–18th Centuries: Iinstitutions and Communities*, (Istanbul: Isis Press 2004), pp. 339–68.

Where the interrelation between the various religious groups was good, the non-Muslims could do much more than the strict rules of the *Sheriât* allowed. This tolerance is not to be found only in written documents, it was a practice in local communities. For example, the many new monasteries in Northern Bosnia, in border zones wrested from the Hungarians in the early decades of the sixteenth century after a protracted period of warfare, were the result of the settlement of Orthodox Christian auxiliaries to the Ottomans: the Vlachs, or Iflak. The monumental and architecturally rich monasteries of Gomionica, Liplje, Mostanica, Ozren, Paprača, Vozuća or Tamna are good illustrations of this point.[8]

Good mutual relations and comradeship in arms were more important than the letter of the Law. Yet in other areas, where relations were strained, nothing more could be done that the minimum allowed by the Law. A special case is the restoration of the independent Serbian church organisation in 1557. Internal problems in the Church had led to the disappearance of an independent ecclesiastical organisation under a Patriarch. In 1557, when the famous Sokollo Mehmed Pasha was Beylerbey (Governor-General) of Ottoman Europe, Sultan Süleyman decreed that the Serbian church should regain its independent status. This ushered in a wave of building and restoration of churches that

---

[8]Gomionica is first mentioned in the Ottoman *tahrir defter* T.D. 432 from 1540 under the name 'Monastery of Zalužje', then again in an Ottoman document of 1560, of which a copy is preserved in the Ahkam Defter No 2775 in the Istanbul B.B.O.A. It is a petition of the Sandjak Bey of Bosnia to Istanbul to grant a *timar* (an estate in usufruct) to the Abbot Andrija of the 'Monastery of Zalužje, alias Gomionica', who for 24 years as the abbot of the mentioned monastery 'ha[d] merits for the stability of the settlement and peaceful and favourable situation in the wider area around the monastery.' Important parts of rich fresco from the second half of the sixteenth century, made by the best artist of the period but later covered by layers of plaster, have been discovered in 1982 in the dome, the choir and the nave of the Gomionica church. In 1994–1996 other high quality frescoes, dating back to the seventeenth century, were discovered in the refectory. But during the recent extensive archaeological excavation underneath the church not a single trace of an older construction was found. The monastery was new and must be regarded as a typical product of the Ottoman manner in dealing with these kinds of problems. A number of these monasteries show profound Islamic influences in their architecture, construction and decoration, especially at Mostanica and Paprača.

went on for decades, in the great monasteries as well in the villages.[9] Sokollo Mehmed, a Bosnian Serb by origin, had his brother Makarije appointed Patriarch of the restored Serbian church and his nephew Savatije Archbishop of the Herzegovina, which in that time included large parts of the present-day Montenegro. In the church of Budisavci in Kosovo a full-scale portrait of the Patriarch dated 1568 is preserved. Near the sources of the river Piva in Montenegro stands the giant church of the Pivski Manastir, erected between 1573 and 1586 at the expenditure of Savatije, who later became Serbian Patriarch himself.

Church building and painting in Serbia and Kosovo went on even during the less prosperous seventeenth century. The real break of this pattern came during the long war against the 'Holy League' of Christian powers (1683–1699), when in 1689 large Austrian and German armies invaded Serbia, Macedonia and Western Bulgaria and almost split Ottoman Europe in two. This invasion was accompanied by untold destruction and loss of life, only to be compared with the destruction of Germany during the Thirty Years War of Religion (1618–1648). Great Balkan cities like Sarajevo, Skopje, Prizren or Novi Pazar and scores of smaller ones went up in flames. During this cruel conflict many monasteries were ruined and remained deserted for long periods of time. Between 1738 and 1739 the same happened on a lesser scale. In the particular case of Kosovo it led to the emigration of many thousands of Serbs and Catholic Albanians and their replacement by Muslim Albanian mountaineers. Yet, despite the destruction, Kosovo or Serbia are still studded by churches and monasteries. In conclusion, attributing the destruction of monuments of culture to religious animosities of particular groups in the Ottoman period is simplistic. It is in the context of war that provides a better explanation, in Kosovo, elsewhere in the region, and in other countries altogether.

During World War II, Croatian Ustashas (Roman Catholic) destroyed almost all Serbian Orthodox monasteries[10] of the Fruška Gora, or

---

[9]For the political background of the restoration of 1557, the stylistic peculiarities of the wall paintings and their program, as well as a gazetteer of the preserved monuments see the epochal work of Sreten Petković, *Zidno Slikarstvo na području Pećke Patriašije, 1557–1614*, (Novi Sad 1965), especially pp. 14–32, which is the key to the rich further literature. (Substantial English summary, pp. 215–27).

[10]At the time of my visits in the 1970s many of these monasteries were still in ruins.

'Frankish Mountains', the wooded hills north of Belgrade that at the time of the First Bulgarian Empire (eighth to tenth century) constituted the border with the Carolingian Empire of Charlemagne. In the sixteenth century, when the area was well within the Ottoman borders, almost two dozen Orthodox monasteries sprang up there; the architectonically richest among them were Rakovo, Petkovica and first of all Novo Hopovo, with a church, completed in 1576, as big as the ones of the Medieval Serbian empire. In 1992–1995 a wave of destruction swept over Bosnia and Herzegovina. In the parts of the country that were dominated or occupied by the Orthodox Christian Serbs every Islamic object, including some of the oldest and most beautiful mosques of the entire Balkans, all officially recognised 'monuments of culture', were systematically destroyed.[11] In the territories occupied by the Roman Catholic Croats some of the oldest and artistically most valuable Serbian Orthodox monasteries and village churches were blown up and the ruins removed. A case in point is the venerable monastery of Žitomislić on the Neretva, 17 kilometres downstream from Mostar, founded in the second half of the sixteenth century by an Orthodox Christian nobleman in Ottoman service, the Sipahi Milislav Hrabren Miloradović. It suffered terribly in 1941, during World War II, when it was set on fire and its monks were killed. In the war of 1992–1995 it was totally razed to the ground. When in 1993 Croat troops regained control of Mostar, they blew up the great Orthodox cathedral built in 1863–1873, one of the most monumental works of architecture in the country, constructed with the financial help of the Ottoman Sultan Abdülaziz. Its giant ruins still 'crown' the town of Mostar. As late as 2001 Macedonian Christian extremists burned down dozens of mosques, including the fifteenth century Çarşi Camii (Mosque of the Market) of Prilep. In Tetovo/Kalkandelen, Macedonia, first security forces, then paramilitary groups fired with machine guns

---

[11]To cite only the most important: Foča on the Drina, Aladža Džamija, 1550 (called: 'the Pearl of the Balkans'); Banja Luka, Ferhadije Mosque, 1579, idem, Defterdarevo Mosque, 1594–1595; Čajniče, Sinan Pasha Borovinić Mosque and mausolea, 1570–1571; Knežina, Sultan Selim's Mosque, 1518–1519. For the destruction of the Ottoman monuments of Banja Luka see the richly illustrated monograph of Aleksander Ravlič, *Banjalučka Ferhadija*, (Rijeka 1996). For the artistic value of the Aladja Mosque in Foča see the rich monograph of Andrej Andrejević (also a Bosnian Serb), *Aladža Džamija u Foπi* (Belgrade, 1972).

at the famous Aladža Mosque, a monument under the protection of UNESCO. The building survived, but the local Macedonian-Christian authorities long prevented its restoration under all sorts of pretexts. The shield stating that the building was under protection of UNESCO has miraculously disappeared. In Kosovo in 1998–1999 Serbs destroyed the whole historical Islamic town centres of Gjakova/ Djakovica, Peja/Peć and Vushtrri/Vučitrn. In the aftermath of the war, Albanians retaliated by destroying or badly damaging works of art, in this case Byzantino–Slavic architecture and priceless fourteenth century frescoes.[12]

These waves of destruction were never exclusive to the Balkans. In the mid-fifteenth century, at the end of the Hundred Years War, the French noblemen Jean Jouvenil de Oursin gave an overview of the countless monasteries and churches that had been destroyed in the Midi, Central and Southern France either by the French or by the English. In the German province of Mecklenburg-Vorpommern we can still see today the churches ruined by the armies of the Thirty Years War (1618–1648) and later repaired in the course of the eighteenth century, when the province started to recover from the conflict that had killed four-fifths of its population. In my own country, Holland, one can still see ruins of churches destroyed in 1574 during the Dutch Revolt against Spain, and from the time of the French invasion of 1672: Bergen N.H., Egmond-Binnen, Heemskerk, or Ammersooien are good cases in point. In the western half of the German federal state of Baden-Würthemberg and the southern half of Rheinland-Pfalz, there are no churches older than the early eighteenth century. Buildings from the Romanesque and Gothic periods had disappeared as a result of the deliberated policy of the French King Louis XIV to destroy the entire land, *brulez le Palatinate*.

---

[12]For these actions and their results see the special report of the UNESCO investigations, *Cultural Heritage in South-East Europe: Kosovo, Protection and Conservation of Multi-Ethnic Heritage in Danger*, Mission Report, 26–30 April 2004, *Cultural Heritage in South-East Europe Series*, no. 2, (Venice: UNESCO, 2004).

8. Was the Albanian opposition to the Serb Kingdom's annexation in 1912 without justification?

Ivo Banac

THE ALLEGATION

What happened in Kosovo after World War I was not just a 'change of occupiers', the Serbian master replacing the Turkish one, as some circles like to portray it. The fact is that after centuries of social immobility, Kosovo suddenly went through a revolutionary change. The Serbian liberation on Kosovo, in a small way, resembled the Napoleonic push through Europe. It opened many doors to Albanians. That they were unable or unwilling to use them is another matter.

(Alex N Dragnich, retired Political Science Professor at Vanderbilt University and Slavko Todorovich, former broadcaster for the Voice of America).[1]

In 1912 the Serbian army advanced into Kosova, defeated the Ottoman forces, and took over the *vilayet*. For Serbia the annexation meant not only the liberation of long lost territory, but also the opportunity to civilize Kosova. This opinion was shared by many western commentators at the time, the British historian G M Trevelyan among them. But for Albanians in Kosova, the annexation represented a violent separation from the other Albanian territories. The decade that followed was punctuated by internal armed resistance even after the end of World War I.

---

[1]*The Saga of Kosovo. Focus on Serbian–Albanian Relations,* East European Monographs. (Boulder: Columbia University Press, 1984), p. 122.

The Answer

The nineteenth-century national movements in the Ottoman Balkans developed belatedly among the predominantly Muslim peoples, most notably among the Albanians. Although the diaspora community of the Catholic Arbëresh in southern Italy promoted Albanian statehood as early as 1876, most Albanian leaders were content to advance purely defensive projects during the period of the Great Eastern Crisis (1875–1878), that is, the projects that would prevent the carve-up of Ottoman Albanian territories (e.g., the turning over of the Gusinje district to Montenegro at the Congress of Berlin). Out of this arose the more obviously political programs which called for a single autonomous Albanian province (*villayet*) that would be governed by the Albanian-speaking Ottoman officials and where the language of instruction in the schools would be Albanian. This was the program of the League of Prizren, an all-Albanian political effort, but typically centered on the north which, with Kosovo and the Shkodër area, was politically the most articulate of the Albanian regions.

It cannot be argued that the north was more traditionalist than the other Albanian regions. The presence of Albanian Catholics made it somewhat more open to the European-based modernist ideas, including nationalism. Its proximity to dangers that were stemming from the independent Balkan states, notably Serbia and Montenegro, as well as to the possible Austro–Hungarian, Italian, and other Power incursions, certainly made it more vibrant politically. Hence the leagues of Prizren (1878) and Peja (1899) and the calls for the unification of the 'four Albanian *villayets*' (Kosovo, Shkodër, Monastir [Bitola] and Ioannina) that were significant posts on the ledger of northern activism. The north and the diaspora (the Frashëri brothers, Terenc Toçi) shaped the idea of Albanian identity and autonomy, frequently at odds with the competing identities—Slavic and non-Slavic.

The traditional Ottoman order in the Balkans was undermined not only by the national revolutionary movements but, too, by the various Westernizing reforms. The latter regularly were viewed with suspicion by the traditionalist Balkan Muslim elites, who preferred a measure of self-rule under the loosest of Ottoman bonds. Hence, the trauma of 1912 in Kosovo was provoked, in addition to the heterodox Serbian nationalist rule, by various modernist innovations that accompanied it. The resistance of Albanians to the Young Turk innovations was renowned. In fact, it was the Albanian revolt, mainly in Kosovo, that compelled the Ottoman government to grant autonomy to the territorially undefined Albania on 18 August 1912, and which in turn provoked the military phase of the Balkan alliance against Istanbul. Still, the Albanians were more interested in being left to their own devices than in having a national state, least of all an alien one that the Serbs imposed on them. Moreover, they were quite unprepared for the ideological implications of Serbian nationalism, which systematically dehumanized them and portrayed them as a minority in their own land.

It should be noted that the Serbian cult of Kosovo, centered on the 1389 battle, was not a central theme of Serbian nationalism—and hence a legitimizing device for the Serbian claims to Kosovo, until the 1860s. As a relatively new addition in the thesaurus of Serbian nationalism, the cult of Kosovo concealed the weaknesses of Serbian claims to this area, until they became wiped away as a result of the Balkan wars. What Milan Rakić and other Serbian visitors to pre-1912 Kosovo saw as pretense would be endowed with authority by the victorious Serbian army. When the Montenegrins and Serbians attacked the Ottoman state in October 1912 they encountered weak Ottoman resistance. The only significant obstacles to Serbian advances were mounted by the Albanian units of Isa Boletini, Idriz Seferi, and Bajram Curri. Serbian behavior in turn was harsh and replete with massacres.

The Serbian war aim was the acquisition of Kosovo and the whole northern Albanian land mass from Lake Ohrid to the Adriatic, thus giving Serbia the littoral area south of Ulcinj to Durrës, and perhaps even to the mouth of the Shkumbin. In the process, some 20,000 to 25,000 Albanians were massacred, notably in the towns of Ferizaj, Prizren, and Gjakova. The aim was to promote the Serbian claims by 'ethnic cleansing' and statistical manipulation before the inevitable Powers' conference that would finalize the new borders. The conference that was convened in London (December 1912) confronted strenuous Austro–Hungarian opposition to any Serbian access to the Adriatic, but also Vienna's support for the independence of Albania. These views as seconded by Italy, and broadly by Britain were quickly adopted by all powers. There ensued a significant haggling over the borders of Albania, with Austria–Hungary arguing for the new state's rights to much of Kosovo and present-day western Macedonia. France and Russia in turn supported the Serbian claims to Peja, Gjakova, Prizren, Debar, and Ohrid. Despite the gains of all of these salients, the Serbian nationalists viewed the results of the war as unfair. Contention over the borders with Albania would continue well after World War I, the first serious foreign adventure of the new Kingdom of Serbs, Croats, and Slovenes being the attempt to seize the Lume area (south of Prizren) from Albania in the late summer of 1920. One of the unintended consequences of this action was the loss of territory to Austria in Carinthia; many Slovene voters were deterred from opting for Yugoslavia, in a territorial plebiscite held in October 1920, for fear of being recruited into the units involved in Albania.

The policies of the Serbian military in Kosovo were denounced by a small band of Serbian socialists and such foreign leftists as Leon Trotsky. Dimitrije Tucović, a Serbian socialist leader, noted in his important book *Serbia and Albania: A Contribution to a Critique of the Serbian Bourgeoisie's Policy of Conquest* (1914) that 'it is nowadays very risky to preach the need of common work with the Albanians. In the pernicious contest to justify a wrong policy the [Serbian] bourgeois press has created a tower of false and tendentious views about the Albanians, while Serbia's policy of conquest with its barbaric methods must have filled the Albanians with a deep hatred toward us. But that was not so in the past. As can be seen from the accounts of Marko Miljanov [Montenegrin military commander and writer], the Serbian and Albanian tribes lived in close contact under the Turkish rule. They were bound by a high degree of social reciprocity that was expressed in many common customs, traditions, and memories, as well as in the common actions against the Turkish authorities.'[2]

Given the nature of Serbian occupation in 1912, the Serbian policy of seizing the Albanian lands and settling them with colonists, introducing various new taxes and humiliations, it is small wonder that Serbian rule was accompanied by major rebellions (Lume rebellion in 1913) and resistance. That is why in November 1915 the Austro–Hungarian occupation forces, and initially even the Bulgarians, were welcomed in Kosovo as liberators. Vienna treated Kosova as a temporarily occupied

---

[2]Dimitrije Tucović, *Srbija i Arbanija: Jedan prilog kritici zavojevačke politike srpske buržoazije*, (Belgrade, 1914), pp. 113–4.

part of Albania and tried to please the local population by opening Albanian-language schools and promoting the new Albanian literary standard. It can be concluded that the Kosovar Albanians had good reasons to resist in 1912. Their resistance would mount with the return of the Serbian rule in 1918.

9. Is the complaint about the Serb state's deportation policy of Albanians between the two World Wars based on myth?

Noel Malcolm

THE ALLEGATION

Most of the land available for homesteading belonged to Turks who had left with the Turkish army, or who had moved to Asia Minor. Some of this migration continued until the late 1930s. About 40,000 Turks left Kosovo and other South Serbian regions, and many from Bosnia as well. Another 40,000 were Albanians who, being Muslims, declared themselves Turks. The official policy of Belgrade was to encourage Turks and Albanians to leave. In the process there were some injustices and abuses, but this was not the intention of the law.

(Alex N Dragnich, retired Political Science Professor at Vanderbilt University and Slavko Todorovich, former broadcaster for the Voice of America).[1]

Discontent with the new state among the ethnic Albanian masses stepped up emigration to Turkey, in whose Muslim environment they felt at home. Many openly admitted that they could not bear being ruled over by members of the former infidel masses, Serbs, whom they pejoratively called Ski (Slavs) ... By the 1930s, thousands of ethnic Albanian and Turkish families had voluntarily moved to Turkey.

(Dušan Bataković, Former Ambassador of Serbia and Montenegro in Greece, historian and advisor of President Boris Tadić on Kosova).[2]

---

[1]*The Saga of Kosovo. Focus on Serbian–Albanian Relations*, East European Monographs. Boulder, (New York: Columbia University Press, 1984), p. 121.
[2]'The Age of Restoration', in *The Kosovo Chronicle* (Belgrade: Plato, 1992) also http://www.batakovic.com [Consulted 4 April 2006].

The contention is that Albanians' complaint of a policy of mass expulsion to Turkey between the two World Wars is not based on reality. If there was any migration, it must have been voluntary.

The Answer

A policy for deportation of Albanians was not only discussed in official circles in Belgrade, but actually embodied in a formal treaty with Turkey; however, the outbreak of World War II prevented the treaty from being put into effect.

The discussions among Serbian civil servants took place in the period 1937–1939 in the 'Serbian Cultural Club' in Belgrade. They were concerned at the failure of the colonization programme to create an absolute Serb majority in the Kosovar population: at best, they calculated that it had raised the Serb element from 24 to 38 per cent. (Ottoman statistics suggest, however, that the starting point was lower than that.) One participant in the discussions proposed bringing in another 470,000 colonists and expelling 300,000 Albanians. The most influential participant was Vaso Čubrilović, a Bosnian Serb, who had been one of the organizers of the assassination of Archduke Franz Ferdinand in 1914. As he pointed out: 'At a time when Germany can expel tens of thousands of Jews … the shifting of a few hundred thousand Albanians will not lead to the outbreak of a world war.' His ideas were set out in 1937 in an unusually detailed policy document, which was intended to act as a blueprint for administering such a mass expulsion.[3]

Čubrilović's proposals would have found many sympathetic listeners and readers in government circles in Belgrade. (Another leading intellectual, the novelist Ivo Andrić, who worked in the Foreign Ministry, also wrote a paper recommending the expulsion of the Muslim Albanians.) The idea itself was not new: in 1926 the Yugoslav government had asked Turkey if it would be willing to take between 300,000 and 400,000 Albanians, and further negotiations on this topic had taken place in 1933–1935. Eventually, in July 1938, a formal treaty was drawn up and initialled by the two governments. Under this agreement, Turkey was to take 40,000 families of 'Turks', receiving a payment

---

[3]Čubrilović, *The Expulsion of Albanians*, (1936), http://www.albanianhistory.net/texts/AH25.html [Last consulted 26 March 2006].

from Belgrade of 500 Turkish pounds per family. A family was defined as 'blood relations living under one roof', which in Kosova would have included many extended families of ten members or more. Since the treaty excluded the inhabitants of towns, and since most of the small Turkish-speaking population of Kosova was urban, it is clear that the measure was in fact aimed at Muslim Albanians, not Turks.

As has been mentioned already, the outbreak of the war prevented this treaty from being put into effect. So it can be said that the (formal) policy was never implemented. Informally, however, a similar policy had been in force for a long time. Full statistical evidence is not available, and estimates vary, but it would be reasonable to say that between 90,000 and 150,000 Albanians and other Muslims left Kosova in the period between the two wars. Many thousands had also left after the initial conquest in 1912.

Those Muslims were responding to a variety of pressures, including forced conversions to Orthodoxy (in the initial period), the suppression of Albanian-language education, the colonization process, heavy reprisals for the kaçak guerrilla actions, and the confiscation of Albanian land. In 1938 more than 6,000 people, the population of 23 villages in the Drenica region of Kosova, were deprived of their land. The official policy was to allow such people only 0.4 hectares per family member. As one Serbian policy document put it: 'This is below the minimum for subsistence. But that is and has been our aim: to make their life impossible, and in that way to force them to emigrate.' The effects of this informal policy were not as great, in numerical terms, as those of the formal policy would have been; but here too the advent of war may have saved the Albanian population from what would otherwise have been a much larger exodus.

10. Is it true that Tito's Yugoslav policies favored Albanians in Kosova?

Ivo Banac

THE ALLEGATION

According to this allegation, Tito's policies of decentralization, and all other decisions that were dictated by his concern with curbing the role of Serbia in the federal system of Yugoslavia, favored Albanians in Kosova. The 1986 impassioned petition to the Assemblies of the Socialist Federal Republic of Yugoslavia and the Republic of Serbia, signed by more than 200 intellectuals, Orthodox clergy and retired army officers, warns that:

Under cover of the struggle against 'Great-Serb hegemonism' a rigged political trial of the Serb nation and its history has been going on for decades ... There is no national minority in the world which has greater constitutional rights [than the Albanians in Yugoslavia], but its leaders and ideologues are leading it into a national adventure in which it can lose all.[1]

This opinion is shared by other observers of Yugoslav politics:

This Josip Broz Tito, the Great-Slovene Communist, concluded before World War II that Yugoslavia could be recreated only on the basis of a weakened and constructed Serbia. Thus Tito prevented the return of one hundred thousand Serbs exiled from Kosovo during the Fascist–Nazi occupation and allowed some seventy-five thousand Albanians who had migrated north in that period to remain in Kosovo, thus shifting the ethnic makeup of the region. He then provided autonomous rights to the Kosovo

---

[1]Branka Magaš, *The Destruction of Yugoslavia. Tracking the Break-up 1980–1992* (London: Verso, 1993), pp. 50–1.

> *Albanians, eventually empowering them in the provincial government, in education and the police.*
> (David Binder, retired Washington, DC-based correspondent for *The New York Times*).[2]

The Answer

Various myths about the nature of the Tito regime include variations on the theme of his personal responsibility—for good or for ill—in various decisions taken by the Yugoslav authorities during his long period in power (1944–1980). Tito has been portrayed as a Croat renegade, crypto-Great Serb, frustrated liberal, and, most significantly, from the point of view of Serb nationalists, Tito was seen as the executor of a Croat–Slovene 'lasting coalition for the political domination' of Yugoslavia.[3] Hence, Tito's option for more autonomy for Kosovo after 1968 supposedly reflected his anti-Serbian bias. Likewise, other leading figures of the early regime, notably the security chief Aleksandar Ranković, were seen as exponents of specific national interests—in Ranković's case that of Serbia.

Milovan Djilas dispelled the various claims about the Tito regime in an aside in his memoirs, in which he ridiculed attempts to 'whiten' Tito by 'blackening his closest associates from the prewar, wartime, and postwar (anti-Soviet) periods ... In the claims of Croat as well as Albanian nationalists that Ranković carried out a special, personal, regime in Croatia and in Kosovo, we are confronted not just with the misrepresentation of events but with the propagandistic exploitation of the fact that Ranković was a Serbian. There never was any "Ranković regime", at least while I was in power. All of it was Tito's regime— the regime of Tito and of the group that coalesced around him before the war.'[4]

And, indeed, the repression that was pursued in Kosovo in the last phases of the war, the suppression of Shaban Polluzha's revolt in Drenica (1944–1945), the prohibition of return of the Slavic colonists to

---

[2]'The Yugoslav Earthquake', *Mediterranean Quarterly*, Winter 2001, pp. 11–21, and p. 16.
[3]Memorandum of the Serbian Academy, 1986.
[4]Milovan Djilas, *Vlast*, (London, 1983), p. 14.

Kosovo (1945), the decision to give 'Kosovo and Metohija' the status of a region (*oblast*) and not, like Vojvodina, that of a province (*pokrajina*) in 1945, the harsh Serbian-dominated regime that lasted until 1966 and which included rigged trials that implicated leading Kosovar Albanian Communists (Prizren trial, 1956), the relaxation and various moves that increased the rights of Albanians and the autonomy of Kosovo (1966–1981), are not indications of inconsistency in the policy of Tito and his government, but rather an aspect of politics that were made outside Kosovo and frequently without regard for Kosovo.

The primary decision of the Tito regime toward Kosovo was the decision to retain this entity within the Serbian federal unit of the Yugoslav federation. There were other options, including the turning over of Kosovo to Albania. That option was ruled out for reasons of practicality, without endangering Kosovo's access to Albania, which was to all intents and purposes unlimited until the Stalin–Tito break of 1948. But the fact remains that Tito's Communists were weakest in Serbia at the end of the war. Tito deprived Serbia of the monopoly of power, of its dynasty, of the established church. He legitimated the Montenegrin identity and the autonomies of Vojvodina and Kosovo. This had to be compensated by the prerogatives that Serbia actually obtained in the 1940s and 1950s and that in turn tipped the balance of power dangerously in the direction of centralism and Serbian dominance. The anti-centralist measures that followed the downfall of Ranković (1966) and culminated in the Constitution of 1974 addressed these imbalances. Still, even during the period of centralism the Communist regime could not do less than maintain the national rights of the interwar period. Hence, the Albanian language, however discriminated, had an official standing and, especially because of the doggedness of Albanian resistance, it was not possible to allow the return of Slavic colonists or to deny the distinct status of Kosovo.

The Tito regime was a strict Stalinist enterprise even after Stalin's break with Tito in 1948. The mistreatment of Albanians in Yugoslavia after 1948 was in part an aspect of the bad relations with Enver Hoxha's Albania that contributed to the typically Stalinist criminalization of the whole Albanian population in Yugoslavia. Not until the early 1950s did the Yugoslav regime start developing ideological alternatives to Stalinism, and even then never in the direction of limiting or abandoning the regime's monopoly of power. Hence, the manufacture of palliatives that rendered an extenuating representation of what was effectively a single-party dictatorship. The choices among these palliatives were the system of workers' self-management in production (instead of free trade unions) and of federalization in governance (instead of democracy). In that sense the Albanians from Kosovo got the maximum of what the regime offered: limited equality with the other regime elites (participation in the rotation system after 1974) and institutional autonomy (provincial party committee and legislative assembly, university, academy of sciences, distinct media). But in Kosovo they did not get the status of a republic, which was contrary to the regime dogma; the status of republic was reserved for the *narodi* (constituent nations) of Yugoslavia, not for the *narodnosti* (nationalities; euphemism for minorities) that realized the fullness of their statehood elsewhere—in Albania, in the case of Yugoslav Albanians.

From the Serbian nationalist point of view all of Kosovo's achievements after 1966 were excessive, as Dobrica Ćosić argued in the Central Committee of the League of Communists of Serbia (SKS) in May 1968. Insistence on equality (province not region, provincial constitution not statute, the right to use the national symbols and flags) or on Albanian-preferred usage (Kosovo not the acronym Kosmet for Kosovo and Metohija) were all seen as attempts that equated the status of provinces (specifically that of Kosovo) to the federal republics. Reactions to such demands, according to the veteran Serbian Communist Dragoslav Marković, 'are harsh among the Serbs and, frequently, nationalistic'.[5] Marković himself, moreover, in Tito's lifetime, initiated the proceedings of a SKS CC working group that was unofficially known as *The Blue Book* (March 1977). This was a polemic against the new constitutional position of the autonomous provinces and led to a clash in the SKS CC in which the Kosovo leader Mahmut Bakalli was joined by the Vojvodina Serbs Dušan Alimpić and Stevan Doronjski, as well as by the Serbian anti-nationalists Miloš Minić and Mirko Popović. The recommendations of *The Blue Book* for the diminution of the provincial prerogatives were not adopted, nor was *The Blue Book* itself sanctioned. The time for a counterattack required a weaker federal center, which would be possible after Tito's death. But as Marković noted in June 1977, 'All is known, all is clear.'[6]

---

[5]Dragoslav Draža Marković, *Život i politika, 1967–1978*. vol. 1, (Belgrade, 1987), p. 64.
[6]Ibid., vol. 2, p. 367.

So, were the Albanians favored under Tito? No, they, like all the other political factors in Communist-era Yugoslavia, were an object of a great game that was fought within an autocratic party that held the monopoly of power, and whose internal relations were governed by an outworn, though occasionally updated doctrine of Marxism–Leninism as interpreted in Belgrade, but also by various ongoing practical concerns. After Tito's death there existed a consensus in the SKS for the revamping of the Yugoslav Constitution of 1974, particularly of those articles that defined the status of the autonomous provinces. The Kosovo demonstrations of 1981 merely presented an opportunity for the political debut of this consensus.

11. Is it true that Albanians collaborated with Nazi Germany during World War II?

Bernd Fischer

[As Albanians are driven out of their homes in the spring of 1999] *many Serbs see this as a fitting revenge: partly for the bombing of Serbia by NATO, but also for the 'cleansing' to which they themselves were subjected in the past.* ... *The majority of the Serb and Montenegrin inhabitants of Kosovo were virtually exterminated between April 1941 and October 1944 by the 'Ballists'. These were Kosovo Albanian fascist and nationalist militias of the 'Balli Kombëtar'. Under both masters* [Italian Fascists and German Nazis] *they committed terrible atrocities against the Serbs.*

(Tommaso Di Francesco and Giacomo Scotti, respectively correspondent for the Italian left-wing newspaper *Il Manifesto* and writer and journalist from Fiume/Rijeka).[1]

The relatively unproblematic occupation of a unified Kosova–Albania territory by the Axis Powers during World War II places Albanians once again on the 'wrong side of history' against their neighbours, and makes them accomplices of the Jewish Holocaust. This argument has a powerful impact on a discourse that explains contemporary violence, in Kosova as well as in all former Yugoslavia, as one stage in the cycle of violence opened by the traumatic experience of World War II.

---

[1]'Sixty Years of Ethnic Cleansing', *Le Monde Diplomatique*, May 1999 (also published in the Italian newspaper *Il Manifesto*, 2 May 1999).

The Answer

The relationship between the Albanians and the Axis during World War II has traditionally been somewhat of a contentious issue, but the arguments seem to have become even more pointed in light of the impending independence of Kosova. Those who oppose independence attempt to support their argument by suggesting that the Albanians of Kosova should not be allowed to join Europe as a separate political entity because they have not earned that status. This contention is supported by the fallacious assumption that Kosova lacks the moral stature of a western nation, as exhibited by the widespread pro-Nazi sentiments expressed during the war.

The Albanian experience with the Axis during World War II was, in many respects, not dissimilar to the experience of its neighbours. Like its neighbours, Albania was invaded and occupied, it provided some collaborators and offered extensive resistance. That there was less than universal support for the resistance is in part a function of the fact that the central issue during the war, in Kosova but in much of old Albania as well, was always the Serb–Albanian national question. The Axis, in particular the Germans, effectively played on this issue and also tended to be less brutal than in Yugoslavia or Greece, in an effort to maximize collaboration. But the Germans found few ideological partners, as they did elsewhere—and even those who collaborated could not be considered pro-Nazi. This was perhaps most effectively demonstrated by the widespread Albanian rescue of indigenous and foreign Jews. All Balkan peoples offered resistance to the Germans, but only the Albanians actively and extensively rescued Jews.

This is not to say, of course, that there was no relationship between Albanians and Germans during World War II—clearly there was cooperation. It must be openly understood in its comparative historical context and should not be ignored as some contemporary Kosovar historians are prone to do. It is not sufficient simply to suggest that those Albanians who cooperated with the Germans need not be discussed because they were not legitimate representatives of the nation. So if we leave aside the two extremes of 'all Albanians were pro-Nazi' and 'no real Albanians collaborated' how can we understand the relationship between and Germans and the Albanians during World War II?

Zogist Albania was the first state to fall to the Axis when, in April 1939, it was invaded by the Italians and eventually absorbed, as a supposedly separate kingdom, into Mussolini's new Roman Empire. With the German destruction of Yugoslavia in 1941, a version of 'Greater Albania' including most of Kosova, (the Germans retained Mitrovica for its mines) was created and ruled by the Italians with the aid of a number of puppet Albanian regimes. With the collapse of Italy in September 1943, Germany was forced to assume the role of the occupation power in Albania. The seriously overburdened Germans had one very clear priority—to secure the Adriatic coastline and interior lines of communications with as few troops as possible. This required an Albanian regime with some genuine authority. In order to encourage cooperation, Herman Neubacher, German Foreign Minister Joachim von Ribbentrop's special representative for Southeast Europe, employed some political skill in placing heavy emphasis on the nationalist card that did much to inform German–Albanian relations. Conversant with propaganda techniques, the Germans initially covered the state with leaflets reassuring the Albanians that nothing would endanger its independence from Italy 'who robbed you and has betrayed us'. Albanian youths were complimented for their struggle against fascist Italian colonial expansion. Soon after arriving in the capital, a German general took the trouble to make a speech in which he apologized first for having occupied the country at all and second for having done so 'without first knocking on the door'.[2]

This was followed by German officials deploying Austrian soldiers and civilians in Albania; they were identified with Austro–Hungarian troops who had protected Albanians from Serbs during the World War I and had generally left a good impression. Then the Germans created what might be described as a 'soft' occupation administration. Rather than the usual formula of appointing a military governor, the German left relations with the Albanians to the German ambassador in Tirana, who proclaimed Albania's independence, along with 'relative' neutrality and 'relative' sovereignty.[3]

Neubacher insisted that the propaganda be backed by a set of policies that proved to be less brutal than those imposed in other areas under

---

[2]US National Archives, USDS, OSS, Research and Analysis Branch, Nr. 1475, Survey on Albania, p. 20, December 1943.

[3]Hermann Neubacher, *Sonderauftrag Sudost, 1940–1945: Bericht eines fliegenden Diplomaten* (Gottingen: Musterschmidt Verlag, 1956), p. 113; Captured German Records, roll T120/340, Nr. 1060, Belgrade, Neubacher, 30 September 1943.

German control. Recognizing that the Italian occupation had made fascism unpopular, Neubacher refused to allow the Germans to construct any fascist organizations. The local press was virtually free from censorship and was permitted to publish Allied communiqués.[4] Neubacher refused to allow the recruitment of forced labour, at least from pre-war or 'old' Albania. He initially was even successful in resisting SS attempts to set up an Albanian SS division, arguing that such a military contingent was incompatible with an 'independent' Albania.[5] The Germans under Neubacher refrained, for the most part, from the hunting and deporting of Jews. The Germans also encouraged their first puppet prime minister to initiate a progressive program of economic modernization and land reform, while announcing at every opportunity that the general goal of the government was to protect Albania's territorial integrity within its ethnic borders. The Albanologist Margaret Hasluck, who at that time was advising the British in Cairo, proclaimed that 'the lines of government policy would meet with our warm approval if we were not at war with the country whose armed forces now occupy Albania'.[6]

Much of this, of course, remained on paper and few had illusions about where the real power rested, but the structure was still more than a façade. The Germans hoped that their concessions would attract quality Albanian leadership that could organize a government with at least some degree of legitimacy, allowing it to unburden the Germans. Neubacher was initially disappointed since few people of stature were willing to step forward. Despite the propaganda, the obvious connection between the Germans and the Italians was clear to all, as was the fact that Germany had staunchly supported the Italian invasion of Albania in 1939. Neubacher also credits British propaganda for this initial reluctance, propaganda which convinced many that Germany could not win the war and that a British invasion of the Balkans was imminent. As hopes of a British invasion began to recede and as Neubacher began to make clear that the alternative to some form of cooperation was a traditional military occupation, some

---

[4]US National Archives, USDS, OSS, Research and Analysis Branch, German Military Government over Europe, Albania, N. 2500.1, 1 December 1944.
[5]Neubacher, p. 116.
[6]Reginald Hibbert, *Albania's National Liberation Struggle*, (London: Pinter, 1991), p. 64.

prominent Albanians did step forward to form a government under the Germans.

The group that the Germans attracted tended to have some connection with either Austria or Germany—either they had studied there or at least were conversant with the language. The group was also dominated by Albanians from the north or from Kosova and this is certainly not surprising. Northerners had positive memories of the Austrians from the first war, and the Kosovars, some of whom had experience working with the Germans in Mitrovica, tended to view the Germans as liberators from the extreme repression Kosovar Albanians had experienced since annexation to Serbia in 1912 and as a power that guaranteed the survival of an ethnic Albania. Many of these people, then, were exclusively attempting to save 'Greater Albania', and were distressed by Allied promises to return Kosova to a reconstituted Yugoslavia. Their willingness to cooperate with the Germans had nothing to do with ideological sympathy for fascism, as was found in Croatia, Serbia and elsewhere, nor did it indicate any interest in the general wartime goals of the Axis. The support was an expression of traditional nationalism—the hope to seize the opportunity of the collapse of Yugoslavia to reverse the colonization and Slavicization policy of the previous two decades and protect ethnic Albania.[7] Few of these leaders equated their actions with collaboration.

Naturally most Albanians disapproved of this cooperation. Although this type of exercise tends to be fraught with danger, one German historian has concluded that perhaps 25–30 percent of the population viewed the Albanian collaborationist government under the Germans in a favorable light.[8] This, of course, leaves the vast majority with a neutral or negative view, expressed by either passive or active opposition. Active opposition to the Germans was complex and controversial. The groups included a series of independent chieftains who tended to have only regional influence and who cooperated with each other and with the other resistance groups only when specific advantage was foreseeable. Included among the more organized

---

[7]Noel Malcolm, *Kosova, A Short History*, (London: MacMillan, 1998), p. 296 and p. 313 on the expulsion of tens of thousands of Serbs and Montenegrins, 'mainly colonists, but including some of the old established Slavs of Kosovo.'
[8]Bernhard Kuhmel, 'Deutschland und Albanien, 1943–1944' (Ph.D. diss., University of Bochum, 1981) p. 448.

groups was the Zogist Legality (*Legalitet*) that hoped to restore the monarchy of King Zog. Led by Abaz Kupi, Legality was pro-British and operated throughout 'Greater Albania'. Next we have the loosely organized National Front (Balli Kombëtar), a platform for anti-Zogist liberals who tended to be pro-western and also operated throughout 'Greater Albania'.

The most important resistance group, however, were the communist partisans under Enver Hoxha who certainly did the most damage to the German position. Since the Yugoslavs played a major role in organizing the Albanian party and its resistance organizations, Yugoslav policy priorities—including the return of Kosova—tended to dominate partisan thinking. As a result, Hoxha operated principally in 'old' Albania, at least until the very end of the war in the Balkans. A separate Albanian partisan movement was ultimately established in Kosova but its activities tended to be limited and it never gained wide popular support, in part because the communist movement was perceived as being Slav-based. In Kosova, the dominant question throughout the war was the Albanian–Serb national question.

As in the rest of occupied Europe, the vast majority of the Albanian population did not participate in armed resistance. Most of the resistance during the war was passive, ranging from sabotage, both symbolic and actual, to public acts of defiance or simple non-cooperation. Workers struck the docks and sabotaged the mines, particularly the chromium mines, upon which the Germans were becoming increasingly reliant. Sabotage of a symbolic nature included the defacing of official portraits and posted announcements. Public acts of defiance included students insulting government officials or singing patriotic songs in movie theaters. Non-cooperation included many incidents of students and others refusing to participate in the public celebration of holidays, and more importantly, young men refusing to be drawn into the various security battalions which the Germans hoped to create— the most notorious of which was the volunteer SS Skenderbeg division.

Although Herman Neubacher initially succeeded in convincing Berlin that an indigenous SS division was incompatible with the notion of Albanian independence, by early 1944, as the Germans and their puppets became increasingly desperate, SS chief Heinrich Himmler received personal approval from Hitler for the creation of an SS division in Albania, with a mandate to protect ethnic Albania. The division was ultimately formed and took part in Kosova's most shameful episode during the war—the arrest and deportation of 281 Jews. But it never became a significant force. The division was never able to muster more than half of the planned 12,000 and of those who become part of the formation, few were actually volunteers. Within months fully half had deserted and the Germans were actually forced to disarm some of the battalions, sending their officers to prison, followed quickly by the dissolution of the entire division prior to the end of 1944.[9] One of the principal reasons for the failure of this most prominent attempt to use Albanians as security forces was again passive resistance through non-cooperation. According to the division's commander, the main obstacle was 'the invisible resistance of the *beys* and *agas*, which resulted in inactivity on the part of the prefects and mayors who were controlled by the *beys*, and in a whispering campaign of propaganda against recruitment.'[10]

Perhaps even the most noted achievement of the Albanians during the war—the saving of hundreds of Jews—can be described as passive resistance and non-cooperation, although these courageous acts often put Albanians at significant personal risk. This risk was increased after September 1944 when the German civilian administration was replaced by the SS that actively pursued Jews throughout Albania. Religious tolerance in the West is often gauged in our time by the treatment of Jews. While others in the Balkans— and obviously in the rest of Europe—institutionalized discrimination, participated passively or often enthusiastically in some of the most horrific crimes against humanity in relation to Jews, Albanians opened their country and often their homes to not only Albanian Jews but to foreign Jews as well, motivated in part by a strong tradition of hospitality as well as an attitude of religious tolerance. The result of this attitude and often personal sacrifice was that fully one hundred per cent of Jews from 'old' Albania were saved. It is estimated that even 60 per cent of the Jews from Kosova were saved, a remarkable achievement when seen in the light of regional comparison. In Yugoslavia, excluding Kosova, the rate of survival for Jews was a mere 18–28 per cent and in Greece no more than 14–22 per cent survived. Because Albania became known as a

---

[9]Christoph Stamm, 'Zur deutschen Besetzung Albaniens', *Militargeschichtliche Mitteilungen* 2 (1981), p. 111; British War Office Records, 204/9428, Reports and Memos, July 1944–February 1945.
[10]Malcolm, *Kosovo*, p. 309.

haven, there were perhaps eight times as many Jews in the country at the end of the war as there had been at the beginning—a remarkable development certainly unrivalled in the Balkans and in Europe as a whole.

Perhaps this fact should constitute the true measure of the content of Albanian character during World War II.

12. Did Albanians in Kosova breach their voluntary commitment to join Yugoslavia in 1945?

Owen Pearson

THE ALLEGATION

When in November 1991 the Arbitration Committee headed by Robert Badinter of France delivered its opinions on the subject of Yugoslavia's political crisis to the European Community Conference on Yugoslavia, it mentioned only the secession rights of the Republics:

— *... the Socialist Federal Republic of Yugoslavia is in the process of dissolution;*

— *... it is incumbent upon the Republics to settle such problems of state succession as may arise from this process in keeping with the principles and rules of international law, with particular regard for human rights and the rights of peoples and minorities;*

— *... it is up to those Republics that so wish, to work together to form a new association endowed with the democratic institutions of their choice.*[1]

Kosova is not a constituent Republic of Yugoslavia, and thus it has no right to secede. The contention that Kosova voluntarily joined Serbia in 1945 before the Federation was established, thereby becoming part of the Republic of Serbia and not a constituent part of Yugoslavia, bears great influence on a legal argument against self-determination.

---

[1]http://www.ejil.org/journal/Vol3/No1/art13.html [Consulted on 26 March 2006].

The Answer

There was no voluntary commitment on the part of the Kosovars to join Yugoslavia in 1945. On the contrary, Kosova was annexed once again to Serbia without the consent of its citizens. In order to understand what happened at the end of World War II we must turn to the tortuous development of Serb 'diplomacy' in the relationship of Kosova with Communist Yugoslavia, going back to the inter-war period.

The Yugoslav Communists agreed that Albanians should be free to choose their own destiny in several of their pre-war congresses. During the conflict, when it appeared that for the Party to gain popularity in Kosova there needed to be a stand in favour of the annexation to Albania, this policy was cautiously upheld. However, as Kosova's Party leader Milan Popović tried to be more explicit on the matter in 1943, he was officially reprimanded by Tito.

In the first days of January 1944 delegates of the two Committees of the Yugoslav Communist Party of Kosova, from Kosovo and the plateau of Dukagjin (western Kosova, called Metohija until 1943), met in Bujan, a village in northern Albania. In the resolution approved at Bujan, the case for Kosova's self-determination is clearly made as the expression of the people's will and in the course of the struggle against the 'injustice of the creation of the first Yugoslavia of King Aleksander and the oppression of the Albanian people under the rule of the hegemonic clique of the Great Serbs'.[2] That decision was reversed in July 1945 by the National Liberation Council of Kosovo and Metohija, a body of 142 members of which 33 were Albanians, representing the 2,000 members of the local Communist Party. This last resolution passed by acclamation in a climate of intimidation, as thousands of Yugoslav troops had been stationed in Kosova to maintain the martial law since February 1945.

On 3 September 1945 the President of the People's Assembly of Serbia passed a law declaring Kosova an autonomous Region of

---

[2]First Conference of the National Liberation Council for Kosovo and the Dukagjin Plateau, 31 December 1943–2 January 1944, pp. 50–1 in Marc Weller, *The Crisis in Kosovo 1989–1999. From the Dissolution of Yugoslavia to Rambouillet and the Outbreak of Hostilities* (Cambridge: Documents and Analysis Publishing, 1999).

Kosovo and Metohija, and part of the Republic of Serbia. In the First Yugoslav Constitution there was no pledge of self-determination for Kosova that the National Liberation Council thought to have obtained in Bujan. All the other Federal Republics, Serbia, Croatia, Bosnia, Slovenia, and Macedonia, retained their right of secession. What follows is a detailed account of the story of how Kosova lost its right.[3]

August 1928

The Yugoslav Communist Party, at its Fourth Congress held in Dresden, endorsed a resolution that Kosova should eventually be returned to Albania. Ugo Sola, the Italian Minister in Tirana, informed Zogu [King of Albania] that ... Italy would guarantee to Zogu that if the Yugoslav state should be destroyed, Albania would receive Kosova within her national frontiers.

August 1940

The Yugoslav Communist Party, at its Fifth Congress held in Zagreb, reaffirmed ... that Kosova should be restored to Albania. This decision was taken to encourage the Albanian Communists to embark upon a more determined campaign of opposition to Italian rule.

October 1940

At the continuing Fifth National Congress of the Yugoslav Communist Party in Zagreb, the Central Committee of the Party presented a document entitled 'Theses of the National Question in Kosova and Metohija', in which the following statement was pronounced: the solution of the national question in Kosova–Metohija can be achieved with the formation of the free workers and peasants' republic of Kosova.

---

[3]All the paragraphs that follow are extracts from volumes I and II of Owen Pearson's diary-chronicle *Albanian in the Twentieth Century* (London and New York: The Centre for Albanian Studies in association with the I.B. Tauris, 2006). Permission to reprint has been granted by Bejtullah Destani of the Centre for Albanian Studies.

20 June 1943

Lieutenant General Svetozar Vukmanovic-Tempo, Chief Political Commissar on the General Staff of the Yugoslav National Liberation Army, a Montenegrin who was one of the closest collaborators of marshal Josip Broz-Tito and his personal representative in Macedonia, made contact with the Albanian Communist leaders Enver Hoxha, Koci Xoxe, Nako Spitru, and others at the village of Kucake, not far from Korc. There they signed with Enver Hoxha a document, drafted in Hoxha's handwriting, entitled 'Conclusions of a meeting of Delegates from the Central Committee of the Communist Parties of Greece, Yugoslavia, and Albania, held on 20 June, 1943'. This document was a proposal to establish a joint General Headquarters of all the Balkan guerrillas, which Enver Hoxha immediately accepted. The following quotation from part of the document clearly held out the prospect of the Communists achieving the unification of Kosova and Diber incorporated with the Albanian state, as the Italian occupation had already imposed:

In Kosova and Metohija there are many Albanians who, because of their chauvinistic hatred of Serbia in the region, do not take part in the national liberation struggle. ... To facilitate the mobilization of the Albanians in this region, the Supreme Command of the National Liberation Army in Yugoslavia has appointed Fadil Xoxha as Commander in Chief of all the national liberation forces in Kosova and Metophija. The struggle which this army is engaged in, under the command of Fadil Hoxha, will be a guarantee to the peoples of Kosova and Metohija that they will decide their future for themselves.

25 July 1943

Svetozar Vukmanovic-Tempo sent a directive to the Yugoslav Communist Party Regional Committee for Kosova and Metohija for the closest possible co-operation in border zones with units of the Supreme Command of the National Liberation Army of Albania ... he particularly stressed the need for it to be explained to the Albanian masses in Kosova and Metohija that it was in their interest to take part, together with the other peoples of Kosmet, in the struggle against the invader and all collaborators, and that, together with the other peoples, a common national liberation army should be organized which should be an army of the brotherhood of all the peoples of Kosmet. Because only in that way would the peoples of Kosmet guarantee that they really would freely decide their future on the basis of the right to national self-determination.

2 October 1943

Svetozar Vukmanovic-Tempo reported that the capitulation of Italy had created a state of anarchy in Diber, where the Albanian partisan unit led by Haxhi Lleshi was not powerful enough to establish its authority. Tempo claimed that power had passed into the hands of tribal leaders who were under the influence of the reactionary Balli Kombetar and were being encouraged to set up a 'Greater Albanian' administration in Diber, which was to be extended to Kosova and Metohija. Tempo addressed the following letter to the Yugoslav Communist party's regional committee for Kosova and Metohija:

Regarding the question of the future borders between Yugoslavia and Albania, it will be resolved by brotherly agreement and co-operation between the National Liberation Army of Yugoslavia and the Council of National liberation of Albania on the basis of the right of self-determination of nations. How the borders will be drawn will depend on the evolution of the political situation in Yugoslavia and Albania. Now we must not make any definite statement on this issue.

25 October 1943

In a letter addressed to the Central Committee of the Albanian Communist Party, Josip Broz-Tito made the accusation that 'between the Communist Party of Yugoslavia and democratic anti-imperialist Albanian there is a problem over Kosovo and Metohija'. After stating that he was not opposed in principle to the 'Albanians of Kosovo having the liberty to go where and how they wish', Tito accused the leadership of the Albanian Communist Party of maintaining 'the stand which the reactionary Albanian bourgeoisie maintain'. He claimed that the Albanian Communists had stated that Kosova, the Dukagjin plateau, and Diber 'should be united with Albania immediately'.

6 December 1943

The Central Committee of the Yugoslav Communist Party addressed a letter, signed by Josip Broz-Tito, to the Central Committee of the

Albanian Communist Party in response to a letter from Miladin Popović on the question of Kosova and Metohija. Tito made the same allegation, using identical words in part, that he had made in an earlier letter which he sent on 25 October; he now wrote as follows:

To raise today the question of unification of Kosovo and Metohia would mean giving a helping hand to various reactionaries, including the enemy himself ... and it is hardly necessary to emphasize that between us and a democratic and anti-imperialist Albanian this cannot possibly be an issue. The new Yugoslavia which is in the making will be a land of free nations, and consequently there shall be no room for national oppression of the Albanian minorities either ...

1 and 2 January 1944

The founding conference of the National Liberation Council for Kosovo and Metohija, meeting at Bujan in the Gjakova highlands, adopted the following resolution:

Kosovo and the Dukagjin Plateau (Metohija) form a region in which Albanian inhabitants [preponderate, who today, as always, still wish to be united with Albanian. Consequently, our duty is to point to the correct course which the Albanian people should follow in order to achieve their aspirations. The only way by which the Albanian people of Kosovo and Metohija can be united with Albanian is through their common struggle with the other peoples of Yugoslavia.

28 March 1944

In a letter to the Regional Committee for Kosova and Methohija, Milovan Djilas wrote, on behalf of the Central Committee of the Communist Party of Yugoslavia, criticizing that part of the resolution of the first conference of the Kosovo Communists at Bujan on 1 and 2 January, which referred to the problem of the union of Kosova and Metohija with Albania, and rejected it. The letter continued:

We instruct you how the national question should be handled. First of all you must understand the decisions of the second meeting of the A.V.N.O.J. (Anti-Fascist National Liberation Council of Yugoslavia), and popularize the essence and aim of these decisions more widely. These decisions guarantee all people equal rights and make possible the right of self-determination. The Kosovo

Communist leadership undertook to amend the relevant passage of the resolution, thus revealing the subordinate position of the Albanian Communists in relation to the Yugoslav Communist Party.

8 to 10 July 1945

The National Liberation Council for Kosova and Metohija held its second conference at Prizren, at which the resolution of 1 and 2 January, 1944, advocating the union of Kosova and Metohija with Albania was amended by the adoption of a new resolution. This was in favour of Kosova and Metohija uniting with the Federal Republic of Serbia, with its status of an autonomous province within a democratic, federal Yugoslavia. The new resolution thus purported to be the most improbable result of the exercise of self-determination by the Albanians of Kosova, supposedly voting freely for forfeiting their age-old dream of an independent united greater Albania.

13. Have Albanians been against a peaceful solution to the question of Kosova's autonomy?

Howard Clark

THE ALLEGATION

With his recent statements to media, saying that Albanians in Kosmet "can no longer live side by side with Slavic fundamentalists" and with similar messages, Rugova encourages separatists and ... "in this way generates and accumulates a destructive emotional explosive for assaults on members of the Serbian security organs."

Because of these statements, Rugova can no longer "prove" he has nothing to do with such acts of separatists, although he invariably states that perpetrators of these attacks have not been discovered.
(*Jedinstvo*, a newspaper published in Kosova, quoted in the BBC Monitoring Service: Central Europe & Balkans, 26 July 1993).[1]

In keeping with the argument that Albanians were conducting a policy of genocide against Serbs in Kosova, every incident that could appear ethnically motivated was recorded by Serb security forces as an act of Albanian terrorism, long before the eruption of the KLA on the political scene. Later on, the accusation of terrorism did not spare the peaceful resistance's leader Ibrahim Rugova.

---

[1]"Serbian-Language Paper Accuses Rugova of Inciting Terrorism", 30 July 1993. http://global.factiva.com/ha/default.aspx [Consulted on 22 February 2006].

The Answer[2]

The nonviolent movement of Albanians in Kosova had different strands—some modernising, some traditional—but it was an authentic movement united around certain key themes. First, the survival of the Albanian society in Kosova. All sorts of pressures were put on Albanians to submit to Serbian domination or leave. There has never been such great social solidarity among Albanians as in the period 1991–1994. Second, legitimacy, contesting the legitimacy of the institutions imposed by Serbia and counterposing the legitimacy of institutions supported by the Albanian population. Third, refusing to be provoked to resort to violence by the vandalism and brutality of the Serbian police and 'emergency management', but rather committed to naming that violence. Fourth, to mobilise international support.

Various actions set the tone for the nonviolent campaign. Chronologically, the first was the miners' march of November 1988—a march not for the extension of Albanian rights but in defence of the 1974 Yugoslav constitution. This was followed in February by the miners' strike against the dismissal of the provincial leadership. These were actions that expressed determination, but without violence or the threat of violence. They provided a lasting image of dignified nonviolence, even though the strategic consensus on nonviolence did not emerge until 1991. In 1990, the petition 'For Democracy, Against Violence' initiated by intellectuals attracted the support of the whole society—some 400,000 signatories, each person giving their full name and address. From 1990–1992 the campaign for the reconciliation of blood feuds, despite police harassment, succeeded in resolving more than 2,000 feuds, nearly half of them involving death, and virtually removing this traditional bane of Albanian society, at least in Kosova and at least until the war.

After 1992, the nonviolent strategy centred above all on maintaining parallel institutions, but in its earlier and more dynamic phase a high level of organizing was needed to establish this as a nonviolent movement, determined both to resist Serbian domination and to avoid war.

The term 'separatist', much used by *Jedinstvo* in the 1990s, is somewhat ambiguous. On the one hand, it signifies people who want a

---

[2]Except where otherwise noted, references for this section can be found in my book, *Civil Resistance in Kosovo* (London: Pluto Press, 2000).

state separate from Serbia. That was virtually the entire Albanian population of Kosova, and Ibrahim Rugova, as president of the Kosova Writers' Association, was one of the first to raise the demand for independence. The starting point for negotiations had to be that Kosova should not be under Serbia, and—in view of the break-up of Yugoslavia and the loss of previous allies in the federation, such as Slovenia and Croatia—the favoured option was independence. On the other hand, 'separatist' signifies separation between people and communities. The Afrikaans word for separation—*apartheid*—came to signify a system of ethnic domination and oppression, and in Kosova *apartheid* was a word widely used to describe what Milošević was seeking to impose.

In resisting this, key bodies established in Kosova espoused universal values, most notably the Council for the Defence of Human Rights and Freedoms (CDHRF) and the Mother Theresa Humanitarian Society. The CDHRF always declared its willingness to have Serbs serve on the Council and at times even reported incidents of Kosova Serbs having their rights violated by the regime. Prominent political prisoners associated with the CDHRF—not least its president Adem Demaçi who has served nearly 28 years in Serbian prisoners, and Hydajet Hyseni, later vice-president of the largest party, the Democratic League of Kosova (LDK)—spoke about the mutual co-operation between Serb and Albanian prisoners, emphasizing that not all Serbs should be seen as enemies. The CDHRF also organised various roundtables with groups from Belgrade as a way to promote Albanian–Serbian dialogue. The Mother Theresa Humantarian Society succeeded in establishing a network of health clinics which by 1994, when the official medical system was in disarray, would even treat Serbs in need.

Also, the constitution drawn up for the independent Republic of Kosova intended to be inclusive. While there was some Bosniak and Turkish participation in the parliamentary elections organised by Kosova Albanians in May 1992, it was too much to expect that there would be any Serbian participation. Nevertheless, the Kosova Albanian consensus was to behave correctly towards Serbs and therefore to reserve a seat allocation for them to show that this was not intended as an ethnically exclusive institution.

As the socialist federation of Yugoslavia broke up, the Kosova Albanians opted for independence. And yet leaders such as Ibrahim

Rugova or Fehmi Agani[3] tried to make this demand as little threatening as possible—for instance, by stating the goal of achieving a demilitarised and neutral Kosova, or by suggesting the process of becoming a UN protectorate as part of a transition towards independence.

This was a period of hardening ethnic lines and also a hardening of the ethnic discipline of each community. By 1989 there was already a severe polarisation between Serbs and Albanians. Symptomatic of this was the fact that very few Serbs in Kosova complained at the dismissal of their Albanian colleagues. However, the situation was to get even worse. One 'trigger' event occurred in March 1990: most Albanians believe, with some expert support, that Serbs used a chemical weapon such as Sarin to poison some 7,000 children. The regime never permitted a proper investigation of what happened, preferring to describe the nausea and dizziness felt by thousands of children as self-induced symptoms of 'mass hysteria'. At that time, Albanians had still to affirm their strategic commitment to nonviolence and there was a spate of perhaps 50 personal attacks on Serbs.

The imposition of 'emergency management' and subsequent mass dismissals of Albanian workers also served to heighten ethnic antagonism. Out of the 164,210 Albanians employed in Kosova in 1990, nearly 90 per cent—146,025 according to the Union of Independent Trade Unions of Kosova (BSPK)—lost their jobs.

Serb spokespeople often suggest that rather than there being mass dismissals, there was an Albanian boycott. That is clearly not true with the first occupation to be hit—the police force. Some people tried to retain their jobs, agreeing to sign the loyalty oaths now required, but then the new 'emergency management' would often find another pretext on which to dismiss them. In the case of other professional groups, such as media workers, medical personnel or teachers, workers were locked out after refusing to implement the new measures being imposed in Kosova or to accept 'emergency management'. One common procedure after either a strike action or an industrial lock-out was for the 'emergency management' to post a public list of who would be allowed to return to work, a list excluding all but a few Albanians. Usually most Albanians listed would then decline to return—either seeing

---

[3]Agani was a sociologist, founder and vice-president of the LDK, killed in May 1999 by Serb police as he was recognised in the crowd of forced evacuees in Prishtina.

that as a breach of solidarity or not wishing to be seen as traitors to their own community. The BSPK collected tens of thousands of testimonies, lodging some 70,000 complaints of unfair dismissal with the Kosova labour court before that court was itself abolished.

In 1991—by the time the Kosova Albanians had made their strategic commitment to nonviolence—most of them were convinced that the Milošević regime wished to provoke violence in order to justify even heavier reprisals and ultimately war. Weapons raids were one of the main instruments of provocation. Police and police reservists would arrive at a village early in the morning, beating up the men of the house and insulting the women until someone disclosed where their weapons (if any) were hidden. The CDHRF and the LDK were very active in responding to such attacks, going to the village to document what had happened—'naming the violence'—but also urging the villagers not to be provoked to respond with violence.

Even according to official figures, in Kosova there was extraordinarily little violence from Albanians in the early 1990s. The Serbian Ministry of Interior web page has a section on 'terrorism in Kosovo and Metohija' with the following statistics for 'Terrorist attacks carried out in the territory of Kosovo and Metohija in the period 1991–December 27, 1998'.

"Terrorist attacks Kosovo–Metohija in 1991–27.12.1998"

	1991	1992	1993	1994	1995	1996	1997	upto 27.12.1998
Attacks	11	11	8	3	7	19	31	1112
Killed	1	3	2	5	6	10	12	287

Source: http://www.serbia-info.com/news/1999-012/7992.html

It is not clear what counts as a 'terrorist attacks', but it is absolutely clear that the main source of violence in Kosova was the regime. Police brutality was increasingly monitored by international as well as local organisations. Paragraph 161 of the February 1993 report of UN Special Rapporteur Tadeusz Mazowiecki gives the following items just for December 1992:

Police action has gone beyond arrest and imprisonment and cases of death as a result of shooting or brutality by the police have been reported. During the first two weeks of December 1992, four incidents were reported from Prishtina and three other small towns during which four Albanians were said to have been killed, and two others and a policeman wounded. It has been asserted that the armed forces also participated in the recent incidents. In two clashes with the Albanian community, the armed forces have allegedly killed two people. Furthermore, the following incidents have also been reported:

(a) On 3 December 1992, in the market of Prishtina, a 19-year-old Albanian was shot dead by the police and his older brother wounded in both legs, presumably while selling goods on the black market;

(b) On 18 December 1992, in Dakovica, [sic] a young man was beaten to death;

(c) On 19 December 1992, a 32-year-old Albanian from Brovina died in the hospital in Prishtina as a result of police brutality and beatings;

(d) On 24 December 1992, the police arrested a group of Albanians in Prishtina outside the Great Mosque, allegedly without giving any reason for the arrest;

(e) On 25 December 1992, in two villages between Prishtina and Peć, police abuse, maltreatment of the inhabitants and destruction of their food supply have been alleged. According to the information received, police brutality and harassment has increased in the town of Peć and the surrounding area with the pretext of seizing and collecting arms held illegally by civilians.[4]

A year later, in February 1994, the International Federation of Human Rights (IFHR) and the CDHRF submitted a memorandum to the UN Commission on Rights reporting that they had 'evidence during the past year of 13,435 cases of mistreatment of Albanians [in Kosova] by the police and the Army of the Federal Republic of Yugoslavia, Serbia and Montenegro. This is only a small part of the mistreatment that has occurred. During 1993, IFHR and CDHRF have evidence of 15 murders, 14 woundings, over 2,300 arrests and over 120 sentences for peaceful political activities in Kosovo'.

Violence against civilians and property

	1991	1992	1993	1994	1995
Deaths in police custody	2	2	2	8	5
Homes raided		not known	1,994	3,553	2,324

The CSCE (Conference for Security and Cooperation in Europe, the forerunner of the OSCE) mission to Kosovo, the Sandzak and Vojvodina reported in June 1993 that 'the situation in Kosovo is stable *and* explosive'. The stability was partly a product of Belgrade's

---

[4]UN reference E/CN.4/1993/50.

pre-occupations elsewhere (especially Bosnia) and partly of the majority population's self-restraint. So great was the Albanian leadership's determination to avoid provocations that, after the widespread education protests of October 1992, it called a moratorium on demonstrations. Instead the movement was to concentrate on international lobbying combined with building and maintaining the parallel system—the educational institutions, the clinics, the voluntary taxation system. However, the continued pressure of Serbian laws and police was explosive—and if the parallel schools were a stabilising factor, the longer students and pupils were constricted to them, the greater their frustration and, ultimately, the greater the explosive potential.

The nonviolence associated with Rugova was based less on pacifism than on prudence—Rugova himself had no objection to military defence or to international military intervention. Also he was well aware that the West preferred Albanians to pursue a nonviolent policy. However, it was too passive a policy, depending too much on the patience and endurance of the people. Others proposed forms of action to reinvigorate the struggle—convening the parliament—and in 1997 the Students Union actually defied Rugova and took action for their own right to study. They took great care in organising nonviolent demonstrations, in the face of police violence, marching from their makeshift 'parallel' University facilities to the buildings of the University. Their action brought international attention and also cooperation with Belgrade's oppositionist students.

In a climate of scepticism about dialogue with Serbs, a number of groups and individuals had always searched for allies among the opposition and civil society in Belgrade, hoping to mobilise opinion and at times resources in favour of a peaceful outcome to the conflict in Kosova. In my book *Civil Resistance in Kosovo*, I argue that the nonviolent struggle would have been more effective if there had been more activity on this front, but the fact was, as Sonja Biserko of the Belgrade Helsinki Committee has put it, 'Albanians had learned to expect little of the Serbian opposition'.

14. Have Albanian terrorism and separatism been the cause of the Yugoslav state policies during the 1990s?

Howard Clark

THE ALLEGATION

In the last twenty years, 200,000 people have been moved out of Kosovo and Metohija, more than 700 settlements have been ethnically 'purged', the emigration is continuing with unabated force, Kosovo and Metohija are becoming 'ethnically pure', the aggression is crossing the border of the nation ... Old women and nuns are raped, frail children beaten up, stables built with gravestones, churches and historical holy places desecrated and shamed, economic sabotage tolerated, people forced to sell their property for nothing.

(From the petition to the Yugoslav and Serb National Assemblies signed in January 1986 by about 200 prominent Serb intellectuals, including former editors of the journal Praxis such as Zaga Golubović, Mihalilo Marković, Ljuba Tadić and Milan Kangrga, as Cowell as the novelist and later President of Yugoslavia Dobrica Ćosić).[1]

Starting from the early 1980s, a large section of the Serb population argued that there was no alternative to the revocation of Kosova's autonomy and stricter law enforcement in order to stop the ethnic cleansing of Serbs. The grievances of Serbs in Kosova, alleging victimisation and persecution by the local Albanian leadership and

---

[1]Branka Magaš, *The Destruction of Yugoslavia. Tracking the Break-up 1980–92* (London: Verso, 1993), p. 50.

society, were addressed very publicly in a series of documents as well as mass protests.

In May 1982 the Serbian Orthodox Church published the 'Appeal for the Protection of the Serb Population and its Holy Places in Kosovo'. A petition signed by 2,016 Serbs from Kosova addressed in October 1985 the Yugoslav and Serb National Assemblies. The intellectuals' petition of 1986 concluded that the only solution to the genocide of Serbs in Kosova would be to revoke Kosova's autonomy.

The pattern of persecution detailed above became the justification for Belgrade's later revocation of Kosova's autonomy and is reaffirmed by western media sources such as *Extra!*, the online magazine of Fairness and Accuracy In Reporting (FAIR).[2] As the late President Milošević's defense at The Hague naturally focuses on the reactive nature of the Serb counter-insurgency conducted against KLA terrorism in the 1990s, a similar argument is made by some observers:

> *Military specialists can recognize the banality of counter-insurgency operations which belong to the repertory of every armed force in the world. Only when carried out by Serbs are these moves automatically described as "ethnic cleansing".*[3]

The Answer

From 1966 onwards, there was a growing polarisation of Serbian and Albanian perceptions of what was happening in Kosova. The fall of Aleksandar Ranković, vice-president and Minister of the Interior, in 1966 marked a shift in the politics of the League of Communists of Yugoslavia. For Serbs,[4] the new federal policy of 'national affirmation' equated to 'strong Yugoslavia, weak Serbia', while at the level of Kosova they were alarmed at what they saw as 'Albanization'.

---

[2]Jim Naureckas, 'Rescued From the Memory Hole. The Forgotten Background of the Serb/Albanian Conflict', *Extra!*, May–June 1999, www.fair.org/index. php?page=1459 [Consulted on 4 April 2006].

[3]Diane Johnstone, (journalist) 'Appraisal of the Two OSCE Reports: Kosovo/ Kosova: As Seen, As Told,' 29 February 2000, http://www.globalresistance. com/article/Johnstone/osce.htm [Consulted on 4 April 2006].

[4]In generalisations, 'Serbs' will here be taken to include 'Montenegrins'.

Ranković, the Serb in charge of the Serbian-dominated secret police force (the Uprava Drzavbe Bezbednosti or UDBa), was a name associated with terror among Albanians in Kosova, but Serbs tended to see him as their protector, especially in retrospect. The post-purge revelations about Ranković and the UDBa were shocking even to those familiar with the practices of authoritarian Communist regimes. *The Times* of London commented: 'the almost daily disclosures of brutal acts of repression, murder and torture by members of Mr. Ranković's police against the Albanian minority are ... astonishingly frank'.[5] Such methods had 'encouraged the emigration' of untold thousands of Yugoslav Albanians.[6]

Throughout Yugoslavia, the federal changes aimed to strengthen the powers of the republics against the central state, but also weakened Serbia by creating two autonomous provinces within Serbia, provinces which from 1974 onwards enjoyed representation on the federal presidency. Ethnic keys (a system for allocating various resources according to ethnic quotas) were introduced throughout the federation. In Kosova in particular this entailed what in the West would be called 'affirmative action' or 'positive discrimination' to redress the pro-Serbian bias in public administration, employment, housing and education. When in 1967 Tito paid his first visit to Kosova in 16 years, it was to announce a new dispensation for Albanians. 'One cannot talk about equal rights when Serbs are given preference in factories ... and Albanians are rejected although they have the same or better qualifications'.[7] Thus the historical context for Kosova's autonomy within Yugoslavia was a period of reaction against domination (that was seen as Serbian domination), a time for 'affirmative action', and even a time for emancipation. For the first time, Albanians began to outnumber Serbs in the League of Communists of Kosova.[8] Albanian (and Turkish) gained equal status to

---

[5]*The Times*, 22 September 1966, quoted in Sami Repishti, 'Human Rights and the Albanian Nationality in Yugoslavia', in Oskar Gruenwald and Karen Rosenblum-Cale (eds), *Human Rights in Yugoslavia* (Irvington, 1986), p. 244.

[6]In the 1950s around 200,000 Yugoslav Albanians emigrated from Yugoslavia to Turkey, see Noel Malcolm, *Kosovo: A Short History* (London: Macmillan; New York: University Press, 1998), p. 323, and Miranda Vickers, *Between Serb and Albanian: a History of Kosovo* (London: Hurst, 1998), p. 157. Some authors suggest even higher figures.

[7]Quoted by Malcolm, *Kosovo*, p. 324.

[8]By 1973, LCY membership in Kosova had risen to 47,791, of whom 29,507 were Albanians (61.7 per cent) while 12,515 (26.2 per cent) were Serbs and 3,824

Serbo–Croatian as official languages of the province. In the haste to expand Albanian-language secondary education, textbooks and even teachers were brought in from Albania. The University of Prishtina was established, and soon grew to be Yugoslavia's third largest university.

There should be no doubt that this was accompanied by abuses, such as widespread nepotism. Throughout Yugoslavia, membership of the League of Communists was less and less motivated by conviction and more and more as a gateway for personal advancement. From 1968 onwards, the Kosova administration applied 'ethnic keys' but their functioning, as elsewhere in Yugoslavia, was opaque, and in Kosova, as elsewhere, gave rise to resentment.

Any process of 'affirmative action' is likely to be fraught with problems, even one carried out with transparency and proper monitoring. Serbs did not want to adapt to the reality of being a minority in Kosova, and what was worse their complaints about these 'new realities' went unheeded. When Dobrica Ćosić first voiced the complaints of Kosovo Serbs in 1968, he found himself removed from the LCY Central Committee. However, the issue would not go away, each time coming back more strongly.

The population statistics showed that Serbs and Montenegrins were an ever-diminishing minority in Kosova—between 1971 and 1981 their numbers diminished in absolute terms while their percentage of the population fell from 20.9 to 14.7 per cent. Most Serbian commentators presented this change of demographic balance as evidence that Albanian maltreatment of Serbs in Kosova was forcing them to emigrate. 'The constant exodus' of Serbs from Kosova had been a repeated theme of the Orthodox Church even during the Ranković era.[9] In the 1980s, however, intellectuals and then the Milošević party machine joined the chorus. Gross exaggerations were the order of the day. Take the 1986 petition of Serbian intellectuals, quoted above. Rather than

---

(8.0 per cent) Montenegrins. Two other observations: only Bosnia had as high a proportion of the population as members of the LCY; the proportion of Serbs and Montenegrins in the LCY remained much higher than their proportion in the overall population (roughly double in the 1970s).

[9]Slavenko Terzić, director of the History Institute of SANU 1987–2002, at the trial of Slobodan Milošević cited bishops' reports from 1951, 1959, 1961 and 1962. http://www.un.org/icty/transe54/041206IT.html, p. 34268. [Consulted on 4 April, 2006]

Table 1: Population of Kosova according to census figures

	1948		1953		1961		1971		1981	
	Population	%	Population	%	Population	%	Population	%	Population	%
Total	727,820		808,141		963,988		1,243,693		1,584,440	
Alb	498,242	68.5	524,559	64.9	646,805	67.1	916,168	73.7	1,226,736	77.4
Serb	171,911	23.6	189,869	23.5	227,016	23.6	228,264	18.4	209,498	13.2
Mont	28,050	3.9	31,343	3.9	37,538	3.9	31,555	2.5	27,028	1.7

200,000 Serbs leaving Kosova as it claimed, the 1981 census indicates 85,012 Serbs and Montenegrins had left since 1961, while the number of settlements without Serb inhabitants had increased not by 700 in that period but by 260.[10] Higher numbers—but lower percentages of the population—moved from Bosnia and Croatia to Serbia in the same period.[11]

Responding to the media vilification of Albanians as rapists, independent investigations indicate that Kosova had low rates of inter-ethnic rape and murder compared with the rest of former Yugoslavia.[12] Meanwhile examining the question of redressing the ethnic balance in employment, the figures indicate that even in 1980 Serbs still fared better than Albanians.

---

[10]The 410 settlements without Serbs in 1961 had risen to 670 in 1981. See Ruza Petrović and Marina Blagojević, 'The Migration of Serbs and Montegrins from Kosovo and Metohija', *Demographic Studies* (Serbian Academy of Arts and Sciences Department of Social Sciences). Presented in 1988 and available on-line at http://www.rastko.org.yu/kosovo/istorija/kosovo_migrations [Consulted on 4 April 2006].

[11]While the 85,012 emigrants from Kosova left a population in 1981 of 209,000 Serbs and Montenegrins, the 111,828 Serbs from Bosnia left a Serb minority of 1,321,000 and the 132,044 from Croatia left 532,000.

[12]According to Christine von Kohl and Wolfgang Libal, whilst in inner Serbia there were 2.43 reported rapes or attempted rapes for every 10,000 men, the rate in Kosovo was 0.96, and mostly within the same nationality. From 1979–1987, only 31 rapes or attempted rapes of Serbian women by Albanians were reported in Kosova, and in 1988–1989 none at all, C. von Kohl and W. Libal, *Kosovo: Gordischer Knoten des Balkan* (Vienna: Europaverlag, 1992), p. 70. They further report that the Mother Superior at Peć assured them she knew of no cases of nuns being raped, contrary to many media stories. Hudelist obtained figures from the Ministry of Interior that between 1982 and 1986 in Kosova, 16 Serbian/Montenegrin women were raped by Albanians, and there were 19 attempted rapes—Darko Hudelist, 'The Kosovo Autumn of 1987', *Start* (Zagreb), 31 October 1987, quoted by Arshi Pipa, 'The Political Situation of the Albanians in Yugoslavia, with particular attention to the Kosovo Problem: A Critical Approach', *East European Quarterly*, XXIII, No. 2, June 1989, p. 180, n.23. On murder, from 1981–1987, there were five confirmed inter-ethnic murders in Kosovo, two by Albanians, three by Serbs. Hudelist, op cit. Also Azem Vllasi in *Vreme* NDA, 25 September 1995.

Table 2: Job to ethnicity ratio, 1968 and 1980[13]

	1968	1980
Serbs:	1:4	1:5
Albanians:	1:17	1:11

The most solid study purporting to support Serbian claims was commissioned by the Serbian Academy of Arts and Sciences (SANU) in 1985. By the time it was published in 1988, the majority of the population of Serbia seem to have believed there was a concerted campaign by Albanians to ethnically purify Kosova as a step towards gaining a republic and thence secession. The SANU researchers—Petrović and Blagojević—interviewed 500 households, consisting of 2,512 people. The most important motives for leaving were 'pressure' and 'indirect pressure', although 78 households also indicated that they would not have left if they had found employment. Whilst 43 households said they had good relationships with the Albanian community, seven considered themselves 'driven out', and 324 reported conflicts, including 34 complaints of serious injury and seven of rape or attempted rape. There were frequent complaints about local authorities. 'We soon lost faith in the authorities and the state. The courts were as though they didn't exist, you had to protect and fend for yourself.'

This summary hardly fits with the researchers' egregious remarks concerning the 'extermination' or 'genocide' of Serbs. Rather Petrović and Blagojević's key finding was that Serbs were most likely to decide to move when their numbers in a locality fell below 20–30 per cent—a threshold now being reached in an increasing number of rural areas, and not only because of emigration but also because the demographic trend towards urbanisation was stronger among Serbs than Albanians. Some 298 of the 500 households traced the change in Kosova back to 1966–1968, yet the researchers did not ask for information about post-Ranković purges or about the fear or reality of other types of 'score-settling' after Ranković's fall.

In 1990 a very different Belgrade study of the situation in Kosova was commissioned by the anti-nationalist association of intellectuals,

---

[13]Figures from Malcolm, *Kosovo*, p. 326.

UJDI (Association for a Yugoslav Democratic Initiative). It offered this perspective:

The core of the Serbian–Albanian relationship has been characterized by a pattern of domination—Serb over Albanian or Albanian over Serb—ever since Kosovo was part of the Ottoman Empire. Under Tito ... whoever held power at any given time held absolute power, controlling the media, the police, the courts and the labour market. Although this dictatorship was theoretically a "dictatorship of the proletariat" it was handily used as a thinly disguised dictatorship of the ruling ethnic group. This absolute domination, which Serbs exercised by controlling the Kosovo Communist Party from 1945 to 1966 and Albanians from 1966 to 1988, exacerbated inter-ethnic intolerance.[14]

Where does the demand for a separate republic fit into this picture?

We have seen the Serbian interpretation that harassing Serbs to emigrate from Kosova was part of the plan to achieve this republic. There is no doubt that most Albanians felt it was unjust that they did not have a republic, but they were seriously divided over how to achieve this. Serbs were not the only nationality alarmed by the 1981 demonstrations, and indeed these were put down not by federal troops—not just Serbian forces. An internal LCY report on the demonstrations estimated that 300 demonstrators were killed.[15] From March to June 1,700 people were arrested and between July and September 226 people, mostly under 25 years old, were sentenced to up to 15 years for 'verbal offences or hostile propaganda'.[16]

After 1981, the demand 'Kosova Republic' became the symbol for Yugoslav Albanian discontent and rising expectations. The federal LCY's 'solution' to the immediate crisis and beyond was to insist that the provincial leadership repress those who raised this demand. There were purges inside the LCY in Kosova, school and university teachers lost their jobs through 'differentiation' (being declared politically unfit), and widespread surveillance and harassment of Kosova Albanians

---

[14]Srdja Popović et al., *Kosovski Cvor: dresiti ili seci?* (Belgrade: Khronos, 1990). Quote taken from Srjda Popović, 'A Pattern of Domination', *Balkan War Report*, April–May 1993, pp. 6–7.

[15]Hugh Poulton, *The Balkans: Minorities and States in Conflict* (Minority Rights Group, London 1991), p. 60.

[16]Sami Repishti, 'Human Rights and the Albanian Nationality in Yugoslavia', p. 263.

again became the norm. From March 1981 to November 1988 a reported 584,373 Kosova Albanians—half the adult population—were arrested, interrogated and interned.[17] Once again, as in the days of Ranković, the whole population seemed under suspicion.

The locally-administered repression still seemed 'weak' to the resurgent Serbian nationalism. With Community authority diminishing throughout Yugoslavia, from 1987 onwards Milošević was able to build himself a new populist base for his own brand of authoritarianism by playing the tune of Serbian nationalism while beating the drum of Kosova. The oppression of Serbs wherever they were a minority became a central theme for Milošević's 'anti-bureaucratic revolution'— and the most symbolic metaphor for this Serbian suffering was the purported oppression of Serbs in Kosova. Therefore Milošević's political machine took Kosova Serbs to other parts of Yugoslavia to rally aggrieved Serbs at 'meetings of truth', and therefore they used the 1989 celebrations of the 500th anniversary of the Battle of Kosovo as a rallying cry for Serbian unity. The federal leadership of the LCY could not contain the forces pulling Yugoslavia apart, and every gesture by any other nationality—above all by Slovenians or Croatians—that challenged the Serbian nationalist narrative about Kosova served to inflame Serbian opinion even further.

---

[17]Cited in Mark Thompson, *A Paper House: The Ending of Yugoslavia* (London: Hutchinson Radius/Vintage, 1992), p. 128. From 1981 until September 1988, official sources recorded that 1,750 ethnic Albanians were convicted of political crimes in regular courts, while more than 7,000 were summarily jailed for minor political offences. The military in the same period claimed to discover 241 illegal groups composed of 1,600 Albanians—Amnesty International EUR/48/08/89.

15. Was the KLA a criminal, terrorist and Islamist organization?

Stacy Sullivan

THE ALLEGATION

Those of us who warned that the West was being sucked in on the side of an extremist, militant Kosovo–Albanian independence movement were dismissed as appeasers. The fact that the lead organization spearheading the fight for independence, the Kosovo Liberation Army (KLA) , was universally designated as terrorist organization and known to be receiving support from Osama bin Laden's al-Qaeda was conveniently ignored.
(Retired Major General Lewis MacKenzie, Canadian, former Commander of UN Peacekeeping Forces in NATO in former Yugoslavia).[1]

The KLA is presented in many media commentaries and political analysis as a criminal, terrorist and Islamist organization.

… [T]he KLA was a conduit for foreign fighters, including jihad veterans from Bosnia, Chechnya and Afghanistan. While mujahedin in Kosovo do not necessarily translate into an Al Qaeda presence, in all likelihood many of those fighters trained in al Qaeda camps in Afghanistan.
(Charles V. Peña, Director of Defense Policy Studies at the Cato Institute).[2]

The Kosovo Liberation Army (KLA) was formed and was financed by criminal enterprises that took root in cities like the Bronx and Brussels,

---

[1]"We bombed the wrong side", *National Post*, 8 April 2004.
[2]"Al Qaeda: The Balkans Connection", *Mediterranean Quarterly*, 16.4 (2005), pp. 65–76.

> Hamburg and Geneva, Rome and Chicago. The KLA engaged in terrorist
> activities whose cause the international community took up.
> (Vuk Jeremić, Senior Advisor to the President of Serbia).[3]

The Answer

Since 1998, when war broke out in Kosova, there have been persistent allegations in the media that the Kosova Liberation Army was a criminal, terrorist and Islamist organization, or more specifically, that it had ties to Al Qaeda and was funded with drug money through Albanian criminal networks. Early on in the war, such mainstream magazines as *Time* reported that US intelligence believed that the Iranian Revolutionary Guard was training its fighters. The Serb newspaper *Nedeljni* reported that mujahideen had set up a training camp in northern Albania to instruct the rebels.[4] In a column in the *New York Times*, William Safire wrote that Chechen fighters had gone to Kosovo to help the Albanian rebels in their fight for independence.[5]

Other common allegations were that the KLA was financed through Albanian criminal networks—the trafficking of drugs and women—that had long been established in Europe. The allegations appeared to have credibility not only because some of them came from reputable sources, but also because the KLA morphed from obscure group of rural militants into to the fasting-growing guerrilla movement in the world in a matter of weeks. Clearly, the rebel movement had to be getting training and support from somewhere.

The possibility that *mujahideen* and Islamic organizations might have been helping the KLA was not completely far-fetched because Al Qaeda had attempted to establish a foothold in Albania in the early 1990s through a network of charities. Additionally, Albanians, because they came from an oppressive regime in the poorest part of Europe, were known to be involved criminal circles in both Europe and the US. So

---

[3]'Past and Future Status of Kosovo,' Testimony Before the House of Representatives International Relations Committee, 18 May 2005, www.house. gov/international_relations/109/jer051805.pdf [Last visited on April 23 2006].
[4]'Mujahideen deployed in Kosovo', *Nedeljni*, 1 April 1998.
[5]William Safire, 'Essay; The Kosovo Dilemma', *The New York Times*, 18 June 1998, Editorial page, p. 35.

when I first began reporting on the KLA in 1998, this was this story that I wanted to find. Instead, I found an Albanian–American contractor named Florin Krasniqi who was running something called the 'Homeland Calling Fund' out of the office of his Brooklyn roofing company, Triangle General Contractors.

Krasniqi, along with several other Albanian–American businessmen had started the US branch of the Homeland Calling Fund in 1997. The fund had actually been established a couple of years before that by a group of Kosovar émigrés in Switzerland who had long advocated waging a war of independence. But since the emergence of the KLA, it had expanded and now had branches in Germany, Austria, Norway, Denmark, France, Sweden, Italy, Belgium, Canada and Australia.

The day I walked into Krasniqi's office in April 1998, about a dozen men from New York's Albanian community stopped in with checks and envelopes of cash, which Krasniqi placed in a cardboard box underneath his desk. Technically, he told me, the Homeland Calling Fund was a charitable organization. On paper, it was meant to aid the needy in Kosova and Albania so all donations to it were tax-deductible. Because of that status, Krasniqi had to try to maintain some pretense that the fund's money was being used for humanitarian purposes. 'I like to think the contributions are going to help refugees who have been displaced by the fighting', he said. 'Of course, I can never be sure where the money goes once it reaches Albania. If it's being used to buy guns, that's none of my business.'

As it turned out, much of the money Albanian–Americans donated to the US branch of the Homeland Calling fund was being used to buy guns, tens of thousands of them which were available in Albania following the 1997 unrest that left the country's armories open for looting. Additional weapons, 0.50 caliber sniper rifles and other guns were purchased legally in the US and exported to Albania where they were smuggled across the border to Kosova.

Between 1997 and 1999, Krasniqi estimates that the US branch of the Homeland Calling Fund raised about $30,000,000. There is no way to verify those numbers, since much of it was delivered in cash and hand-carried to Albania, but Homeland Calling receipts and bank transfers account for at least $10,000,000.

There are an estimated 400,000 people of Albanian descent in the US, concentrated mostly in the tri-state New York area, Chicago and

Detroit, and they are a tight-knit group profoundly dedicated to their homeland. Until 1998, they were a little known émigré community, but a very well-to-do one that had more than its fair share of small businessmen with restaurants and construction companies, as well as doormen and building superintendents. For eight years during the reign of Ibrahim Rugova, president of the self-styled Republic of Kosova, they contributed 3 per cent of their income to supporting government, schools and hospitals Rugova's party created, so the community was already accustomed to contributing funds, so it is not far-fetched that they could have contributed the sums Krasniqi claims.

Is it possible that some of the millions that Albanians donated to the coffers of Homeland Calling branches in the US and Europe could have included some dirty money? Of course it is. The minority of Albanian émigrés involved in criminal activities was not immune to patriotism and most certainly donated to the cause. But the vast majority of money came from doormen, building superintendents, taxi drivers, mechanics, restaurateurs and construction workers, many of whom attended fundraising dinners I covered.

Paul Hockenos, who has studied Balkan Diasporas in Europe, came to a similar conclusion. Although he acknowledged that hundreds of kilograms of heroin passed through Albania and Macedonia, to the extent that by 2000 the Interpol estimated that Albanians controlled 40 per cent of the European heroin trade, he concluded that it was not drug barons who bankrolled the KLA. '... The predominant source of the KLA's guns and money was not big-time criminals but the enormous disenfranchised Diaspora population spawned by Milosević's policies. The contributions for the KLA weaponry came from the same migrants who had deposited hundreds of millions of German marks into [the LDK's] accounts for the shadow state. A portion of the KLA's funding may have been dirty money, but it did not explain the KLA.'[6]

As for the allegations that the KLA was receiving money and fighters from Islamic groups, I simply never saw any evidence of this. In June 1998, I went to northern Albania to investigate rumors that the Iranian revolutionary guard was training the KLA. For weeks, I traveled around remote regions visiting several training camps which the KLA

---

[6] Hockenos, Paul. *Homeland Calling: Exile Patriotism and the Balkan Wars* (Cornell University Press, 2003), p. 255.

had established. What I found there were primitive border camps full of men who ranged in age from 15 to 70 and in profession from farmers to doctors. Most of them had fled a Serb advance and crossed the border into Albania looking for a weapon and some training in how to use it so they could return to protect their homes. The men were subsisting on bread, cheese and tomatoes, all courtesy of the local villagers, and received only the most rudimentary training, mostly from Albanian army officers, before returning to Kosova.

In the two years that I covered the conflict in Kosova, never once did I see the mujahideen fighters I saw in Bosnia, or hear KLA soldiers even allude to any kind of commitment to Islam. Most said they were offended by such allegations, bragged about how they were Catholic before the Ottomans came and converted them, and said their only religion was Albanianism.

It would later emerge that in April 1998, an Egyptian-born Frenchman named Claude Chiek Ben Abdel Kader, who claimed to be an operative for Al Qaeda, had approached the KLA's Supreme Command in Tirana and offered to provide guns, money and fighters. Although the KLA was desperate for all three, the Supreme Command refused. Through its channels to the Albanian government, the US had made it clear that it would not tolerate the rebels receiving any assistance from Islamic fundamentalists.

Krasniqi recalled being furious about the refusal at the time. 'I would have taken money from the devil at the time, so I wanted them to take it', he said. 'I had no interest in establishing an Islamic state or working with terrorists, but I wanted freedom for my people so I was angry that they refused the help.' In retrospect, however, Krasniqi says it was the right decision.

To date, there has not been report offering any specific details about Islamic connections to the KLA and Kosova remains an avowedly secular entity in spite of the KLA's powerful influence in the post-war era. When several KLA commanders and fighters were put on trial for war crimes at the UN Tribunal in The Hague for killing Serb civilians, the history of the rebel army was thoroughly examined and the question of criminal money and ties to Islamic fundamentalists were roundly dismissed.

16. Is it true that there is no right of self-determination for Kosova?

Jennifer Ober and Paul R. Williams

THE ALLEGATION

To argue that secession from an internationally recognized state is an unacceptable principle, but to claim at the same time that the very same demand should be acknowledged in the case of the Kosovo Albanians because they suffered so much under the Milošević regime, is to ignore not only international law but also the political consequences of such a unilateral decision being imposed upon Serbia and Montenegro.
(Statement by the President of the Republic of Serbia Boris Tadić at the UN Security Council Meeting, New York, 14 February 2006).[1]

Any attempt at imposing such a solution [Kosovo's independence] through a de facto legalization of a partition of Serbia, i.e. through forcible secession of a part of its territory, would be tantamount not only to legal violence against a democratic state, but against international law itself.
(Statement by Vojislav Koštunica, Prime Minister of the Republic of Serbia at the UN Security Council meeting on Kosovo, 24 October 2005).[2]

The right of self-determination is denied on broad legal and political grounds, as a violation of the principle of state sovereignty. Because Kosova was never granted the status of a constituent Yugoslav republic, as the argument goes, it remains part of Serbia and does not have the right to become a state.

---

[1]http://www.kosovo.com/news/archive/2006/February_17/2.html [Consulted on 4 April 2006].
[2]http://www.kosovo.com/news/archive/2005/October_24/5.html [Consulted on 4 April 2006].

The Answer

According to the principle of self-determination, when a country commits gross human rights violations against a population, or denies its people the right to self-determination, that country divests itself of the right to govern the oppressed population. In the case of Kosovo, as will be discussed below, the international community acted upon the principle of self-determination to divest the Federal Republic of Yugoslavia of control over Kosovo, and began a process of earned sovereignty, whereby it slowly transferred governing functions and authority to Kosovo. It is anticipated that this transfer will eventually result in a fully independent Kosovo.

Beginning in 1912, with the illegal occupation of Kosovo by the Republic of Serbia, through to 1999, Serbia engaged in a systematic campaign of violence, coercion, ethnic cleansing and genocide. Serbian abuses in Kosovo posed such a risk to regional stability that the UN Security Council felt compelled to invoke Chapter VII of the UN Charter and intervene militarily. UN Security Council Resolution 1244 displaced the sovereignty of the Federal Republic of Yugoslavia and placed Kosovo under a UN trusteeship—the largest and most extensive in the history of the UN. Within this authority, the UN Security Council established a framework that conceived of independence for Kosovo after a temporary period of international administration. The authority to exercise Kosovo's sovereign responsibilities thus rests with the UN, which has established a structure to transfer that sovereignty back to Kosovo.

Self-determination arose as an internationally accepted legal principle during the decolonization period after World War II. With the collapse of colonial empires, the international community recognized a need to codify the principle of self-determination; namely that territories subjugated by colonial powers have the right to their own independence. The principle has traditionally been conditioned upon respect for territorial integrity and national unity. Despite this conditionality, territorial units of a state have legitimately disassociated themselves from the parent state and created or resumed their own international status.[3]

---

[3]Paul R. Williams, et al. *Intermediate Sovereignty as a Basis for Resolving the Kosovo Crisis*, Europe Report No. 46, The International Crisis Group,

International law attempts to preserve the balance between the principle of territorial integrity and the fact that territorial units may under some circumstances legitimately disassociate from their parent state by indicating that the people of a territorial unit seeking disassociation from the predecessor state must have been denied the ability to exercise their right of self-determination; further, disassociation must respect the principle of *uti possidetis*.[4] Developments in international law support the proposition that the territorial integrity and sovereignty of a government is entitled to respect only so long as it represents the equal rights and interests of the whole population without discrimination on racial, ethnic, or religious grounds.[5] Sovereign states who degrade the basic rights of the population, including the denial of the right of democratic self-government, forfeit their claim to sovereignty and territorial integrity.[6] The General Assembly reaffirmed this principle in the UN' 1970 Declaration on Friendly Relations. The Declaration also reaffirmed the principle of territorial integrity, but with an important caveat:

Nothing in the foregoing paragraphs shall be construed as authorizing or encouraging any action which would dismember or impair, totally or in part, the territorial integrity or political unity of sovereign and independent States *conducting themselves in compliance with the principle of equal rights and self-determination of peoples* as described above and thus possessed of a government representing the whole people belonging to the territory without distinction as to race, creed or color.[7] [Emphasis added]

By this act, the General Assembly indicated that states are entitled to invoke the right of territorial integrity so long as they possess

---

9 November 1998, citing the separation of the Baltic states from the former Soviet Union, the subsequent dissolution of the Soviet Union and the attainment of statehood by its former republics, the separation of Czechoslovakia into the Czech Republic and Slovakia, and the dissolution of the SFRY leading to statehood for Slovenia, Croatia, Bosnia and Herzegovina, and Macedonia [hereinafter Crisis Group Report].

[4]Ibid.

[5]Ibid.

[6]Ibid.

[7]Declaration on Principles of International Law Concerning Friendly Relations and Co-operation among States in Accordance with the Charter of the United Nations, GA Res. 2625 (XXV) (24 October 1970).

'a government representing the whole people belonging to the territory without distinction as to race, creed or color'.[8] Where such a government is not present, 'peoples' within existing states will be entitled to an unlimited right to self-determination.[9]

More recently, in considering whether Quebec could properly secede from Canada, the Canadian Supreme Court held that secession might only arise under the principle of self-determination where: (1) 'a people' is governed as part of a colonial empire; (2) 'a people is subject to alien subjugation, domination or exploitation'; or (3) possibly where 'a people is denied any meaningful exercise of its right to self-determination within the state of which it forms a part'.[10] The Court then went on to declare that a state whose government represents the whole of the people

---

[8]See Crisis Group Report, supra, note 3, at 10, citing Antonio Cassese (*Self-Determination of Peoples. A Legal Reappraisal*, Cambridge University Press, 1995), p. 112: 'If in a sovereign State the government is "representative" of the whole population, in that it grants equal access to the political decision-making process and political institutions to any group and in particular does not deny access to government to groups on the basis of race, creed or color, then that government respects the principle of self-determination; consequently, groups are entitled to claim a right to self-determination only where the government of a sovereign State denies access on such grounds.'

[9]See Crisis Group Report, supra, note 3, at 10, arguing that the savings' clause in the Friendly Relations Declaration might arguably be read as applying only to governments that are unrepresentative by virtue of distinctions based on 'race, creed or color.' Distinctions based on political opinion, for example, might not trigger the clause. Whatever the persuasiveness of this reading, it is important to note that the 1993 Vienna Declaration of the World Conference on Human Rights, which was accepted by all United Nations member states, reiterated the savings clause but without this limiting language. Paragraph 2 of Part I speaks of states, 'possessed of a government representing the whole people belonging to the territory *without distinction of any kind*' (emphasis added). This version of the clause withholds the assurance of territorial integrity from states whose governments exclude citizens for any reason whatever.

[10]Decison of the Supreme Court of Canada in the Matter of Section 53 of the Supreme Court Act, R.S.C., 1985, C. S-26; and in the matter of a Reference by the Governor in Council Concerning Certain Questions Relating to the Secession of Quebec from Canada, as set out in Order in Council P.C. 1996–1997, dated 30 September 1996 at para. 154 [herinafter Decision of the Supreme Court of Canada.].

or peoples resident within its territory, on a basis of equality and without discrimination, and respects the principles of self-determination in its internal arrangements, is entitled to maintain its territorial integrity under international law and to have the territorial integrity recognized by other states.[11] As the Court found that the people of Quebec had not been 'denied meaningful access to government to pursue their political, economic, cultural and social development, they were not entitled to secede from Canada'.[12] Implicitly, however, had the Court found that the people of Quebec were denied any such a right of democratic self-government and respect for human rights, then secession from Canada might have been permissible.[13]

As a government's legitimacy derives from a people's exercise of the right of self-determination and from its conduct in accordance with its obligation to protect and promote the fundamental human rights of its entire people, the question must therefore be asked whether a government has been imposed on people by force, or by an exercise of self-determination.[14]

Serbia's illegal occupation of Kosovo began between November 1912 and November 1915, prior to the creation of the Kingdom of Serbs, Croats and Slovenes. The Serbian constitution of 1908, in force during the occupation, decreed that no change could be made to the borders of Serbia without the agreement of a special, enlarged Grand National Assembly. No such assembly was convened to ratify the annexation of Kosovo.[15] Under international law, territory conquered by one state from another becomes legally a part of the victorious state only when the transfer is formally agreed to by the two belligerents in a treaty after the war.[16] After the Balkan war two such treaties were drafted: the Treaty of London in 1913 and the treaty of Istanbul in 1914. Serbia failed to ratify either treaty. Kosovo was no more a legitimate part of

---

[11]Crisis Group Report, supra note 3, at 16, citing Decision of the Supreme Court of Canada, at para. 154.
[12]Ibid., at 16.
[13]Ibid., at 16.
[14]Ibid.,at 16.
[15]Noel Malcolm, *Kosovo: A Short History* (London: Macmillan, 1998).
[16]Hugo Grotius, *The Rights of War and Peace* 193 (A. C. Campbell trans., M. Walter Dunne, 1901) (1670); *Oppenheim's International Law* (7th ed. 1952) vol. II at pp. 219–20.

Serbia in 1912–1915 than it was a part of Austria–Hungary or Germany or Bulgaria (the later occupying powers) in 1915–1918.[17] Importantly, the Serbian government never passed any legislation to provide Albanians in Kosovo with Serbian citizenship; they gained a new citizenship for the first time only when they were made citizens of the Yugoslav state in 1928.[18]

In 1963, Yugoslavia adopted a new constitution which promoted Kosovo to the status of Autonomous Province of Serbia. In 1968, the Yugoslav Constitution was amended to provide autonomous provinces the status of *socio-political communities*. This status is identical to the other republics constituting Yugoslavia.[19] Kosovo was deemed to be one of the eight constituent units of Yugoslavia: six republics (Serbia, Croatia, Slovenia, Montenegro, Macedonia and Bosnia–Herzegovina) and two autonomous provinces in Serbia (Vojvodina and Kosovo). In 1974, Yugoslavia adopted another constitution which effectively provided the Autonomous Provinces of Kosovo and Vojvodina sovereign status nearly equivalent to that of the other six republics of Yugoslavia. Kosovo adopted its own constitution, appointed its own representative on a rotating Federal Presidency and elected parliamentarians to the Federal Parliament on the same basis and with the same legislative rights as all other federal units.[20] As an autonomous province, Kosovo had its own administration, assembly and judiciary and it was a member of Serbian institutions and federal institutions, the collective presidency and a Federal Parliament in which it had the right of veto.[21] Under the 1974 Constitution Kosovo was constitutionally proclaimed to be an integral part of the Yugoslavia Federation.[22] Thus, for instance, the

---

[17]Noel Malcolm, *Kosovo*, note 13, at 266.

[18]Ibid., The Yugoslav Nationality Law of 1928 established citizenship for Albanians who lived in Kosovo between 1913 and the establishment of Yugoslavia in 1918.

[19]Paul R. Williams, 'Earned Sovereignty: the Road to Resolving the Conflict of Kosovo's Final Status', *Denver Journal of International Law and Policy*, vol. 31:3, 2003, pp. 395–6.

[20]Ibid.

[21]Independent International Commission on Kosovo: *The Kosovo Report*, available at http://www.oxfordscholarship.com/oso/public/content/politicalscience/0199243093/toc.html.

[22]1974 Constitution, articles 1 and 2.

constitution provided that Kosovo was expected to participate in the joint realization of the interests of the federation,[23] and that like the other republics it would be equally responsible for implementing, enforcing, and amending the Yugoslav Constitution,[24] as well as the ratification of international agreements and the formulation of Yugoslavian foreign policy.[25]

In the 1980s, Slobodan Milošević rose to power amidst waves of Serbian nationalism. With Milošević at the helm, the Serbian regime forced through illegitimate constitutional amendments which revoked the autonomy of Kosovo and removed Kosovo's control over the police force, judicial system, civil defense, and over economic, social and education policy. To force these amendments through, as required by the Federal Constitution, members of the Serbian security forces surrounded the Kosovo Parliament with tanks and armed personnel carriers.

In the 1990s, Serbia issued a series of legal decrees forbidding the sale of property to Albanians, outlawing Albanian language newspapers, and closing the Kosovo Academy of Sciences. In response, the Kosovo Assembly adopted a resolution proclaiming for itself equal status with the other Yugoslav Republics. Serbia responded by expelling Albanians from state employment in Kosovo and forcibly dissolved all remaining Kosovo governmental institutions deriving from the 1974 constitution. As a result, Kosovo was ruled directly from Belgrade. Had this involved state actors it would be akin to an illegal armed attack expressly prohibited by Article 2(4) of the UN Charter.[26] In response, the members of the dissolved Albanian Assembly held a secret meeting, created a constitutional law for the Republic of Kosovo, and held a referendum on the question of whether Kosovo should be declared a sovereign and independent Republic. 87 per cent of eligible voters participated in the vote, with 99 per cent voting in favor of independence.

---

[23] 1974 Constitution, article 244.

[24] 1974 Constitution, articles 276–9, 398–403.

[25] 1974 Constitution, article 271.

[26] 'All members shall refrain in their international relations from the threat or use of force against the territorial integrity or political independence of any state, or in any other manner inconsistent with the Purposes of the United Nations.'

Serbia rejected the referendum. Instead, Serbia asserted that this act changed Kosovo's legal status vis-à-vis both Serbia and the Socialist Federal Republic of Yugoslavia. This assertion ignored the framework of the existing Yugoslav constitution and law, which required the unanimous consent of all eight federal units, including Kosovo, to any change in Kosovo's status under the federal constitution.

From 1963 to date, the only country that has had a legitimate rule over Kosovo has been the Socialist Federal Republic of Yugoslavia (SFRY), the governance of which Kosovo participated in, alongside Serbia. In light of the fact that Kosovo has never been legally incorporated into the Republic of Serbia, Serbia may make no claim to sovereignty over Kosovo, and can make no claim of territorial integrity. In addition to the violation or revocation of intrastate autonomy agreements, when an entity has suffered systematic persecution at the hands of the central authorities, the central government is divested of its right to territorial unity in relation to the territory.[27] The Belgrade government exercised oppressive rule over Kosovo through a series of civil and human rights abuses to such an extent that it can be argued that a right of self-defense was triggered on the part of the Kosovo population, a right they chose to exercise almost exclusively through non-violent means during the first half-decade of Serbia's rule in Kosovo.[28] These abuses amounted to a de facto apartheid regime in Kosovo. Virtually all Albanians were deprived the right to education, employment, and use of social services, as detailed above. Through successive decrees made by the Republic of Serbia, thousands of Serbs moved to Kosovo. These policies were design to create 'ethnically clean' Serb-only communities.

In response to these policies, Albanians chose a route of peaceful resistance in Kosovo. Having been shut out of their own parliament and all educational, medical, economic and governmental institutions, the people of Kosovo created their own parallel state. Serbian military, police and para-military forces, heavily present in Kosovo from the beginning of the 1990s, engaged in widespread acts of violence, arbitrary arrest, and torture. By 1997, Serbian military and police forces

---

[27]Ved Nanda, 'Self-Determination and Secession Under International Law', 29 *Denv. J. Int'l L & Pol'y*, p. 505 and pp. 306–7 (2001).
[28]Independent International Commission on Kosovo, supra note 21.

were actively engaged in a brutal resistance campaign which resulted in many civilian deaths and disappearances.[29] Hundreds of thousands of Albanians were forcibly driven from their homes.[30] In 1999 Serbia escalated the campaign and engaged in a massive armed and genocidal attack on the Albanian civilian population. The Independent International Commission on Kosovo estimated that between 24 March and 19 June 1999, 10,000 people were killed, the vast majority of the victims being Albanians killed by Serbian forces.[31] There is evidence of widespread rape and torture as well as looting, poaching, and extortion.[32]

As a result of Serbian aggression, a group of Albanian separatists formed the Kosovo Liberation Army (KLA), which began a campaign of resistance to the Serbian authorities. In the winter of 1997, the Serbian forces began a brutal crackdown on the KLA which spilled over into Kosovo's civilian population. As the situation deteriorated, the UN called on both sides to end hostilities and pursue a diplomatic solution to the burgeoning conflict.[33] The violence continued, prompting the US and its Allies to convene the Rambouillet peace talks in February 1999. When these talks broke down and Serbian aggression continued, NATO commenced a bombing campaign against Belgrade and Serbian positions in Kosovo. Against this backdrop, United Nations Security Council Resolution 1244 (UNSCR 1244) was adopted. UNSCR 1244 provided for the creation of the United Nations Mission in Kosovo (UNMIK), which assumed responsibility for nearly all of Kosovo's sovereign authority and functions, leaving only a few functions to be exercised by the Federal Republic of Yugoslavia (FRY). UNSCR 1244 also established a NATO security presence to bring

---

[29]*See Kosovo Focus on Human Rights*, at http://www.hrw.org/campaigns/ kosovo98/reports.html.

[30]*Kosovo/Kosova As Seen, As Told; An Analysis of Human Rights Findings* of the OSCE Kosovo Verification Mission from October 1998 to June 1999, available at http://www.osce.org/kosovo/item_11_17755.html.

[31]Independent International Commission on Kosovo, *The Kosovo Report*, note 21.

[32]*Ethnic Cleansing in Kosovo: An Accounting*, US Dep't of State 3 (December 1999).

[33]S.C. Res. 1199, 53rd Sess., 3930th mtg. at para. 1, UN Doc. S/Res/1199 (23 September 1998); S.C. Res. 1203, 53rd Sess., 3937th mtg. At Prmbl., paras. 3–4, UN Doc. S/Res 1203 (24 October 1998).

stability to the region and called for the UN to facilitate a political process to determine Kosovo's final status. Over time, the UN representative worked to create a Kosovo Constitutional Framework providing for a parliament and a president.[34] The UN Special Representative in Kosovo then embarked on a process of devolving specified powers to the Kosovo institutions and excluding the exercise of any authority by FRY institutions.

Despite the clarity of UNSCR 1244 regarding the interim transfer of sovereignty to the UN administration and the legitimacy of a process for determining the final status, some states have argued that UNSCR 1244, by its preambular reference to the sovereignty and territorial integrity of the FRY, precludes an eventual independent final status for Kosovo. This argument does not rest on a sufficient legal foundation. The Preamble of UNSCR 1244 affirms, 'the commitment of all Member States to the sovereignty and territorial integrity of the Federal Republic of Yugoslavia ... as set out in the Helsinki Final Act and Annex 2.'[35] Affirming the sovereignty and territorial integrity of the FRY while invoking the Helsinki Final Act is significant given that Helsinki equates the state's rights to sovereignty and territorial integrity with the minority people's right to self-determination.[36] The Helsinki Final Act states:

By virtue of the principle of equal rights and self-determination of peoples, *all* peoples *always* have the right, in full freedom, to determine, when and as they wish, their internal and external political status, without external interference, and to pursue as they wish their political, economic, social and cultural development.[37]

Similarly, UNSCR 1244's affirmation of the sovereign rights and territorial integrity of the FRY with reference to Annex 2 weakens arguments claiming UNSCR 1244 precludes Kosovo independence. Annex 2

---

[34]*Constitutional Framework for Provisional Self Government*, UN Mission in Kosovo, 15 May 2001, UN Doc. UNMIK/REG/2001/9 (2001), available at http://www.unmikonline.org/constframework.htm [Last visited 10 January 2004]; United Nations Security Council Resolution S.C. Res. 1244 (1999).
[35]S.C. Res. 1244, supra note 18, at Prmbl.
[36]*See* Helsinki Final Act, sec. 1(a)VIII, 1 August 1975 available at http://www.seerecon.org/region/sp/ helfa75e.pdf [Last visted 26 April, 2006].
[37]Ibid., (Emphasis added).

expressly places the respect for the sovereignty and territorial integrity of the FRY within the context of the 'interim political framework agreement providing for substantial self-government for Kosovo'. Importantly, through its adoption of the Rambouillet Accords, Annex 2 envisions a final solution based on the will of the Kosovar people, not deference to the sovereignty or territorial integrity of the FRY.

The international civil presence in Kosovo, which took the form of a Special Representative to the Secretary General and accompanying staff, was authorized to provide an interim civil administration for Kosovo.[38] The Security Council made it clear, however, that the UN administration was only an interim entity and that, pending settlement of the final status of Kosovo, its primary task was to promote the establishment of substantial autonomy and self-government in Kosovo, based on the Ahtisaari Agreement and the Rambouillet Accords.[39] To accomplish this objective the UN civil administration was charged with 'organizing and overseeing the development of provisional institutions for democratic and autonomous self-government pending a political settlement, including the holding of elections'.[40]

The UN administration was then to oversee the transfer of authority from Kosovo's provisional institutions to new institutions established under a political settlement.[41] The Security Council did not provide an express timetable for resolving the question of the final status of Kosovo, but indicated that this process should be governed by the Rambouillet Accords, which set a three-year time frame (which expired in 2002). Importantly, UNSCR 1244 in no way intends for the deployment of a UN administration to supplant the process for a settlement of

---

[38]The mandate of the UN administration included the authority to: perform basic civilian administrative functions; support the reconstruction of key infrastructure and other economic reconstruction; support, in coordination with international humanitarian organizations, humanitarian and disaster relief aid; maintain civil law and order, including establishing local police forces, and meanwhile through the deployment of international police personnel to serve in Kosovo, protect and promote human rights; and assure the safe and unimpeded return of all refugees and displaced persons to their homes in Kosovo. See UN Security Council Resolution 1244 (1999), para. 11.
[39]UN Security Council Resolution 1244 (1999), para. 10a.
[40]UN Security Council Resolution 1244 (1999), para. 11.
[41]Ibid.

Kosovo's final status. Rather, UNSCR 1244 is very clear in its mandate to the UN administration to assume control of sovereign functions, negotiate a constitutional framework, and then begin the transfer of sovereign functions to Kosovo institutions. Simultaneously, the UN is mandated to pursue a resolution of the final status of Kosovo.[42] The authority to exercise Kosovo's sovereign responsibilities rests with the UN, not Serbia. When a country continuously violates a people's right to self-determination and engages in systematic and wide-scale human rights abuses, that country must forgo any sovereignty it exercises over those people.

---

[42]Ibid.

17. Was the former 1999 NATO intervention an illegal war against the Former Republic of Yugoslavia?

Catherine Croft and Paul R. Williams

THE ALLEGATION

For the first time, NATO abandoned its defensive posture and attacked a country that posed no threat to its member states, outside the NATO treaty area, and without seeking UN Security Council authorization. International law was circumvented in the name of an alleged higher moral imperative. A precedent was set.
(Diana Johnstone, British journalist and commentator).[1]

For some commentators, NATO intervention was an unmitigated violation of international law. In the absence of a legal decision on its legality (the International Criminal Court did not rule on the merit of the arguments presented by Serbia and Montenegro against NATO countries in 1999), the issue is still open to debate.

There is a range of opinions among those who deny the legality of NATO's actions. The Italian jurist and former Presiding Judge at the International Crime Tribunal for the Former Yugoslavia Antonio Cassese argued that intervention was illegal under the international law, but may indicate the emergence of a new

---

[1]*Fools' Crusade Yugoslavia, NATO and Western Delusions*, New York: Monthly Review Press, 2002, available at http://www.monthlyreview.org/foolscrusade. html [Consulted 4 April 2006].

doctrine that allows the use of force to stop a state's large-scale atrocities within its territory.[2]

The Independent International Commission on Kosovo called the NATO intervention an illegal but legitimate action.[3]

The Answer

The US and its NATO allies defended the air strikes against Yugoslavia on moral grounds (to stop atrocities) and security grounds (to prevent the conflict from spilling over to neighboring European countries). Curiously, however, the NATO countries did not provided a legal justification for the intervention despite acting without the approval of the UN Security Council. The failure of NATO countries to articulate a legal basis for their humanitarian intervention is especially puzzling since it was justifiable on several grounds. Here, we analyze the legal rationale for the 1999 NATO humanitarian intervention in Kosovo.[4]

Article 2(4) of the UN Charter provides a general proscription against the use of force, but international law recognizes this general prohibition must be balanced against the realistic needs of preventing human rights abuses and maintaining peace and security. In the case of the humanitarian intervention in Kosovo, five compelling legal arguments support the legality of NATO action. First, NATO action was consistent with several Security Council resolutions on Kosovo. Second, the intervention was a necessary exercise of the right to collective self-defense of Albanians in Kosovo. Third, NATO action was consistent with the stated purposes of the UN Charter. Fourth, NATO countries were acting in fulfillment of their international legal obligations to prevent the crime of genocide. Finally, the inability of Albanians in Kosovo to exercise their right to self-determination

---

[2]Antonio Cassese, 'Ex iniuria ius oritur: Are We Moving towards International Legitimation of Forcible Humanitarian Countermeasures in the World Community?' The European Journal of International Law, 10, 1999, pp. 23–30.

[3]Independent International Commission on Kosovo: The Kosovo Report, available at http://www.oxfordscholarship.com/oso/public/content/politicalscience/0199243093/toc.html.

[4]This chapter draws from Paul Williams and Michael Scharf, 'NATO Intervention on Trial: The Legal Case That Was Never Made', Human Rights Review, 103 (2000).

overcame Yugoslavia's right to territorial integrity and established a legal justification for the resort to force.

Critics argue that NATO's humanitarian intervention in the former Yugoslavia was unlawful on the basis of Article 2(4) of the UN Charter (Charter). Article 2(4) prohibits 'the threat or use of force against the territorial integrity or political independence of any state, or in any other manner inconsistent with the Purposes of the United Nations'. Chapter VII of the Charter provides two exceptions to the strict prohibition of use of force. Article 39 of the Charter permits the Security Council to authorize the use of force to maintain or restore international peace and security, and Article 51 recognizes the 'inherent right of individual or collective self-defense'.

When the use of force is either authorized by the UN Security Council or is necessary for the exercise of self-defense, such force does not violate Article 2(4). Although the Security Council did not expressly authorize NATO action in Kosovo, NATO action was consistent with the Security Council's declared objectives and took place in the face of the Security Council's own inability to take action to maintain regional peace and security. Moreover, Albanians were incapable of exercising their right to self-defense against Serbian forces without international assistance. Even though the Security Council had not explicitly authorized NATO's intervention in the former Yugoslavia, NATO action took place against the backdrop of Security Council resolutions recognizing the increasing violations of human rights and impending humanitarian catastrophe in Kosovo.[5] The Security Council determined that the actions of Yugoslavia in Kosovo constituted a threat to peace and security in the region and, pursuant to Chapter VII of the Charter, demanded a halt to such actions.[6] The Security Council, however, was unable to achieve the objectives set forth in these resolutions due to political deadlock. It was clear that the Security Council resolutions on the situation in Kosovo passed with no threat of action behind them, as a Security Council authorization of force was unlikely

---

[5]See UN Security Council Resolution 1199, S/Res/1199, 23 September 1998 [hereinafter UNSCR 1199]. See also UN Security Council Resolution 1160, S/Res/1160, 31 March 1998 [hereinafter UNSCR 1160] and UN Security Council Resolution 1203, S/Res/1203, 24 October 1998 [hereinafter UNSCR 1203].

[6]See UNSCR 1199 and UNSCR 11203.

no matter how desperate the situation in Kosovo became. NATO countries acted upon the failure of the Security Council to achieve its stated goals of ending human rights violations and stemming the flow of Kosovo refugees.

United States Secretary of State Madeline Albright articulated this reasoning in a speech in Washington in March 1999, declaring: 'Acting under Chapter 7, the Security Council adopted three resolutions ... imposing mandatory obligations on the FRY; and these obligations the FRY has flagrantly ignored. So NATO actions are being taken within this framework, and we continue to believe that NATO's actions are justified and necessary to stop the violence.'[7] Even if these facts do not create an implicit Security Council authorization for humanitarian intervention in Kosovo, they do lend considerable legitimacy to NATO actions in the absence of express authorization.

The right to self-defense is the second exception to the prohibition of the use of force encompassed by Article 2(4) of the Charter. Article 51 of the Charter recognizes 'the inherent right of individual or collective self-defense if an armed attack occurs against a Member of the UN, until the Security Council has taken measures necessary to maintain international peace and security'. This question becomes more complicated when it relates to whether the right to self-defense includes a right to call upon other states to engage in collective self-defense against the aggression of a totalitarian and oppressive regime. The International Court of Justice rejected the Reagan Administration's attempt to assert such a rationale for intervening in Nicaragua in 1985, stating: 'The Court cannot contemplate the creation of a new rule opening up a right of intervention by one State against another on the ground that the latter has opted for some particular ideology or political system.'[8] However, the question the ICJ considered in the Nicaragua case is different from the situation in Kosovo in that NATO did not intervene to impose democratic government in Yugoslavia, but to protect Albanians in Kosovo from ethnic cleansing and genocide.

Intervention designed to prevent grave abuses of human rights is not prohibited by Article 2(4) of the UN Charter. The phrase 'or in any

---

[7]Secretary of State Madeline K. Albright, Press Conference on Kosovo in Washington DC, 25 March 1999.

[8]Case Concerning Military and Paramilitary Activities in and Against Nicaragua (Nicaragua vs. United States), 1986, ICJ 14, 133.

other manner inconsistent with the Purposes of the United Nations' is not limited to the above-mentioned exceptions to the prohibition against the use of force. The 'purposes' of the UN, as articulated in Article 1 of the Charter, include maintaining international peace and security and developing relations among nations based on respect for the principle of equal rights and self-determination of peoples. The Security Council passed two resolutions declaring that the situation in Kosovo threatened regional peace and security.[9] The resolutions called for the former Yugoslavia to 'cooperate with international efforts to improve the humanitarian situation and avert the impending humanitarian catastrophe' and create conditions that would allow refugees and displaced persons to return to their homes in safety.[10] NATO action in Kosovo was consistent with the Purposes of the UN, both as stated in Article One of the Charter and in the text of Security Council resolutions on Kosovo. The primary justification NATO countries offered for their operations in Kosovo was a concern that the peace and stability of Europe was threatened by the conflict's potential to spill into neighboring countries.[11]

There are also international obligations to prevent genocide. The 1948 Convention on the Prevention and Punishment of the Crime of Genocide (Genocide Convention) obliges state parties to 'undertake to prevent and punish' genocide.[12] Further, the crime of genocide has attained the level of a preemptory norm of international law (*jus cogens*), superseding other treaty rights and obligations.[13] The NATO countries, as parties to the Genocide Convention, had an obligation to intervene. Moreover, as a party to the Genocide Convention, the Federal Republic of Yugoslavia has, by implication, waived its right to invoke territorial integrity to shield it from international action to halt genocide.

International law recognizes that a state's territorial integrity is subject to that state's ability to protect the right of its people to self-determination.

---

[9]See UNSCR 1199 and UNSCR 1203.
[10]See UNSCR 1203 at para. 11–2.
[11]See Press statement by Javier Solana on 23 March 1999.
[12]Article 1 of the Convention on the Crime of Genocide, 78 U.N.T.S. 277, entered into force 12 January 1951.
[13]See generally, Frowein, 'Jus Cogens', in *Encyclopedia of Public International Law*, Installment 7, at 327 (Bernhardt ed. 1984).

The UN General Assembly reaffirmed this principle in the UN's 1970 Declaration on Friendly Relations, declaring:

Nothing in the foregoing paragraphs shall be construed as authorizing or encouraging any action which would dismember or impair, totally or in part, the territorial integrity or political unity of sovereign and independent States *conducting themselves in compliance with the principle of equal rights and self-determination of peoples* as described above and thus possessed of a government representing the whole people belonging to the territory without distinction as to race, creed or color.[14] [Emphasis added]

Even Ian Brownlie, who served as counsel for Yugoslavia in its case before the International Court of Justice, recognized that self-determination has become a peremptory norm of international law.[15]

The territorial integrity of the Federal Republic of Yugoslavia was subject to the right of Albanians to exercise self-determination in Kosovo. In the events leading up to NATO's intervention, Albanians had been stripped of any ability to exercise their right to self-determination. The Serbian government exercised oppressive rule over Kosovo through a series of civil and human rights abuses that amounted to a de facto apartheid regime in Kosovo. As a clearly defined group of people with a distinct identity who have been sys-tematically denied fundamental human rights and the opportunity to engage in collective democratic self-governance, Albanians are entitled to self-determination. In the very unique circumstances facing the people of Kosovo, the internationally recognized right of self-determination includes the right to resort to force.[16]

Critics of the humanitarian intervention in Kosovo fear that justifying NATO's actions will encourage other countries to intervene in less altruistic circumstances. It was for this reason that the Western

---

[14]Declaration on Principles of International Law Concerning Friendly Relations and Co-operation among States in Accordance with the Charter of the UN, GA Res. 2625 (XXV) (24 October 1970).

[15]Ian Brownlie, *Principles of Public International Law*, 4th ed. (New York: Oxford University Press, 1990), pp. 513, 515.

[16]Antonio Cassese, *Self Determination of Peoples: A Legal Reappraisal*, (Cambridge University Press, 1995), p. 151. The United States, for example, has taken the position that the resort to force, other than by terrorism, by liberation movements is not unlawful.

countries condemned the Indian invasion of Bangladesh in 1971 and the Tanzanian invasion of Uganda in 1979.[17] While these invasions put an end to mass slaughters, in each case the self-interest of the invading state was clear.[18] The unique circumstances of the Kosovo case limit its precedential value as a legal justification for future humanitarian interventions. The intervention in Kosovo was consistent with three UN Security Council resolutions condemning the violence in Kosovo and warning of an impending 'humanitarian catastrophe'. The threat of death to tens of thousands of refugees was imminent, and the Security Council was helpless to prevent it. NATO's objectives were consistent with the goals of the Security Council as stated in its resolutions.

In addition to the UN resolutions, other features of NATO action in Kosovo distinguish it from future potential humanitarian crises. Unlike the Tanzanian and Ugandan cases, NATO countries lacked any political self-interest in Kosovo. The multilateral nature of NATO's intervention in Kosovo adds further legitimacy to NATO's intervention. Ensuring that multilateral coalitions carry out humanitarian interventions 'filters out worst forms of national self-interest'.[19] Fears of abusive invocation of the doctrine of humanitarian intervention must be balanced against the compelling need for a contemporary and realistic interpretation of Article 2(4), especially in light of the Security Council's paralysis in the face of mass atrocities.

To conclude, NATO's humanitarian intervention in Kosovo was consistent with Article 2(4) of the UN Charter. The two exceptions to Article 2(4)—Security Council authorization and self-defense—apply to NATO action in Kosovo. First, NATO acted within the framework of Security Council resolutions that warned of an imminent humanitarian catastrophe and in the face of the failure of the Security Council to accomplish its own goals. Second, Kosovo was incapable of effectively

---

[17]See Oscar Schachter, 'The Right of States to Use Armed Force', *Michigan Law Review*, vol. 82, April–May 1984, pp. 1620, 1628–1633.

[18]Ibid.

[19]Clara Portela, 'Humanitarian Intervention, NATO and International Law: Can the Institution of Humanitarian Intervention Justify Unauthorized Action?' Berlin Information—center for Transatlantic Security, December, 2000, citing Michael J. Glennon, 'The New Interventionism', *Foreign Affairs*, 78(3), May–June 1999.

acting in its own self-defense. Moreover, NATO action was consistent with the Purposes of the UN, specifically the maintenance of international peace and security. The Security Council itself determined that the situation in Kosovo was a threat to regional peace and security, and NATO acted in order to prevent the conflict in Kosovo from spilling over into neighboring countries.

The Charter's general prohibition against the use of force is balanced against the interests of preventing future impotence in the face of wide spread atrocities. The UN was clearly unable to act to prevent mass atrocities in Kosovo. As members of the Genocide Convention, NATO countries had an obligation to intervene on Kosovo's behalf in order to prevent ethnic cleansing, and the inability of Albanians in Kosovo to exercise their right to self-determination eroded the territorial integrity of the former Yugoslavia. That NATO acted in Kosovo without political self-interest further strengthens the legal foundation of NATO's humanitarian intervention.

18. Is it true that the NATO bombing and the KLA were responsible for the Albanian refugee crisis in the spring of 1999 and that the number of Albanians killed during the war has been grossly exaggerated?

Excerpts from AAAS/ABA-CEELI Report

THE ALLEGATION

During the bombing, NATO officials reported as many as 225,000 Albanian men missing. After the bombing, officials said the Serbs had murdered 10,000 Albanians. The ICTY now believes over 11,000 people, mostly Albanians, were killed in war crimes. But so far investigators have found the bodies of only 2,108 presumed victims, including some Serbs ... Pathologist Emilio Perez Pujol, who headed a team of Spanish investigators, recently told The Times of London, 'I calculate that the final figure of dead in will be 2,500 at the most. This includes lots of strange deaths that can't be blamed on anyone in particular'.[1]

The war of the body count of civilians killed during the NATO bombing started when the first discoveries by war crime investigators turned out to disappoint expectations. It has never really ended. As that initial number was later upgraded, with exhumations proceeding in a total of more than 500 sites, criticism did not abate.

---

[1]Brian Mitchell, 'How Many Really Died in Kosovo?' *Investor's Business Daily*, Wednesday, 17 November 1999.

The war crimes tribunal in The Hague is beginning to panic over its case against former Serbian president Slobodan Milošević according to a Vancouver detective sent to unearth mass graves in and a Canadian filmmaker who documented the exhumations ... Calgary filmmaker Garth Pritchard and Sgt. Honeybourn are critical of Ms. Arbour, now UN High Commissioner for Human Rights, and her claims that the Serbs, directed by Mr. Milošević, murdered as many as 200,000 civilians during its ethnic cleansing of. ... This was a massacre that never happened, Mr. Pritchard maintains ...

I was telephoned by an RCMP officer seconded to the Hague tribunal's investigative unit, a corporal named Tom Steenvoorden, who told me the total number of bodies they have recovered amounts to 5,080, which is a far cry from 200,000, he told the Citizen.

I want someone like Peter Mansbridge or Ms. Arbour to tell me where the other 195,000 bodies are. This is a massacre that never happened.
(Bruce Garvey, writer for the Canadian newspaper *The National Post*).[2]

Critics never took notice of the possibility that destruction of evidence—and bodies—might impede the speedy and final recovery of all the missing. Nor did they pay much attention to the Belgrade-based Humanitarian Law Center's recent denunciation of the cover up of war crimes by Serb forces,[3] indicating that the 1999 discovery of a refrigerator truck in Serbia full of corpses from Kosova might not have been an isolated accident.

Disagreement about the number of killings during the NATO war is linked to a broader disagreement on the intervention. If we cannot talk about mass killings, how do we justify the war? Human Rights Watch writes that, 'within three weeks of the start of NATO bombing, 525,787 refugees from Kosovo had flooded the neighboring countries, according to the United Nation High Commissioner for Refugees (UNHCR). All told, government forces expelled 862,979 ethnic Albanians from Kosovo, and several hundred thousand more were internally displaced, in addition to

---

[2]'Massacres in Kosovo never happened, say Canadians who investigated mass graves', *The Ottawa Citizen*, 29 August 2004.
[3]Nataša Kandić, 'Members of the State Security Took Part in the Destruction of Evidence of the War Crimes in Kosovo.' 23 December 1004. http://www.hlc. org.yu/english/Facing_The_Past/press_Releases/index.php?file=1004.html. [Last visited 26 April 2006].

those displaced prior to March 1999. More than 80 per cent of the entire population or 90 per cent of Kosovo Albanians were displaced from their homes.'[4] As the flow of refugees started to cross the borders with Albania, Montenegro and Macedonia at the same time as the NATO bombing in March 1999, the question has been raised: what came first, the humanitarian crisis or the war? War critics such as Noam Chomsky[5] or the British journalist Eve-Ann Prentice, a defense witness in the trial of the late Slobodan Milošević,[6] have no doubt that the war precipitated the humanitarian crisis and not *vice versa*.

The Answer

We looked for an answer to this allegation in the independent report presented to the International Tribunal for the Former Yugoslavia on 3 January 2002, 'Killings and Refugee Flow in Kosovo, March–June 1999'. The report is authored by Patrick Ball, Wendy Betts, Fritz Scheuren, Jana Dudukovich and Jana Asher, under the auspices of the American Association for the Advancement of Science and the American Bar Association/Central and East European Law Initiative.[7] This study is a statistical analysis of patterns of killings and refugee flows during the NATO's bombing campaign, based on a scientific estimate of the number of deaths and refugees. Because those two phenomena show distinct temporal and regional patterns, the researchers conclude that they did not occur independently and could thus be explained by a common cause. But which one?

---

[4]*Under Orders, War Crimes in Kosovo*, Human Rights Watch, 2001, p. 4 also http://www.hrw.org/reports/2001/kosovo.
[5]Among others articles and books, 'A Review of NATO's War over', *Z Magazine*, April–May 2001, also in http://www.chomsky.info/articles/200005-html.
[6]Michael Furquhar, 'Through the Looking Class. British Journalist Tells Milošević Trial that western politicians and press created distorted image of the conflict', IWPR, Tribunal Update No. 438, 2005–February 2006, http://www.iwpr.net/ index.php?m=p&o=259362&s=f&apc_state=henftri259362.
[7]To read the complete report, go to http://archives.aaas.org/ docs/2002-.pdf. Similar conclusions are reached independently by Human Rights Watch, see *Under Orders* (2001), especially Ch. 15, 'Statistical Analysis of Violations'. This is only partially accounted for by the fact that Human Rights Watch provided its interview data for the AAAS-ABA/CEELI report, 17 per cent of the total interviews.

Was the KLA the reason for people to leave their homes, whether because they were ordered by the guerrilla or they were fleeing the conflict between the Yugoslav forces and the KLA? Or was it NATO the main culprit, directly, as the bombing killed and displaced people, or indirectly, because it instigated Yugoslav authorities to take revenge on Albanian civilians? A third hypothesis is that there was a systematic campaign to expel Albanians from Kosova and the killings were either used to accelerate the exodus or were caused by it. The study finds that only the third hypothesis, or the Yugoslav authorities' campaign of killings and deportation, is consistent with the data. The other two are rejected. This is not a definitive proof of guilt, but it is a scientifically sound analysis that resonates with the many reports by nongovernmental organizations on the humanitarian crisis of 1999.

How do the Researchers Come to that Conclusion?

First, the data. They count the refugees, by using the Albanian border guard registries of people entering Albanian through Morina and supplementing them with records obtained from the UNHCR and the Albanian government as well as survey data from human rights organizations. This number is not the conclusive data on all those who left their homes, as it included only people who crossed the border and not the internally displaced. The total number of the dead, 10,356, is estimated on the basis of a widely-used demographic statistical technique and using data from the American Bar Association/Central and East European Law Initiative (ABA/CEELI); Human Rights Watch; the Organization for the Security and Cooperation in Europe (OSCE); and records of exhumations conducted by international teams for the ICTY.

The researchers discover that the refugees left their homes in waves.

'From late March through late May 1999, ethnic Albanians left their homes in Kosovo in three distinct time periods, or phases. These phases were: 24 March to 6 April; 7 April to 23 April; and 24 April to 11 May. The essential characteristic of this phase structure is the presence of low points in the number of refugees leaving their homes on 6 to 8 April and 23 to 25 April, the phase transition dates. During the 6 to 8 April phase transition, refugee flow falls to approximately 6,000 people, down from the phase one peak of slightly more than 52,000. During the 23 to 25 April phase transition, refugee flow falls to approximately 1,000 from the phase two peak of more than 16,000. The third phase sees refugee flow rising to two peaks of approximately 8,000 and 6,000 in early May, representing the last surges. Refugee flow declines to fewer than 100 people per two-day period after 11 May.'

This pattern of flights could not be happening by chance, the researchers conclude.

'The mass exodus of Kosovar Albanians on this scale and in this pattern could only have been driven by a common cause.'

When they turn to analyzing the patterns of killing over time, the researchers find a similar flow.

'The data show a peak in the number of killings in late March, and another peak in mid-April. Most noteworthy is that, similar to the refugee flow data, the incidence of killings fell to nearly zero on 6 to 7 April and again on 22 to 24 April. Thus, not only does the number of killings exhibit the same extreme contrasts between the high and low points as observed in refugee flow, these high and low points occur at the nearly same times as those in the refugee flow. These surges would not occur by chance.'

And when they analyze the number of killings and displaced people by region—north, east, west and south—they find similar patterns as well.

'In all regions, the 6 to 7 and 22 to 24 April dates mark low points in both the flow of refugees and the number of people killed ... The analysis shows that these events occurred in similar patterns in each of the four regions. The analysis does not prove what caused either pattern, not that one of the patterns caused the other. The analysis does show that acts of violence—killings—were associated in time and space with the refugee departures from their homes.'

How to Explain these Patterns?

If these patterns are explained by KLA activities, it is appropriate to assume that KLA actions did precede the thousands of expulsions and killings recorded at the high peaks of the patterns.

'However, this analysis shows that KLA activity followed the peaks in the killing and refugee numbers in more places than it preceded them. Thus there is no clear cause and effect relationship between KLA activity and the pattern described here.'

The hypothesis that NATO may be the cause of these patterns is also rejected.

'[A] noteworthy fact regarding NATO air strikes was that during 2–4 April, attacks were greatly reduced due to bad weather. Yet this period, during which there were relatively few NATO strikes, includes substantial peaks of Kosovo-wide killings and refugee flow. As with the findings regarding the KLA, the analysis of data on NATO shows that the air strikes more often followed the peaks in the killings and refugee numbers than preceded them.

Therefore, the hypothesis that NATO air strikes directly or indirectly caused the patterns in killings and refugee flow should be rejected. The findings of this study are consistent with the hypothesis that action by Yugoslav forces was the cause of the killings and refugee flow. In particular, one of the findings of this study shows a circumstantial link between Yugoslav army activities and the observed pattern in killings and refugee flow. The extreme decline in the number of killings and refugee flow observed during the period 6–7 April coincides with the unilateral ceasefire declared by the Yugoslav authorities in recognition of Orthodox Easter. During the period when Yugoslav forces ceased hostilities, the number of killings and refugee departure fell drastically.'

19. Were Albanians responsible for "reverse ethnic cleansing" after the war?

Vjosa Dobruna

THE ALLEGATION

'Ethnic cleansing' is indeed an appropriate description for what happened in the days after March 17. An anti-Serb rampage by ethnic Albanians left 28 dead and 900 injured (including 80 peacekeepers), made refugees of 3,500 more and destroyed 280 houses and 30 churches. And 'pogrom' a term bandied about by Vojislav Koštunica, Serbian prime minister, is an appropriate metaphor for the course of the violence.
(Christopher Caldwell, editor of the US conservative magazine *The Weekly Standard*).[1]

The exodus of Serbs from Kosova after the war has been interpreted as 'reverse ethnic cleansing,' an understanding which has been reinforced by the March 2004 riots.

Convinced that they can act with impunity and tired of waiting for independence, Albanians in the province are growing restless. Last year, violent race riots erupted in Kosovo, revealing the ethnic tensions that lie just below the surface in Kosovo. For three days, a pogrom against the Serb minority raged out of control while many of the KFOR troops stayed in the camps, doing nothing to intervene. By the time it was over, 19 people were dead, thousand were injured, and almost 600 buildings had been destroyed.
(Alkman Granitsas, journalist).[2]

---

[1]'Nato's Kosovo Dream is Dead', *The Financial Times*, 29 March 2004.
[2]'Paradigm Slip', *The New Republic*, 11 April 2005.

The Answer

After the end of the 1999 war, followed by NATO deployment in Kosova, the mass migration of tens of thousands of Serbs to Serbia and Montenegro has changed the local demographic character. That this phenomenon occurred in a climate of intimidation and violence cannot be disputed. But is 'reverse ethnic cleansing' really an appropriate definition of what happened? Ethnic cleansing is a general term, although an agreement exists in the international arena on what it means: it is the process by which an area is rendered 'ethnically homogeneous by using force or intimidation to remove persons of given groups from the area'.[3] Usually, it is accompanied by military operations. Commonly, it is called a 'policy', a systemic campaign, it implies a plan and a conspiracy to it by groups who represent or are backed by political or military authorities. In Kosova, ethnic cleansing was carried out through arbitrary detentions, torture, rape, killing, destruction of property and mass deportation by the Serb state led by Milošević. To call postwar violence against Serb civilians and individual violations of human rights of Serbs in Kosova 'reverse ethnic cleansing' is tantamount to establishing political and moral equivalence between two very different phenomena. This judgment uses general ethnic categories to frame groups and events that are far more complex and deserve closer scrutiny.

In 1999 there was no policy developed by any structure of the Albanian society to expel Serbs from Kosova. In fact, there was no Albanian-organized political structure at all, with the authority and/or the capacity to conduct a campaign of ethnic cleansing. The first Special Representative of the Secretary General in Kosovo, Bernard Kouchner, said, 'It is not fair to make comparisons with the situation before or during the war ... It is no longer a matter of policy ... the crimes we see are the acts of individuals.'[4] There was simply no state policy or political conspiracy to make Kosova a 'pure' Albanian state. Human rights

---

[3]'Ethnic Cleansing' in Roy Gutman and David Rieff (eds) *Crimes of War: What the Public Should Know* (New York: Norton, 1999) also http://www.crimesofwar.org/thebook/book.html.

[4]Bernard Kouchner, Special Representative of the UN Secretary General Kofi Annan, http://www.osce.org/publications/odihr/1999/11/17756_515_en.pdf [Consulted 4 April 2006].

organizations such as Human Rights Watch, that have thoroughly investigated violations of individuals and groups rights, have found evidence 'that some KLA units were responsible for violence against minorities beginning in the summer of 1999, and continuing throughout 2000 and early 2001'.[5] They have established that postwar violence against Serb civilians has been politically motivated, besides being the manifestation of a desire for revenge and retaliation, where 'the removal from Kosovo of non-ethnic Albanians ... [would] better justify an independent state'. However, they have found 'no evidence ... of a coordinated policy to this end of the political or military leadership of the former KLA, which has made public statements condemning attacks against minorities.' No evidence was ever produced of a possible responsibility of former KLA commanders in leading or backing such violence. There was no conspiracy among postwar security forces in the name of a real or imagined 'ethnic solidarity', due to the simple fact that international organizations such as the United Nations Mission in Kosovo (UNMIK) and the NATO Mission KFOR were and still are responsible for local security, law and order.

Very few individuals were involved in the violence, as the large majority of Albanians focused on rebuilding their homes and their lives from scratch, enjoying the peace. The best evidence for this is the outcome of postwar elections, where Kosovars consistently gave large margins of victory[6] to the party lead by Mr. Ibrahim Rugova, the Democratic League of Kosova (LDK). Mr. Rugova ran on a platform advocating an independent Kosova as a state for all its inhabitants, the Kosovars, respectful of minority rights. Rarely in history have those who fought in a liberation war performed badly in the first postwar elections. In Kosova, the more militant parties that were founded by former Kosovo Liberation Army (KLA) fighters, and those advocating 'Ethnic Albania' have won a smaller number of seats in Parliament.

Do Albanian leaders have any responsibility for what happened after the war? Of course they do. Their failure of leadership cannot be

---

[5]All the quotations in this paragraph are from 'Abuses after June 12, 1999', in *Under Orders: War Crimes in Kosovo*, Human Rights Watch, 2001 also http://www.hrw.org/reports/2001/kosovo [Last visited 26 April 2006].
[6]Results of the 2000 municipal election, the first after the war: the LDK won by 58.0 per cent of the votes. Source: Statistic Office of Kosova, OSCE Mission in Kosovo.

underestimated. In the immediate aftermath of the war, they showed poor judgment and lack of political courage. Former KLA commanders did distance themselves from violence against minorities, but did not publicly and actively engage in stopping it. When human rights activists and some individuals dared publicly and forcibly criticize those actions, they found no support. More recently, in March 2004, Albanian political leadership has been taken by surprise by the mob rule that spread like wildfire all over the province. Some politicians forgot that they had been charged with leading a vulnerable society and 'followed' the mob, using the riots for their own opportunistic reasons. The active intervention of Prime Minister Bajram Rexhepi and a few others to stop the violence was an exception to the more general passive and confused reaction. Still, failure to lead, as unforgivable as it is in such circumstances, does not amount to 'ethnic cleansing', especially when the political leadership has very little or no authority on law enforcement.

Is the Albanian society responsible for the postwar violence? There were Albanian perpetrators who committed acts of violence against individuals and property in the aftermath of the war and in 2004. But even more than in the case of the leadership, it would be wrong to attribute collective responsibilities to an entity which is complex, differentiated, and should not be seen in essentialist terms, as a unified group. Yet, there are personal and political observations that suggest some interpretive comments on the failure of the society to show a stronger condemnation of the violence.

Despite the history of discrimination against Albanians by different Serbian regimes from 1912 onwards, Serbs and Albanians have lived side-by-side with very few exceptions. Conflict over territory has always been a problem for nationalist Serb structures such as the Orthodox Church and the Academy of Science, but not the main issue between Serbs and Albanians.[7] The decade of apartheid (1990–1999) and the war of 1998–1999 have changed this. The conflict that was perceived as rooted in the oppression of Albanians by the Serb state began

---

[7]It is interesting to note that Albanians have not publicly blamed the Serbian people for the atrocities committed against them; they have merely condemned the Serbian government. Justin Godard, of the Carnegie Commission, pointed out that all nations ought to be able to make the distinction between government and people, as the Albanians did.

to acquire strong ethnic connotations, because of the mass support and involvement of individual Serbs in implementing the discriminatory policies of the Milošević regime. Even after the war, the majority of the remaining Serbs in Kosova voted for Milošević and the Radical Party of Serbia, the same people and organizations that planned and executed atrocities against Albanians in Kosova.

Upon their return to their destroyed homes in June 1999, Albanians tried to come to terms with what had happened to them. They came back to burned houses, or apartments still standing but emptied of everything of value, even undergarments and items of sentimental value, such as family pictures. They were missing traces of their past lives. More tragically, they were missing family members and friends, disappeared in the frenzy of the war against civilians waged by Serb troops, with the complicity of many Serb civilians. Dealing with the trauma of a decade of apartheid and a violent war consumed a great deal of the majority population's energy, at a time in which they found themselves to be also the political majority: Albanians did not fully understand their new role because they had never experienced it in their history. Personally and politically, they did not have the awareness that as a majority, they had more responsibility for their neighbors, no matter what their ethnic identification. When Serbs withdrew into their 'enclaves', initially for serious security reasons, later to boycott Kosova's provisional institutions and hopes for independence, the situation was no better for either side; the group that had represented oppression and violence was out of sight, and further, mutual mistrust built up. It was not just a matter of perception, but of justice denied. With a police and court system working at best erratically, very few charges for past violations of human rights against Albanians were made after the war, resulting in minor sentences for crimes such as mass murder.[8] Nothing is known of the fate of 3,525 missing persons.[9] This issue remains an open wound in Kosova, but is also a symbol of wider grievance, particularly among Albanians, who blame its lack of solution on Belgrade's intransigence and the inaction of UNMIK. The

---

[8]'Observations and Recommendations of the OSCE Legal System Monitoring', http://www.osce.org/documents/mik/1999/12/963_en.pdf, [Consulted 4 April 2006].

[9]ICRC statement, 'Persons Unaccounted for in Connection with the Kosovo Crisis', 10 April 2001.

public sensed that there would be no justice for past violations of human rights and that the truth about what happened during the war would never be known. An environment in which impunity triumphed became the background for further violations of human rights, this time the rights of minorities: the great majority of violence against them has gone unpunished.

The March 2004 riots were the result of a general mood of fear and mistrust. The violence was sparked off by a tragic event, the drowning in the river Iber of three Albanian children, who were believed at first to have jumped in the water to escape pursuit by Serb residents of a nearby village. As the news of the incident spread, it fed the belief that the war was not over yet. Although unprofessional media, which immediately reported the drowning of the three children as an ethnically motivated incident, contributed to and further deepened the already poisoned atmosphere, the riots were not the result of media reporting; the violence was related to the common perception among the Albanian population that only evil can come from the Serb side.

The strong suspicion that Serb enclaves in Kosova were being used by Belgrade to consolidate political and territorial control over parts of the province, scared and enraged many Albanians, even those who did not join the demonstrators. Because of the rich history of ethnic cleansing of Albanians by Serbia and the recent experience in which a willing local Serb population participated, these latter become target of the March 2004 violence.[10] Most of the protesters were young students, children from secondary schools, who joined in spontaneous violence against ethnic Serb neighbors, whose presence is a catalyst for serious problems. As an outside observer has also noted, 'failure to restore some vitality to Kosovo's economic life and offer a positive perspective for a future political settlement acceptable to both sides' has led to a situation where 'both communities have provided thousands of young recruits to an army of the dispossessed and unemployed. With no money and the prospect only of further misery, frustration and anger

---

[10]During the 2004 March protest, 19 people—8 Serbs and 11 Albanians–were killed. 550 homes and 20 Serbian Orthodox Churches were burned, leaving approximately 4,000 Serbs, Roma and Ashkali displaced. See Human Rights Watch Report, *Failure to Protect: Anti-Minority Violence in Kosovo*, 26 July 2004. http://hrw.org/reports/2004/kosovo0704/ [Last visited 26 April 2006].

have now reached a breaking point.'[11] There is no alibi for failing to protect minorities, or for failing to integrate them. Yet, the March 2004 riots were not 'reverse ethnic cleansing'. In their aftermath, Kosova's Provisional Institutions of the Self-Government (PISG) made a commitment to rebuild homes, monasteries and churches destroyed in the rioting with government funds: 4.2 million Euros for the reconstruction of religious sites and over 10.0 million Euros for the reconstruction of Serb and Ashkali communities.

Twenty years ago, Serb strategies to cleanse Kosova of Albanians were announced by the Serbian Orthodox Church with the Academy of Science and Arts of Serbia. Different Serbian political leaders simply adopted the existing platform, as Milošević did. Ethnic cleansing started in March 1998. 250,000 Albanians were driven out of their homes prior to the October 1998 cease-fire.[12] In the spring of 1999, about 863,000 Albanians were deported from Kosova and 590,000 were internally displaced within the province. 90 per cent of the Albanian population was displaced during the war.[13] They represented the entire population of Kosova, people of all ages, genders, and professions. They were able to return to their homes only under the protection of NATO troops and those who used to live in the northern part of Kosova are still displaced. Although the expulsion of Albanians from Kosova by the Serb state has been compared to a Biblical event for its sheer size, it is not a new phenomenon. Other deportations, although smaller in size, have been planned and executed throughout history.

The Serbs who fled Kosova after the war in their thousands are part of this history. Up to now, there is no accurate data on their number.[14] Who were they? In his recent novel, publisher and politician

[11]Misha Glenny, 'The UN and NATO are failing Kosovo', *The International Herald Tribune*, 22 March 2004.

[12]OSCE, *Human Rights in Kosovo: as Seen as Told*, vol. II, 14 June–31 October 1999, ch. 14, also http://www.osce.org/item/17756.html [Consulted 5 April 2006].

[13]UNHCR rough estimates as of 13 May 1999, quoted in OSCE, *Human Rights*, ch. 14.

[14]According to a study by the European Stability Initiative (*The Lausanne Principle. Multiethnicity, Territory and the Future of Kosovo's Serbs*, 7 June 2004, http://www.esiweb.org/pdf/esi_document_id_53.pdf) [Last visited 26 April 2006] which compares figures from the 1991 census and current estimates of Serbs still living in Kosova, the number of internally displaced Serbs could be as low as 65,000, less than half the Serb government figures.

Veton Surroi writes from the point of view of a Serb man who stayed behind and reflected on the predicament of his community after the war: 'Those who stained their hands with blood needed no escort, they left even before NATO came. Afterwards, those who had been connected to the government packed up and left. And then, those who thought that Serbs have the right to rule over Albanians, left. And then, those who had offended the Albanians, left. And then those who had not done a thing, but could not speak Albanian. And then those that couldn't bear the fear, the stories on persecution, and the sole idea that armed Albanians could come into their houses and kill them.'[15] Surroi's work is a novel of political fiction, but it well describes reality. There was mass migration of Serbs after the war, but no mass expulsion. After the NATO air strikes ended, many Serbs left with the Yugoslav Army forces (JNA) and paramilitaries. They left for fear of retribution or because they were affiliated with the Milošević regime. Many left because under pressure from their military structures. As a woman from Gjakova who had been protected by her Serbian neighbors for about three months recounted, 'Serbian soldiers came to the house and ordered the women to leave with them'.[16]

This was not the first time in the history of Kosova that Serbs left in large numbers after a change of regime. And there is no historical evidence that their migration was the result of ethnic cleansing orchestrated by Albanian political groups or Albanian-led institutions. In 1966, after the fall of Alexander Ranković, the Former Minister of the Interior notorious for his anti-Albanian repressive policies, many Serbs who worked for the security state apparatus left Kosova. Serb nationalists described what happened then as the result of discrimination and harassment: 'Gradually the Albanians took over almost all government organs and socialist enterprises in Kosovo, oppressing the Serbian minority who obtained little support or protection from the central government.'[17] But the reality is quite different, as a protagonist of those events remembers: 'After the fall of Ranković, many Serbian cadres in power during his tenure wanted to go to Belgrade. The ethnic

---

[15]Veton Surroi, *Azem Berisha's one and only flight to the castle* (Prishtina: Koha, 2005), p. 74.

[16]Interview with SB, 18 June 1999.

[17]Andrei Simić, *Special Issue: War among the Yugoslavs*, Anthropology of East Europe Review, vol. 11, nos. 1–2, Autumn, 1993.

homogenization of Kosova had already started. They asked us Albanians to nominate them for Federal and Republican posts in Belgrade, and we would do that gladly. It was a common interest; they wanted to go out of Kosova, we wanted to run Kosova.'[18] This process of ethnic homogenization was not happening only in Kosova. 'Despite all efforts by the Titoist government to create a sense of Yugoslav identity, after a rather short period of formal reconciliation there was an intensification of feelings of ethnic distance and opposition. Among other indicators, contrary to expectations that the republics would become increasingly heterogeneous, there was a growth of migration by individuals into the republics dominated by their own ethnic groups.'[19]

After the independence of Kosova it would be appropriate to establish a commission to address the grievances of the people of Kosova in regard to past violations of human rights as well as write a new history of Kosova that would not be based on half-truths. It will be a new start for the relations between Albanians and Serbs in Kosova.

---

[18]Interview with Ekrem Murtezai (Principal adviser to Central Committee of League of the Communists of Yugoslavia, LCY; chief of the cabinet of Fadil Hoxha, member of the Executive Bureau of LCY), February 2006.
[19]Svetislav Spasojevic 'Kuda se Selimo?', *Nin* , October 28, 26–8.

20. Is it true that an independent Kosova will inevitably be a mono-ethnic state, unless Serb communities and their territories become autonomous?

Albin Kurti

THE ALLEGATION

If the province does gain statehood ... he says a mass of Serbs will leave, joining 100,000 exiles who fled to Serbia in 1999. : 'If they don't leave— he says—there will be more killings.'
(Oliver Ivanović, Serb political leader from Mitrovica).[1]

It is clear to everyone that a multi-ethnic paradise in Kosovo is unworkable, more so even than the communist utopia of a society without classes. If that were still feasible, a multi-ethnic society in Kosovo is not.
(Voijslav Kostunica, Prime Minister of Serbia and Montenegro).[2]

The plan passed unanimously today by the Serbian Assembly wants to protect these values of a multi-ethnic and multicultural society. They should be protected through a specific principle, that of an autonomy within autonomy. It is considered that the Serb community can survive and that displaced Serbs can return to Kosovo–Metohija only if they have

---

[1]Quoted by Vivienne Walt and Dean Anastasijević, 'Divided they stand. Kosovo seems headed for independence, but Serbs and Albanians are still at odds over their future', *Time International*, 28 November 2005.
[2]VIP, 29 March 2004.

certain prerogatives of power—prerogatives in legislative, executive and judicial power.
(Aleksandar Simić, Serbia and Montenegro Federal Constitutional Court judge and member of the working group for drafting a plan for Kosova).[3]

Serb leaders, both in Kosova and Serbia, argue in favor of substantive decentralization of Serb-majority municipalities as the only solution to the problem of cohabitation of Serbs and Albanians in Kosova. The same 'realist' perspective contemplates also the partition of Kosova.

Granting northern Kosovo to Serbia while the rest of the province becomes independent would relieve Prishtina of the futile task of trying to assert control over a region that, come what may, intend to maintain its links to Belgrade ... As long as Prishtina is disabused of any hope of swapping northern Kosovo for Albanians enclaves in Southern Serbia, partition would also present a compromise of sorts, enabling Belgrade to claim it has not been left empty-handed. As one of president Tadić's advisers stated, 'If we are looking for a compromise solution, partition seems to be the easy way out'.
(Charles A. Kupchan, Professor of International Affairs at Georgetown University and Senior Fellow at the Council on Foreign Relations).[4]

The Answer

It was Milošević who desperately wanted to make the conflict in Kosova an ethnic conflict, although it really was the result of Serbia's hegemonic aspirations, turned into aggression and terrible crimes by the regime. Strangely, this 'ethnic' approach is still alive today with UNMIK and its favorite buzzword, 'multi-ethnicity', a term whose meaning has no definition: there are no models we are supposed to pursue, and no concrete examples from experience or history we should rely on. There is no idea of how to measure the achievement of 'multi-ethnicity', except the belief that simply by

---

[3]Interview with Belgrade-based B92 TV on 29 April 2004.
[4]'Independence for Kosovo', *Foreign Affairs*, November–December 2005.

repeating a meaningless phrase it will suddenly become meaningful. From the very beginning UNMIK tried to accomplish multi-ethnicity in an ethnically-based manner, by naming groups—Albanians, Serbs, Romas, Turks, Egyptians, Bosniacs and Ashkalis—as in a *terra nullius*. Even today UNMIK does not see human beings, individuals, citizens, or students in Kosova. It sees only Albanians, Serbs and other communities. To UNMIK, individuals are random samples of particular collectivities; the Serb community is singled out among them to the point of discriminating against others. As a result of this, the existing dualism of Kosova–Serbia has been replaced by the dualism of Albanians–Serbs, representing the conflict in Kosova as inherently ethnic as well as shaping it as such; power categorizes and labels people, and over time they become those labels. Milošević did something similar. During the 1990s young people tried to tell Milošević that they were students, but Milošević told them: 'no, you are Albanians!' Presenting and shaping the conflict in Kosova as an ethnic conflict is wrong and harmful. If the conflict and the problem are ethnic, then Milošević is absolved of all crimes and there is only one option: partition. But it is not the solution. Multi-ethnicity, as cohabitation and cooperation of people from different ethnicities, cannot be achieved ethnically.

The problem with UNMIK's ethnicized discourse is that it defines people as groups, starting from differences and not from what is common, such as people's need for freedom, dignity, employment, education, health care, and social security. No wonder. For all these, development is needed. The lack of integration of the Serb minority is not related only to a bitter past, but also to the future. The highest level of integration of Serbs with Albanians has already taken place regardless of the law: first, in numerous local UNMIK and KFOR offices throughout Kosova, where Albanians and Serbs have worked together without a single incident for six and a half years; and second, in organized crime and informal business, where good profits are being made. This high level of integration does not happen because it is situated outside the law, but because there is development, well being and a shared feeling of progress among people. The South East European University (SEEU) in the mostly Albanian area of Tetovo, Macedonia, is an example of how quality European education integrates communities: no Macedonians enrolled in this university at the beginning, now they constitute 15 per cent of the student body.

Lacking independence and sovereignty, Kosova has been administered since 1999 by UNMIK, which has not developed our society and certainly continues to be a mission that cannot develop it. On the contrary. 2,5 billion Euros were poured by the international community into Kosova since the war: Why are there still Serbs, Romas and others in extreme poverty? If international organizations (especially UNMIK and KFOR) ceased for only one month to erect billboards all over Kosova, each of which costs 400 Euros which is twice the average salary, and instead used the money for the social and economic improvement of poor minorities, the condition of these latter would substantially change. But no, poor people from minorities are invited to conferences and seminars where they eat fancy meals in fancy hotels and then they go back to their homes, where they can hardly afford bread and milk.

Underdevelopment characterizes Kosova in all fields. Poverty, unemployment and dissatisfaction are on the increase. 15 per cent of the population is in extreme poverty, another 40 per cent are poor, and unemployment is over 60 per cent. 45.914 people were registered as newborns in the year 1987. They reached the age of 18 last year; became mature and unemployed. The per capita GDP is 964 Euros which is 22 times less than Germany! There is no economic investment or any significant domestic production. The trade deficit is large: the export/import coverage is only 4.38 per cent. In the year 2004 imports were worth 1.030 million Euros, while exports amounted to only 45.1 million Euros. In the past we used to export people—asylum seekers. Now they are being deported back. Instead, poor Kosova exports money to the European Union: 74 per cent of the bank deposits of Kosovars are in two foreign banks, over 150 million Euros of Pensions Trust Fund are also abroad, as are nearly 200 million Euros of Post and Telecom of Kosova, all this namely for some security reasons. There is a status quo in Kosova, but this status quo is only for the people in power, not at all for the majority of population which is regressing economically. While international and domestic politicians keep talking about fulfilling standards, the standard of living for the people of Kosova is sliding from bad to worse. At the edge of existence, when their very survival is at risk, even brothers and best friends become hostile to each other. If Albanians, Serbs and others worked in factories, for instance, with 300 Euro monthly salaries, they would communicate and cooperate.

In the first two years after the end of the war nearly one million people who were deported by Serbian police and military forces returned home and rebuilt 120,000 houses destroyed by the Yugoslav Army. After this humanitarian, emergency and peace-building phase, we should have moved to the development phase. That didn't happen. UNMIK has been an interim administration without a deadline, even though it is precisely the existence of a deadline that constitutes the definition of interim. It has no vision, no plans for the future and no idea that development is a key factor for integration. Despite all this, with the exception of most of the Serb minority, five other minorities are integrated in postwar Kosova: for example, there are many cases of mixed marriages between Albanians and Turks and Albanians and Bosniacs. In Kosova, in fact, there are no minorities, there are only ethnic communities. They have no particular legal status, no specific standing in the society, as there is no democracy and no majority rule. Actually, Kosova is ruled by the latest minority that we in Prishtina jokingly call 'domestic internationals'.

Minorities are typical of nation states—Kosova is neither a state nor a nation state. We can talk about a Serb minority in Croatia, but not in Kosova. Why then is the category of minorities pushed forward? The concern for minorities is a psychological substitute, therefore a diversion from the real concern for the status of Kosova and the fear of the domino effect in the region and beyond. This has created a cosmic viewpoint on Kosova, a viewpoint from the planet Mars which also encompasses, Taiwan, Tibet, Chechnya and other crises. Again: no wonder. Kosova, a small place in Europe, has a planetary address: the UN Security Council. Yet, all Kosova's neighboring countries, with the exception of Serbia, want an independent state of Kosova, or at least are not bothered by it.

Belgrade wants to make the independence and statehood of Kosova impossible; just that. This is exactly the meaning of the formula 'more than autonomy, less than independence'. And it wants to replace talks about the final status of Kosova with negotiations over the territorial autonomy of Serbs in Kosova. This shouldn't be a surprise: in Kosova the demand for more competences, for more responsibilities and for more political power dominates, in Serbia the demand is for more territories. Serbia is already present in Kosova with its parallel structures. For over six and a half years Serb teachers, doctors, officials have received two wages: one from the budget of Kosova and another from the budget of Serbia. Serbia's parallel structures in Kosova have their own annual budget line in the Serbian government's budget plan. As in the past, and not only during the Milošević era, Serbia sees and treats Kosova merely as a territory, a perception which will continue to militarize the Serbs of Kosova just as it has done in the past. Milošević wanted Kosova, but especially in the year 1999 he wanted it without Albanians. Today, Belgrade doesn't allow Serbs to integrate into Kosova to integrate, because then it will lose its political influence. A certain percentage of Serbs must remain in territorial enclaves and not be integrated in the society of Kosova, so Serbia can use them as a backdoor for its plans. The former Mayor of Strpce, Sladjan Ilic, was badly beaten in Belgrade because he showed loyalty toward Prishtina. He didn't come back to Kosova.

Decentralization before status is the first and most important step toward partition. As early as 6 November 2004 Miroljub Labus, Deputy Prime Minister of Serbia, wrote in the newspaper *Politika*, 'In the area of Kosovo and Metohija two entities shall be created. The Serb entity would include these zones: Northern Kosovo (the municipalities of Leposaviq, Zubin Potok, Zveçan and northern Mitrovica) and Anamorava in Kosovo (the municipality of Kamenica, Novobërda, Graçanica and parts of Gjilan and Lipjan).' In the west, Miroljub Labus is considered a moderate and a democrat. Labus mentioned in detail the municipalities and the parts of municipalities that should belong to a Serbian entity, including the eastern part of Kosova in order to encircle the southern part of Serbia, the Presheva Valley mainly inhabited by Albanians, and isolate it from Kosova. (The President of Serbia, Boris Tadić, reiterated this after his meeting with Vladimir Putin in Moscow.) In the Presheva Valley, in the village of Boroc in Bujanoc, Serbia is building a large military base for its Army that has 1,000 beds and will serve as a logistical and command centre. The reason for this base was revealed openly by Nebojša Cović, who on 20 January 2005 declared on B-92 radio that the armed presence of Serbia in the Presheva Valley is necessary so that Serbs of the Anamorava region in Kosova can feel secure! In the municipalities of Gjilan and Kamenica there is communication and cooperation between Albanians and Serbs, however it is exactly Belgrade's policies of decentralization that will destroy this.

On 1 February 2006 the daily newspaper *Politika* announced that municipalities from Serbia, Vojvodina and even from the Republika Srpska in Bosnia will help the Serbs to return to Kosova and to the new Serb municipalities which are about to be created in Kosova through the decentralization process. Decentralization is the most effective means for the implementation of the Serbian government's plans to fragment Kosova, before retaking it. Through decentralization, Serbia intends to expand and define the borders of enclaves, to create continuous territory between enclaves, and legitimate its parallel structures in Kosova. Since the Serbian structures in the enclaves have not been dismantled in advance, decentralization will not offer local citizens the opportunity to govern themselves, but will shift power to Belgrade. The final result of decentralization will be the creation of internal territorial borders within Kosova. Decentralization will cause the final territorial partition of Kosova, while creating a strong Serb entity inside Kosova.

The Albanian villages that Serb negotiators intend to place inside Serb municipalities are those which did not lose many people or suffer too much material damage during the war. The Serbian government believes that those villages can be more easily incorporated in the new Serb municipalities, but these Albanian villages are threatened by the model of the north of Mitrovica. On the nights of 3 and 4 of February 2000, in the north of Mitrovica, 11 Albanians (6 men and 5 women) were killed. Later, during the same month 1,564 Albanian families, with a total of 11,364 members, were expelled. This atrocity occurred in the presence of the KFOR forces and the police. In the north of Kosova a total of only 4,000 Albanian residents have remained. Serbian officials from Kosova and Serbia very often declare that the north of Kosova is a multi-ethnic area. This is what they mean by multi-ethnicity: areas with an overwhelming majority of Serbian population, controlled by the structures of Serbia, and with Albanians as a minority or, alternatively, as a majority that needs to be expelled or killed so that they become the minority!

Part of Serbia's attempt to strengthen its plans for an internal territorial rearrangement of Kosova is the ex-territoriality of the Orthodox churches and monasteries. The Coordinating Centre of the Government of Serbia for Kosova has marked 21 churches and monasteries in Kosova as having a so-called 'strategic interest' for Serbia. The expansionist politics of the Serbian state throughout history has been built on three pillars: the church, the army and the academy. The Church has blessed, the army has oppressed, and the political academy has planned re-colonization. Today, the Serb state intends to transform Orthodox religious sites in our country into a means for the re-colonization of Kosova. In the areas where churches and monasteries will be given ex-territorial status, the Serb government plans to realize the so-called 'sustainable return' of Serbs in Kosova. Belgrade does not want thousands of Serbs to return to Prishtina, or where they have lived before, because they will probably remain a simple minority dispersed throughout Kosova, without significant influence on the future of the country. In order to have enough influence and keep Kosova hostage, they want Serbs to live where they will form a majority and Albanians a minority, or where they will create concentrated and ethnically cleaned Serb residential areas.

In Serb areas within Kosova, Serbia wants to establish Kosova Police Service (KPS) sub-stations. On 6 December 2005, Sanda Rašković-Ivić, who leads the Coordinating Centre of Serbia for Kosova, signed an agreement in Belgrade with Jean Dussourd, the head of the First Pillar of UNMIK in charge of the police and the judicial system, to establish 14 new KPS sub-stations, 12 of which will be in places where Serbs are the majority. This was agreed just before the Special Representative of the Secretary General Soren Jessen Petersen gave the green light for the formation of two new ministries in Kosova's Provisional Government (the Ministry of Interior Affairs and the Ministry of Justice). The Goverment of Kosova gets more symbolic ministries, Serbia gets more solid substance. Through these new police sub-stations Serbia claims to guarantee security for Serb returnees, but in fact is protecting its plan for the re-colonization of Kosova: since each police sub-station has its own operation zone, their combined area of authority will represent the foundation for the future boundaries of a Serb autonomus entity inside Kosova. Serbia does not protect its own people, only territory. There are many Serbs in extreme poverty in Kosova; all Serbs are encouraged by their government to use Serbia's car plates, because not only there is no concern for their security, the attempt is to make them a potential target. Instead Serbia cares a great deal for its security forces in Kosova, such as the 'bridgewatchers' of Mitrovica, a criminal paramilitary formation which prevents Albanians crossing to the north side and that now staffs the KPS. Serbia wants the return of Serbs not for their sake but for the sake of its expansionist plans.

By means of negotiation Serbia is attempting to justify its ambitions to re-establish de facto control of our population and territory, even through partition. There is neither penance nor regret in the Serbian political and intellectual establishment for the 12,000 killed, 3,000 kidnapped, thousands raped, one million expelled and 120,000 houses destroyed in Kosova. There has been no justice for the victims. Serbia was never identified as the aggressor who exercised repression and terror for more than a century. On the contrary, after the fall of Milošević, Serbia was rehabilitated automatically (without fulfilling any conditions or standards) and was admitted into international institutions and bodies. There are many issues which can and should be negotiated with Serbia, but only once the one non-negotiable precondition, the will of the people of Kosova, is accepted. Lack of sovereignty causes a two-fold problem for Kosova. First, it pushes Kosova backward to a degradation that threatens internal security. Secondly, it feeds Serbia's appetites for Kosova and nurtures the continuation of nationalist and chauvinist regimes in Belgrade. This threatens external security. Sovereignty for Kosova that disables Serbia's intrusion and allows freedom for development is key to both integration and security for all communities.

21. Is it true that a human rights culture, respectful of minorities, is a remote possibility in Kosova?

Julie Mertus

THE ALLEGATION

The lack of confidence in the possibility of a human rights culture that is respectful of minorities in post-war Kosova ranges from disbelief to moderate pessimism, as in the following impassioned statement by the Ombudsperson at the end of his mandate.

According to recent statements made at the February UN Security Council meeting on the question of Kosovo, much work still must be done to improve the overall situation of the minority communities in the province. ... What does it mean to protect ethnic minorities? Good laws can be promulgated and special programs can be designed, but if there is no sincere societal will to adopt these changes in everyday life then there is little perspective to alter the dismal status quo.
(Marek Antoni Nowicki, International Ombudsperson in Kosovo, 2000–2005).[1]

The Answer

Slobodan Milošević is gone. He had been the most extraordinary interpreter and manipulator of the 'Myth of Kosovo', or the myth of

---

[1]Kosovo Pro-Memoria, 24 February 2006. http://www.southeasteurope.org/ subpage.php?sub_site=2&id=16495&head=if&site=6 [Consulted on 15 March 2006].

Serbia's loss of its holy land that fueled Serbs' image of themselves as victims. In the story of this man, extraordinarily gifted in manipulating collective myths to suit his individual goals, there is a broader lesson to be learned: how the explosive combination of self-centered political entrepreneurs, nationalism, and 'Truths' about the other creates an irreconcilable enmity between individuals and groups. In order to develop a human rights culture, in Kosova as in Serbia, there should be no place for a cynical exploitation of history as myth and as experience. But neither will it be enough to have new leaderships, new laws and a human rights language, if the people do not fully understand human rights norms; if they do not stop looking at the other in Manichean terms as the enemy; and if humane values do not become part of the identity, interests and expectations of individuals and groups.

By exploiting feelings of insecurity and victimization, Milošević mobilized an entire country to war and become responsible for much misery and bloodshed in former Yugoslavia. But is he the only one to blame? He did not create the 'Myth of Kosovo', nor was his idea to use it for justifying Serb political claims on Kosova. That bright idea came from within Serbia's academic elite, when in 1986 the Memorandum of the Academy of Arts and Science, established the 'truth' of Serb victimization and the need for constitutional revisions to allow for greater centralized control of the Kosova; that stridently defiant document became Milošević's blueprint for war. An understanding that Serb nationalism exists, that it is the sort that promotes Serbs' self-image as victims, and that it predates the war in Yugoslavia explains why Milošević's appropriation of 'the Kosovo myth' was so successful: there was something there to be manipulated.

In my 1999 book on Kosova,[2] I argued that Serb nationalism always had some degree of autonomy that preceded and shaped the political struggles of Milošević's time. At the same time, Milošević was able to use nationalism as a theory of political legitimacy to justify political reality. To recognize this reality is to reject *both* the notion that politics is the cause of everything and that nationalism has nothing to do with it, *and* the notion that conflict is simply the result of age-old primal Balkan hatreds and there is nothing anyone can do until 'those people stop killing each other.' In the book I explained how myths and truths

---

[2]*Kosovo: How Myths and Truths Started a War* (University of California Press, 1999).

can start a war, taking Kosova as a case study for a lesson that could be applied to all. We all have identities, as individuals and as members of groups that are defined through the telling of stories. Accordingly, we understand ourselves as heroes, martyrs, or victims, for example. A dangerous thing, the identity of victim. Once one sees oneself as a victim, one can clearly identify an enemy and elaborate the most demeaning 'truths' about him. As victim, one can more likely find some moral justification to be a perpetrator.

Kosova is one of those places where the identities of two competing nations have been for a long time shaped by a sense of victimization and the construction of 'truths' about the other. There are competing notions of borders, history, language and culture; national stereotypical identities in opposition to each other, whereby Serbs see themselves as 'cultured' compared to the 'primitive' Albanians and Albanians see themselves as 'peaceful' compared to the 'aggressive' Serbs; and narratives of victimization that in recent history happen to collide. But even at the most difficult times, when ethnic tensions were boiling, there were some positive signs. In my clandestine trips to Kosova in the early 1990s, when Milošević's Serbia ruled Kosova as a police state, but Albanians had found some accommodation with the regime by living in a parallel society, I was impressed by how diffused a human rights language was among Albanians. They understood that the repression by the Serb state was not just an expression of brutal force but a violation of fundamental rights that they were entitled to as human beings. The Universal Declaration on Human Rights had already replaced the Socialist state's Constitution as the most influential charter in their society. Later developments in the conflict silenced the 'passive resistance' in favor of armed resistance, but for a full decade a human rights culture was slowly building in Kosova.

It is unfortunate that the 1999 NATO's bombing campaign, dubbed 'humanitarian intervention', never clearly articulated in legal terms the case for justifying intervention on the basis of human rights. The subsequent political developments in Kosova, with the establishment of the UN-led international administration, also failed in fostering a culture of human rights. Since the war, life in Kosova has experienced revenge and violence; it has gone back to mutual suspicion between Serbs and Albanians, and a heightened sense of insecurity for all.

Now Milošević is gone and he can no longer fan the flames of hatred through his references to Serb victimization. The Serbs of Kosova cannot alternatively lament his demise or blame him for all their troubles. Albanians no longer have to fear the return to a police state and to the social and political oppression as a disfavored ethno-national group. There is a real chance for both sides to abandon chauvinist nationalism; set aside myths and truths; and embrace a culture of human rights that would allow Serbs and Albanians to relate to each other not through opposition, but through their shared human experience. As in other countries, included the US, a human rights culture will flourish only with a strong involvement of the civil society and local communities. Memory and storytelling, that were so important in shaping antagonistic identities and fueling deep mistrust, can have a positive role in building community trust in the context of human rights.

22. Would an independent Kosova be an Islamist state?

Dom Lush Gjergji

> Working for Kosovo's independence is to prepare, consciously or unconsciously, the ground for a militant jihad and terrorism in the heart of Europe, which will out at risk all democratic values of Europe and of America itself ... At a time when money and radical propaganda pour into Kosovo from around the Islamic world, I ask: does it make sense for America to hand them a great and unnecessary vestry? Even aside from what may happen to my people—which is my first responsibility—what can be gained from such an outcome in terms of peace in the Balkans, or in Europe?
> (Serbian Orthodox Bishop Artemije of Raška and Prizren).[1]
>
> In this perspective, Kosova's majority Muslim population becomes the exclusive marker of Kosova's religious and cultural identification. The consequence of this perceived exclusive religious make-up, the specter of an Islamist state in an independent Kosova is agitated as a special threat in the dangerous post 9/11 world.

The Answer

Blessed are the meek because they shall inherit the earth (Matthew, 5,5)

Today's world, our time and space, is 'mixed'. It is religiously, ethnically and culturally very complex, a new, still unknown reality

---

[1]Quoted in Srdja Trifković, 'A Bishop's Lonely Struggle', 2006, *Chronicles Magazine* (http://www.chroniclesmagazine.org) [Consulted on 24 April, 2006].

to many, a challenge, an opportunity for cooperation but also clash. The 'clash of civilizations' seems a reality, especially after 9/11 and other conflicts in the world. We are asking ourselves: how is peaceful coexistence possible, how is it possible to cooperate in a brotherly fashion as Christians and Muslims; are we destined to settle, at best, for mutual tolerance? Is it better to be far or close, because love from a distance somehow works, while being close might be utterly impossible? Must we hate each other until we destroy the other with our self-destruction? I am the witness of a Kosova experience which is, thank God, rather different from others, and offers substantial hope for pluralism and cooperation.

We Albanians, descendants of the Illyrians, are Christians from the time of the Apostles.[2] We had our first martyrs, San Floro e San Lauro, in the first part of the second century AD in Ulpiana. Archaeology and ancient Christian literature confirm that Christianity was rooted in our region. There was a great change in the fifteenth century, after the death of our national hero Gjorgji Kastrioti, also known as Skanderbeg (1405–1468). For 24 years he defended the territory of today's Albania and Europe from Ottoman incursions, but later, inevitably, the Ottomans prevailed until 1912. Islamization started then, whether forcibly or by the granting of privileges. Currently in Kosova 96 per cent of Albanians are Muslim, 4 per cent Catholic. In Albania the situation is different: 60 per cent are Muslims and 40 per cent Christian, Orthodox and Catholics.

The historical fact that Islam arrived later and through Ottoman domination creates the first important aspect of our religious life. Many contemporary Albanians, especially the youths and intellectuals, have great respect and sympathy for Christianity, especialy the Catholic church, that they call 'our ancient faith'. Why? Without Christianity there would be no Albanian people, language, culture, or traditions. The desire to know our past through history, our classic literature that is almost completely Christian, creates a sort of 'cultural baptism', that is, the recovery of those Christian values and content, at least from the cultural point of view. Albanians consider Christianity their patrimony, their spiritual and cultural inheritance, even though traditionally or because of conviction they are Muslims. Christianity is the key to understanding ourselves and our 2000 year history, but also to

---

[2]See. 1 Rom 15, 19; 2 Tit 3, 12; 2 Tim 4, 10.

understanding European culture, and reaching the fundamental decisions about who we were, who we are now, and who we want to be now and in the future.

For these reasons, we find an Islam in Kosova that is mostly traditional, inherited from our history of Ottoman domination; it is rather moderate and open, pro-European. With Islam we cooperate well on common issues, such as peace, justice, cohabitation, interreligious dialogue, and solidarity. Religious divisions and belonging have never touched what it means to be an Albanian, that is, our brotherhood, or the root of inter-ethnic and interreligious tolerance, and furthermore, of brotherly cohabitation and collaboration. We have historically inherited and currently cultivate a double brotherhood: a national one as Albanians, and a religious one as monotheistic believers. This brings us closer and unables us to share several national and religious values.

Mother Theresa of Calcutta was born and reared in this historical experience. An Albanian from Skopje, she lived in an environment that was already open to the world in her family and her parish. 'To love and help everybody is our Christian value' said her father, Kolë Bojaxhiu, who often repeated: 'God has been generous with us, he has given us everything, so we can give it to others, especially the needy.' Drane Bojaxhiu, her mother, helped everybody. Mother Theresa said: 'many poor people in Skopje and its surrounding vicinity knew our door. And nobody returned empty handed ... Every day we had some guest for lunch. When I grew up, I understood that those were poor people without anything, whom my mother fed ...'[3]

It is not widely known that the Ecumenical Patriarch of the Orthodox Church in Constantinople, Atenagora I (1886–1972) was of Albanian descent. He had experienced religous divisions and later bravely became the 'prophet of unity' of all Christians. He promoted interreligious dialogue, with his three historical meetings with Pope Paul VI. Thanks to the climate created by these meetings, the mutual excommunication declared in 1054 was null and the road was open to ecumenical dialogue. This experience of brotherly collaboration and openness to the world was shared also by Ibrahim Rugova (1944–2006), the first President of Kosova, who created and courageously followed a strategy of non-violence and peace, of cohabitation among different ethnic groups and religions; he was the 'Gandhi of our times.'

---

[3]Lush Gjergji, *Madre della Carità* (Bergamo:Velar, 1998), pp. 38–68; 223–9.

After the death of Tito in 1980 and until 1989, the year of the abolition of the autonomy of Kosova, there has been a systematic destruction of Kosovar institutions, and their virtual 'Serbianization.' Serbia wanted to maintain the monopoly of domination over everybody and everything at all costs, even at the cost of war. There was war in the 1990s, with Serbia's military intervention. Our recent history is painful and unfortunately it is not yet concluded.

These challenges and injustices led to the birth of three great popular movements:

1) The movement for Albanian people's reconciliation, or the fight against blood feuds, a century old custom based on the customary law of the Lekë Dukagjini: 'blood is never lost nor forgiven'. This movement for reconciliation was given impetus by Albanian youths and intellectuals, supported by both the Catholic Church and the Islamic community. 1,275 cases of blood feuds have been reconciled with ceremonies that were held everywhere: churches, mosques, public squares, and open fields. About half a million people participated in these events. There were often large crowds, as in 1 May 1990 in Verrat e Llukës. This movement for peace and forgiveness was led by prof. Anton Çetta, Albanian, Catholic, and the head of the central council in Prishtina, of which I was also a member.

2) The fight against illiteracy, with the creation of a parallel school system, in order to preserve Albanian language, culture and tradition, from elementary school through to university. A parallel health system was set up, with more than 150 clinics, providing free health care to everybody.

3) The solidarity movement spearheaded by the Mother Theresa Humanitarian Society, founded on 10 May 1990 to rescue people from hunger, extreme poverty and massacres. For 10 years (1990–1999), many people were able to survive thanks to the Mother Theresa Society and the creation of a network of grassroots associations inside Kosova in partnership with our fellow citizens abroad, as well as with varying non-governmental associations, such as Caritas and others. In these past 15 years we have given assistance to everybody, without any ethnic or religious distinction, in the style of the life and the works of Mother Theresa, showing once more that our daughter and mother is deeply rooted in the minds

and the hearts of our people, and is the best expression of our human and Christian nation, culture and tradition. Mother Theresa is our 'Ambassador'. After her death in 1997 we organized 'The days of Mother Theresa' under the auspices of the Presidency of Kosova, an important cultural event in Kosova, Macedonia, Montenegro, Serbia, Croatia, Slovenia, Italy and Switzerland. We want to propose Mother Theresa as a cultural, religious and humanitarian model for the Balkans and the world.

These three movements became the basis for non violent strategy led by Ibrahim Rugova, by consolidating brotherhood and solidarity and creating an interethnic and interreligious dialogue. They were the pillars for a just and long-lasting peace. With the war and 1999 NATO intervention, following the strategy of Milošević to expel all Albanians through a campaign of ethnic cleansing, destruction and rape, one might have thought that the strategy of non violence and peace was dead, or at least not possible. But despite all, we never lost our trust in this strategy, because no army or police can ensure a just and long lasting peace. It can just work as a surgical intervention, and it was useful to throw out the Serb police and army. At best, armed intervention can create the foundation of peace, because just and true peace is born only from a change in people's minds and hearts, from the capacity of freeing oneself from the 'dictatorship' of hate, which never ends by itself. We are free only if we can really forgive, love and live in peace and justice without any national or religious distinction. People in Kosova have fully answered to this appeal for peace: we are problaby the only case in the world that during the free and democratic election after the war did not award victory to the generals, the former combatants, but to the pacifists led by Rugova.

After the war, with the help of the Italian Caritas, the Association Mother Theresa built 25 houses in the municipality of Vita. We built them in large part for Muslim Albanians, for the war widows and orphans. This is how it happened: I personally visited our municipality with my collaborators to understand the situation after the war. Afterwards, we decided to meet with 55 widows and 150 orphans younger than 10 at least once a month, on the first Saturday, in my parish of Binça. We talked, shared their suffering and pain for the death of their beloved; we walked together toward freedom from hatred and vengeance. Today these women have become examples of peace and forgiveness, the most beautiful and encouraging example of how one can win over evil with goodness. They are a concrete testimony of how one can come out of the hell created by hatred and divisions.

Furthermore, we have recovered the dignity of women who, according to local traditions, would be forced to go back to the houses of their parents, leaving their children behind with their husbands' families. They would be forced to marry again, without having been given the chance to overcome the trauma of their husbands' death. They were victims of three evils: beyond the loss of their husbands, killed by the army and the police of Milošević, these women were also losing their children and their homes, while the children became orphans twice, without their missing or murdered fathers, and with their mothers forcibly married to someone else. I have strongly opposed this inhuman 'tradition', which is not even ours, but 'imposed' from the period of the Ottoman domination. Working together first with the widows, then with the parents of the husbands, we managed to defeat a tradition that at first looked untouchable. No woman has been forced to abandon the house of her husband and the children in order to remarry. We have created new relationships, giving women the freedom to choose and the dignity to be themselves, showing once more that with love and patience, sharing, and participating, everything becomes possible and the common good prevails.

23. Would Kosova survive economically as an independent state?

Henry Perritt

THE ALLEGATION

An independent Kosovo would be economically isolated from Serbia and would not have any chance of surviving economically, so it would soon turn into a place of social riots and blood feuds among Albanians themselves.
(Serbia and Montenegro Foreign Minister Vuk Drasković interviewed by Beta News Agency).[1]

That state could live only by smuggling drugs, people and weapons.
(President Boris Tadić in an interview to Radio Free Europe/Radio Liberty).[2]

Doubts over the capacity of Kosova to survive economically are often voiced in the most negative terms, building on the real difficulties that the local post-socialist and post-war economy faces. The argument is that Kosova would never be able to survive because of isolation and cultural backwardness.

---

[1]Quoted in Kosova Report, Monday, 20 June 2005, http://kosovareport. blogspot.com [Consulted on 15 March 2006].
[2]Patrick Moore, 'Analysis: Serbia's President Rejects Independence for Kosova', RFE/RL, 28 January 2005, http://www.rferl.org/reports/balkan-report/2005/ 01/4-280105.asp [Consulted on 15 March 2006].

The Answer

I was in Kosovo for the first time in December 1968, when Serbia was still in charge, and back just after Serbs had left, and about twenty times since then. When ruled by Serbia, all of Kosovo was a depressing trash heap. No one had washed a window in Prishtina in years, garbage and stray dogs were all over the place, I could not send a fax or get money changed. The hotel had doors hanging off their hinges and stopped-up toilets. The food was vile, and the waiters surly. About the only activities that seemed prosperous were the army and the police who stopped us at almost every traffic intersection and rudely pointed automatic weapons at us and pawed through our luggage. Within weeks after the war, Kosovars had cleaned up Prishtina, washed the windows, bought portable generators and set up shop. Everyone welcomed visitors with smiles and enthusiasm. Small businesses had burst out all over like flowers in spring.

Before NATO intervention, Kosovo was well on the way to ruin, corruption, and decay, a backwater of Socialist failure. After the Serb army withdrew, underlying pride and entrepreneurial spirit began to build a market economy, and have continued ever since then to strengthen it. There is a long way to go, but it is clear that much is possible when ordinary people are freed to build a country with cheerfulness and pride, rather than being prisoners of sour, backward looking, defensive isolation, which exalts racism and ethnic hatred as a way to get ahead in politics—characteristics which were hallmarks of the Milošević regime in Kosovo.

Opportunities for business, investment, and job-creation abound. This essay develops the argument that Kosovo not only is viable economically, but has a bright economic future if foreign investors recognize its potential and if its future political leadership, encouraged by the international community, pursues business-friendly policies and regional economic integration.

Kosovo's infrastructure for business is acceptable, though much remains to be done in the electric power sector to assure reliable electricity supplies. Internet connectivity is among the best in the world. It has a nationwide broadband wireless backbone, which allows businesses and individuals to obtain high-speed Internet connections at prices at or below those available in Western Europe and the US. The connections are reliable. Internet cafes abound in the cities, making it easy for individuals, including those of modest means, to maintain regular access to email and Web pages. High quality education and training on information technology is available from the IPKO Institute and the American University in Kosovo. Most Kosovars rely on cellphones rather than landline telephones. However, the fixed telephone system has been upgraded since the war and is reliable. The service provided by the public PTK has been unreliable in the past, although it is usually possible to complete calls after several tries, even when congestion is a problem.

The airport in Prishtina is modern and served by several major airlines with daily flights to hubs throughout Europe and Turkey. Major road construction projects sponsored by the European Union have left Kosovo with a good highway backbone of mostly two-lane paved roads. Rural roads are less satisfactory, many of them unpaved and poorly maintained. Plans are well developed for a new high-capacity highway between Prishtina and the Albanian port of Durres. The government of the Republic of Albania has agreed to invest substantial capital in the portion through the mountains of Albania, and the US Government has promised support. The government of Kosovo needs to overcome EU objections and begin construction on the portion through Kosovo, which also would relieve congestion on the Prishtina-Prizren road. A well-organized and inexpensive system of intercity buses allows the population without automobiles to move about freely all over Kosovo. Kosovo has a basic railroad network, but it is poorly maintained and little used for freight.

The biggest infrastructure problem is an unreliable electricity supply. As noted below, Kosovo has the largest lignite (soft coal) reserves in southern Europe, so it could be an exporter of electricity. But dilapidated power-generating facilities located near lignite mines in the outskirts of Prishtina were not replaced as they should have been after the war because of various bureaucratic impediments in funding for rehabilitation from the European Union. Plans were developed by USAID for a complete rebuilding of the electricity generating complex and associated coal mines but have not been implemented. Plans also exist to tie Kosovo's electric grid in Albania, which would connect Kosovo to the European grid with sufficient capacity to allow Kosovo to export electricity throughout Europe. Until these plans are implemented, rolling power outages even in the major cities will remain common. Most small businesses and many larger facilities have standby generators to assure uninterrupted power supplies.

Kosovo has an ample supply of labor, due to its rapidly growing youth population. A significant fraction of those under 35 have spent time in Europe or the US, working, getting university degrees and learning English. The primary and secondary school system in Kosovo does a good job of inculcating basic skills. The public university is very weak and has so far resisted efforts at dramatic reform. The gap is being filled by a large collection of private institutions, the best of which is the American University in Kosovo, which enrolls about 100 new students annually in degree programs in business administration and information technology. All instruction is in English. No 'brain drain' is evident. Most young Kosovars who have worked or been educated abroad are eager to come home to participate in building a prosperous, democratic independent Kosovo. Young people are resourceful and enthusiastic, especially in their contacts with Americans. Those who have work experience with international organizations have a good work ethic. Some others respond well to good management that emphasizes the importance of meeting deadlines, focusing on achieving results, and being on time for appointments. Wage levels are higher than one might expect, given the oversupply of labor, because international employers bid up wage levels. As the international presence declines, wage levels should soften.

One of the hallmarks of Kosovar society is the strong orientation toward entrepreneurship. Largely excluded from the formal economic system during 10 years of repression by the Milošević regime, Kosovars learned to survive by setting up business ventures with little capital and access to infrastructure. Informal business networks exist throughout the region, into northern Europe and North America. Almost every family is in some kind of business, concentrating more on service and retail trade rather than manufacturing and processing. This pool of entrepreneurs offers significant opportunity to those who have the capacity to tie entrepreneurship to sources of adequate capital and modern business methods.

Kosovo has a good banking system. Internal savings rates are high, and Kosovars proved more willing than many expected to deposit their savings in the array of well-run banks established after the war. The major banking enterprises are tied to banking concerns in Western Europe, and use best practices in terms of internal auditing and conservative loan policies. A significant source of capital in the past has been 'remittances' from Kosovars working abroad. For decades, it has been the custom for at least one younger member of extended families to go abroad to find work and to send money home. While much of this money is consumed meeting the daily needs of family members still in Kosovo, it adds to the overall capital stock. Whether the stream of remittances will remain as high in the future as in the past is uncertain, as Kosovo attracts more of its young people to return and as host countries tighten immigration policies.

Many wealthy individuals with family, social or past-business ties to the Balkans have made significant investments in medium-sized enterprises and building and highway construction. Multinational corporations and individuals lacking any previous connection with Kosovo have expressed interest, but have been more reticent, mostly because of uncertainty about the legal status of Kosovo. Conclusion of final status negotiations should remove these barriers.

Privatization of 'socially owned' and 'publicly owned' enterprises has been controversial, but largely successful. The 14th round of public bidding was launched on 16 March 2006. The privatization agency, Kosovo Trust Agency, recovered well from a year-long hiatus in 2003–2004 due to maladministration by a senior European official who was sent to supervise privatization. Recent rounds of bidding typically have offered 10–12 enterprises in each round and have attracted more than 100 bids in each round, the highest of which typically totaled on the order of €12–15 million per round. A special court has been set up to adjudicate claims arising from privatization and the court is functioning.

Accounting and auditing services are available and professional. A public agency sets accounting standards and licenses accounting professionals. Legal services are improving as well-designed reform of bar associations and lawyer licensing implemented after the war add more better-educated and more professional lawyers to the practicing bar. There still is an acute shortage of well-qualified business lawyers, however, knowledgeable about the new legal framework and oriented toward market transactions. The Chamber of Commerce of Kosovo and the Kosovo–American Chamber of Commerce both are under new leadership, which is western-educated, and energetic in communicating with potential investors about opportunities in Kosovo, providing services to businesses operating in Kosovo and in helping business interests to be well represented before governmental institutions.

Kosovo's economic prospects are brighter if it continues on its path of integrating its economy with others in the region. Already, substantial financial and trade ties with Slovenia and Croatia augment capital and open up markets for products and services from Kosovo. The large ethnic Albanian populations in the Republic of Albania, Macedonia, Serbia and Montenegro make available informal channels for investment and trade. These will strengthen naturally. Present and past governments have had good leadership in developing ties with European policy-makers in charge of EU enlargement and it is important that momentum in this direction continue.

The perspectives for comparative advantage are also good. Kosovo has some of the largest lignite (brown coal) reserves in Europe. Lignite accounts for approximately 50 per cent of total coal consumption in Europe, usually exported in the form of electricity rather than being shipped for long distances. The primary opportunity for substantial capital investment that would produce significant export revenue for Kosovo is in the energy sector, given the need to build new mine and electric generating capacity to take advantage of these reserves.

Kosovo still is a predominantly agricultural economy, with most agricultural production taking place on small family-owned, or village-run subsistence farms. Substantial reform in the methods of farming would be necessary for Kosovo to become a significant exporter—or even to be self-sufficient—in raw agricultural products. Agricultural process-ing, on the other hand, is a significant investment opportunity. Already wine production, soft-drink and beer processing and bottling, and dairy-product processing have attracted significant foreign investment.

Tourism is a largely untapped opportunity for Kosovo. Its geography is beautiful, varied, and largely unspoiled. A state-of-the art ski resort operates in southern Kosovo. Hotels and restaurants in the cities are of high quality. Those features, combined with Kosovo's history and prominence in the news, present the possibility for attracting a significant number of foreign tourists. Investment in tourism is attractive because of the large job-creation potential, relatively low capital costs and the opportunity to earn significant foreign exchange.

Kosovo's good Internet infrastructure, the large number of young professionals with good information-technology skills and the now widely recognized potential of e-commerce to allow small enterprises access to world markets represents another largely-untapped opportu-nity. Most Kosovar businesses and non-profits of any size have web pages, but little has been done so far to establish e-commerce and other forms of Internet intermediation and software services in Kosovo.

Kosovo has made good progress in establishing a rule of law in the economic sphere as well as in the political and human-rights spheres. The main legal obstacle to economic development has been uncertainty about Kosovo's final status, and independence will resolve that. Kosovo's legal climate for business is sound. Laws for business organization, corporate governance and investor protection, for resolving business claims, and for bankruptcy reflect best practices in Europe and the US. The court system still is slow and unreliable, but commercial arbitration is widely used as a substitute.

Macro-economic and tax policies are among the most business-friendly in Europe, focused on minimizing the legal barriers to starting businesses, simplifying and minimizing the tax burden and facilitating free trade. Going forward, the government of Kosovo must resist pressures to erect trade barriers and to impede business formation through non-transparent municipal licensing requirements, always desired by inefficient local businesses which fear competition.

In conclusion, as Kosovo is allowed to break free of a century of subjugation by foreign masters, it presents huge economic opportunities. The right kinds of partnerships between business and government, and between outside investors and managers and local entrepreneurs and workers, can result in significant job creation and significant rates of return on investment. With the right leadership, Kosovo could become the Ireland of southern Europe.

24. Is it true that Kosova cannot govern itself and needs further international tutelage or conditional independence?

Besnik Pula

THE ALLEGATION

The Contact Group's Guiding Principles state that such supervision will be needed '[f]or some time,' while Eide argued that 'entering the future status process does not mean entering the last stage, but the next stage of the international presence'.
(International Crisis Group, a conflict prevention and resolution non-governmental organization).[1]

The idea that an international civilian presence will be necessary even after Kosovar independence seems to be entrenched among international institutions and in diplomatic circles.

The Answer

The notion of 'conditional independence' for Kosova has circulated among international political and diplomatic circles for several years. In essence, the idea has resulted from a struggle by political

---

[1]*Kosovo: The Challenge of Transition*, Europe Report No. 170, 17 February 2006, p. 14. Kai Eide is the Norwegian diplomat appointed as special envoy to Kosova by the UN Secretary General to give a comprehensive review of Kosovo in preparation for status negotiations.

activists in the West, sympathetic to Kosova's independence, to find a workable formula that would enable the West to carry out diplomatically a careful, almost surgical removal of Kosova from the political map of Serbia (implied by the 'independence' part of the notion), while minimizing the political costs of such an act. That political cost would be borne first and foremost by the people of Kosova, for whom freedom would come with strings attached; namely, that their government would be limited in its ability to actually govern Kosova, and that their laws and other policies would be subject to review and possible veto by an externally appointed administrator or body.

Conditional independence was first proposed in late 2000 by the Independent International Commission on Kosovo, a fact-finding group sponsored by the Swedish prime minister and endorsed by UN Secretary General Kofi Annan.[2] The Commission was chaired by Richard Goldstone, the former Chief Justice of the Hague War Crimes Tribunal. In its report, the Commission argued that Kosova should be effectively separated from Yugoslavia (the former name of the Union of Serbia and Montenegro) through a new UN Security Council resolution that would supersede Resolution 1244, the resolution which established UNMIK and placed Kosova under the UN's temporary control. The Commission proposed that Kosova turn into a UN trusteeship until it developed the capability to govern and defend itself effectively, at which point Kosova's future would be determined through a popular referendum. However, while the Commission's groundbreaking, 300-page report gained a broad audience in the diplomatic community, its recommendations were largely ignored. During this particular juncture, at the time when Slobodan Milošević's fall from power had created among European diplomats an atmosphere of jubilance and an unwarranted degree of confidence that Serbia was now irreversibly becoming 'democratic', there was a conspicuous lack of political will in the West to address Kosova's status, leading to the many political complications that arose due to seven years of socially and economically catastrophic UN governance.

In 2002, the International Crisis Group (ICG), an international policy think-tank based in Brussels, took up the notion of 'conditional

---

[2]Independent International Commission on Kosovo: *The Kosovo Report*, available at http://www.oxfordscholarship.com/oso/public/content/politicalscience/0199243093/toc.html.

independence' in one of its reports on Kosovo.[3] According to the ICG, 'conditional independence' meant a political and diplomatic arrangement that 'preclude[s] Kosovo's return to Yugoslav or Serbian sovereignty, while keeping it under a form of international trusteeship, albeit with substantial autonomy, with a continued international military presence, for as long as the external and internal situations demanded'.[4] The concept of 'conditional independence' as proposed by ICG suggested that the focus of Western diplomacy should turn Kosova into a semi-independent state, but not internationally recognized—a 'state on trial' so to speak. During this period, Kosova's political institutions would have broad autonomy in the conduct of domestic policy, though with the continued oversight of an internationally-appointed governor— much like present-day arrangements under UNMIK. While the Commission had originally argued for Kosova's swift separation from Serbia, the ICG advocated that 'conditional independence' become an interim status for Kosova until Belgrade and Prishtina could agree, through dialogue, on an acceptable solution for both sides.[5] However, the ICG report attempted to provide a more specific framework that would constitute the conditions of 'conditional independence'. Thus, the powers held by the international administration would be conditional on two factors: at the international level, the diplomatic process leading to the resolution of Kosova's final status, and at the domestic level, the progress in Kosova on a set of 'benchmarks' that purport to measure Kosova's progress on the protection of ethnic minority rights other criteria. It is possible that the proposal for

---

[3]International Crisis Group, *A Kosovo Roadmap (I): Addressing Final Status.* Balkans Report No. 124. 1 March 2002. Available online at http://www.crisisgroup.org/home/index.cfm?id=1640&l=1 [Last accessed, 27 March 2006].
[4]Ibid., p. iv.
[5]The ICG has since changed its position and now advocates independence as the solution of Kosova's status issue. See ICG, *Kosovo: The Challenge of Transition.* Europe Report No. 170. 17 February 2006. Available online at http://www.crisisgroup.org/home/index.cfm?id=3955&l=1 [Last accessed, 27 March 2006]. In this report the ICG argues that the international community 'must accordingly prepare for the possibility of imposing an independence package for Kosovo, however diplomatically painful that may be in the short term, rather than hoping to finesse Prishtina's and Belgrade's differences with an ambiguous solution, or one in which key elements are deferred'.

'benchmarks' was instrumental in influencing Michael Steiner, Kosova's international governor from 2002–2003, in developing his policy of 'standards before status', namely, UNMIK's policy which established a set of bureaucratic conditions that Kosova would have to fulfill before its status would be up for review. However, while Kosova was politically coerced into focusing all of its energies on a set of rather arbitrary bureaucratic benchmarks (known as the 'standards'),[6] UNMIK could not promise or guarantee that the status would ever come up for review—for the simple reason that the UN, although given a partial mandate for this purpose by Resolution 1244, was unable to raise the status issue without the full diplomatic and political backing of the West.

In 2005, the notion of 'conditional independence' was revived again, though this time in a proposal which sought to gradually confer sovereignty to Kosova, but only within the framework of the European Union (EU). This particular idea was proposed by the International Commission on the Balkans (ICB), an independent group of current and former high political officials and other policy-oriented actors, chaired by Giuliano Amato, former prime minister of Italy. With regards to the resolution of Kosova's status, the ICB proposed a gradual approach, to be managed primarily by the EU, which would address Kosova's status in stages. From its present condition under UNMIK, Kosova would progress to the phase of 'independence without full sovereignty', a rather peculiar notion from the standpoint of international law. At this stage, Kosova would be treated 'as independent but not as a sovereign state [...], allowing it to develop a capacity for self-government.'[7] However, this 'capacity for self-government' was limited by EU monitorship of a set of policy fields related to standards of human rights and minority protection. This period would last until Kosova is considered by the EU to be an appropriate candidate for EU membership. At that time, any international presence in Kosova would be scaled down or pulled out, and Kosova would be given full independence and admitted

---

[6]The official UNMIK standards implementation document is available at http://www.unmikonline.org/pub/misc/ksip_eng.pdf [Last accessed, 27 March 2006].

[7]International Commission on the Balkans, *The Balkans in Europe's Future*. April 2005, p. 21. The full report is available online at http://www.balkan-commission.org [Last accessed, 27 March 2006].

to the EU simultaneously. The rather rigid and unspecific formula for the resolution of Kosova's status has not been adopted as the official policy of the EU or any of its member states. However, given that its recommendations build on a series of prior proposals for 'conditional independence', the argument has likely resonated among Western policy circles and the rather murky notion of 'conditional independence' is likely to be the principle guide of future Western policy in Kosova.

Western political control over Kosova's domestic policies would be performed ostensibly to protect 'minority rights', and purportedly in the interest of Kosova's ethnic Serb minority, but as experience has shown with UNMIK, international administrations and their members, given complete legal immunity, unchecked power and the ability to behave like colonial masters, often tend to supersede their mandate, and their own abuses of power tend to escape scrutiny. Fundamentally, the notion of 'conditional independence' is not only undemocratic but anti-democratic, because it subjects the will of the people and the political representatives chosen by democratic vote to outside review, and the domestic political process to undue interference by outside agents given the mandate to block or veto the decisions of political institutions, placing the entire body politic under a permanent state of emergency, to be enacted at the whims of a international administrator and the collective diplomatic body he represents.[8]

True, a transitional period to independence is necessary due to the legal and institutional complexities under UNMIK, but the terms and modalities of that transition should be negotiated by the UN with the Kosovar authorities as a purely technical process, without including within it a fresh set of political requirements that must be met in order for full sovereignty to be attained. Otherwise we cannot meaningfully speak of independence for Kosova, only a new form of collective subjection of a population, though seemingly benign in its means and purely technical and a political in its declared intentions.

On the other hand, the idea that Kosova must not be subject to specially-tailored 'conditions' for independence does not imply that Kosova ought to become a fully sovereign state that permits no outside

---

[8]It is ironic that one of the 'issues' that Western administrators have occasionally raised in the Balkans is that of gender equality. Yet, all Western administrators appointed to governing regions and territories in the Balkans have so far been exclusively male.

involvement, some kind of a pariah state isolated and unaffected by the developments in Europe and the world. On the contrary, membership in the international community of states and especially in the European community of states, by its very nature involves a set of conditions and limitations on the domestic and international exercise of sovereignty, as obligated by international treaties, conventions and international and European law. The international community of states is a highly exclusive club, and membership entails a diverse set of obligations and responsibilities. These include standards for human and minority rights, as well as for social equality, economic development, political democracy, international peace and security and environmental sustainability. Moreover, one cannot fail to point out that Kosova is by no means exempt from the social and economic pressures of globalization, which for Kosova has meant massive migration, rapid economic liberalization, impoverishment and dependence. Furthermore, there is a general popular consensus in Kosova that Kosova's main political objectives are to gain participation in international politics through the UN, obtain membership in collective security arrangements such as NATO and multilateral institutions such as the OSCE and the Council of Europe, and finally, closely cooperate with neighboring Balkan states to integrate the entire region within the EU. Taking these into account, one fails to see any reasons beyond purely political ones, for the need for the construction of any special political mechanisms, under the control of the UN, EU or any external body, to institute (or, more precisely, invent *de novo*) some form of 'conditional independence' and permit the continuation of colonial-style tutelage in Kosova.[9]

---

[9]For more extensive arguments against 'conditional independence' see Forumi 2015, *Why Independence for Kosovo? The Status Issue, Political Challenges and the Path to European Integration.* October 2005. Available at http://www. newkosovo.org/Why%20Independence%20For%20Kosovo.pdf [Last accessed, 27 March 2006].

25. Is it true that Kosova is a clannish society still regulated by the *Kanun*, or the customary law, and does not belong to the West?

Besnik Pula

The justice system that governs the family's life is, in theory, the modern legal framework set up and overseen by the UN administration which is in charge of Kosovo. But while the new legal system does function, it has to compete with Leke's code in spheres such as family honor.
(Jeton Musliu and Bajram Lani, journalists with the Institute for War and Peace Reporting).[1]

As the argument goes, customary law, codified in the *Kanun* of Leke Dukagjin, still plays an important role in Kosova. In some quarters customary law is the lens through which the entire society of Kosova is understood.

The old book of Leke Dukagjini was found on many UN officers' desks and it was frequently referred to if anything needed to be explained about Kosovo society.
(Kvinna Till Kvinna, Swedish non-governmental organization supporting women in areas of conflict).[2]

---

[1]'Feuds Hold Kosovo Families in Thrall', *Balkan Crisis Report* No 565, 14 July 2005.
[2]*Getting It Right? A Gender Approach to UNMIK Administration in Kosovo*, (Halmstad, Sweden: Bulls Tryckeri, 2001).

The Answer

The *kanun* conventionally refers to the practice of customary law, prevalent until the early twentieth century primarily among the highland populations of Albania, southern Montenegro, and Kosova. From an anthropological perspective, the *kanun* represents the ancient constitution of a regionally-based social system, with masculine honor, hereditary patriarchal authority, and communal democracy as its key principles. With the rise of modern nation-states in the Balkans and the historical pursuit of nationalizing, centralizing and modernizing policies, the practice of the *kanun* has been on the wane. With the rise of modern *governmentality*, revolutionary political ideologies and cultural modernity in the Balkans throughout the twentieth century, the *kanun* as a meaningful social system has ceased to exist. In Kosova, its practice subsists in isolated rural regions, though mostly in the form of blood feuds. However, present-day blood feuds could arguably be a consequence of the failure of modern states to deliver a legitimate mechanism of justice, as well as the state's historical negligence, repression, or abandonment of marginalized and dispossessed social groups.

A stereotypical interpretation of the *kanun* as a largely tribal system of law that is based on clan organization, supports general allusions that Kosovar society is 'clan-based'. These comments, made commonly by nationalist politicians and media outlets in Serbia and reiterated by some Western journalists and so-called 'experts', are nothing more than intellectual atavisms. They find support in an earlier colonial mentality that sought to brand particular cultural and ethnic groups as somehow deficient in their culture and thus deemed undeserving of modern statehood, giving rise to the ill-famed, colonial 'White man's burden' (as a regional imperialist, Serbia always sought to gain a share in the burden). Hence, claims that Albanian society in Kosova is 'clannish', suggesting that clan, family, or blood line is the primary or exclusive basis of solidarity in Kosovar society, can be considered not only as uninformed and baseless, but as ill-intentioned and blatantly racist.

In the western Balkans, the *kanun* was active until the early twentieth century, until the final disintegration of the Ottoman Empire. While its origins are believed to pre-date in the Ottoman Empire, the authorities largely tolerated its practice and in many ways integrated it within the larger imperial cultural and political system, which may also explain the origin of the term *kanun*, which in Turkish simply means 'law'. For instance, in the Catholic region of Mirdita in northern Albania, the hereditary 'chieftain' of the region served a dual role of imperial official and local authority.[3] The 'chieftain', whose authority was nonetheless limited by the *Kuvend*, or the assembly consisting of all household heads, thus served as a sort of intermediary between imperial authority and the local community.

In the Ottoman era, the *kanun* was practiced primarily by Albanian populations where religious authority was comparatively weak, the population was largely pastoral, and in regions where feudal relations of authority, based on the Ottoman *çiflik* system of peasant labor, had not penetrated deeply (in comparison to the agricultural plains of the Balkans). The *kanun* was in essence an evolving body of collective knowledge on rules of arbitration, conflict resolution, marital procedures, property protection and inheritance, inter- and intra-family relations, personal honor, and other fundamental questions of the organization of collective life. It was, essentially, a 'state without a state', in that there was no distinction between moral and political authority, and the latter was lodged within the community and did not exist as a separate bureaucratic organization standing outside of society. In addition, historically there was no single *kanun*, but rather a variety of traditions existing within separate communities, reflecting each community's historical experience.[4] Decision-making under the *kanun* was a collective process, involving the, 'chieftain' as the head of the 'first door'

---

[3]The term 'chieftain' is not used by the *kanun* and is here used only for reasons of brevity, recognizing the risks that such usage may bring due to its common association with the backward and despotic 'tribal authority' of Western colonial primitivism.

[4]The first version of the *kanun* to be codified was based on the ethnographic work by an Albanian Franciscan priest by the name of Shtjefën Gjeçovi. Students of Albanian history and society sometimes refer to Gjeçovi's rendition as if it is the only version of *kanun* practice that existed, and as if there was complete agreement by the various social agents on the interpretations given, which in actuality were constantly contested, reinterpreted and subject to new situations that had no known precedent. Gjeçovi's particular version of the *Kanun of Lekë Dukagjini*, named after the medieval Albanian feudal lord believed to be its progenitor, is also available in English translation as *The Code of Lekë Dukagjini*. Trans. by Leonard Fox. (Bronx, NY: Gjonlekaj Publishing, 1989).

(*dera e parë*), the name by which the most prestigious household was known, as well as the community elders, and finally through the assembly constituted by the entire (male) community. Decisions were enforced collectively, as no separate executive authority existed, nor did the 'chieftain' have control over any troops or agents charged with the implementation of decisions. During the Ottoman era, regions practicing the *kanun* maintained a relative autonomy from the authority of the Porte, accepting its authority only to a limited extent and on the basis of local interpretation, while excluding the right of the Sultan to legislate on issues of local community organization. Communities practicing the *kanun* also constrained the interference of religious authorities in moral questions, explaining the limited influence of the Roman Catholic Church in northern Albania, as well as that of Islamic *Sharia* law among the nominally converted Muslim populations. No doubt, the relative social isolation furnished by the highly mountainous terrain was a factor as well.

As the historian Pal Doçi has argued, the principal unit subject to administrative authority under the *kanun* is not the clan, nor the family, but a delimited *territory* with a particular population in it.[5] Each separate territory, known in *kanun* tradition as the *mal* ('mountain' in Albanian) or *bajrak* ('flag' in Turkish), had its own internal authority structures and autonomously legislated issues. The population of the *bajrak* was subdivided on the basis of individual households based in distinct village settlements, and each male head of the household (usually the eldest member) was chiefly responsible for defending the household's honor against infractions by others. While households were related to each other on the basis of patrilineal clan names, clans in themselves never constituted legitimate collective agents under the *kanun*. Under *kanun* practice, there was no such thing as *clan* honor. Clan name designations were significant primarily for the purposes of marriage, which according to *kanun* practice were performed outside of the patrilineal or matrilineal blood line. Thus, members of the nominally same clan could reside in separate villages and even different *bajrak*s and were therefore subject to a different *kanun* tradition, thereby eliminating the possibility of any inter-clan alliance. In fact, it was possible and not uncommon for members of the same clan to be involved in

---

[5]Pal Doçi, *Vetëqeverisja e Mirditës: vështrim etnologjik e historik.* (Tirana: Shtëpia Botuese Enciklopedike, 1996).

a blood feud due to some prior infringement of a family member's honor.

According to *kanun* tradition, the unnatural death of a family member must be avenged by the victim's family through the killing of the perpetrator or a male member of the perpetrator's household. In some cases, such feuds carry on inter-generationally, as one death provokes another. Given the historical context of the *kanun*, this manner of justice, though crude, is understandable given that households were generally mandated to carry out their own justice in the defense of their honor.[6] Addressing the problem of blood feuds is therefore a complex social issue that can only be accomplished within a polity that has a fundamental interest in building a uniform system of justice within its territory and addressing the fundamental social causes of the problem. Several campaigns against the blood feud have been carried out by official authorities as well as by grassroots activists, which are ongoing and continue to this day. The last, most far-reaching campaign against the blood feud was carried out by a broad coalition of Albanian social activists and intellectuals during 1990 and 1991, when hundreds of feuds were settled or suspended. It would be absurd, if not downright ridiculous, to suggest that a historically racist and chauvinistic state such as Serbia would have the will and the adeptness to address this

---

[6]The *Kanun of Lekë Dukagjini* regulated the manner in which vengeance for blood would be carried out. The *kanun* stipulated the rules of engagement (e.g., shooting the target in the back was impermissible), places or situations in which the target could not be killed (such as inside the home, during a funeral or at an assembly meeting), the type of legitimate target (women, young children and religious figures were usually not permissible as targets of vengeful murder), and the manner in which the body of the victim had to be handled after the killing. Vengeful murder was according to the *kanun* a form of restoring the victim's family's honor, and the *kanun*'s rules of vengeance were neglected at the cost of honor as well as at the risk of communal ostracism and punishment. Vengeful murder was therefore, under *kanun* practice, a communally sanctioned and regulated form of behavior, which is certainly not the case today in the era of penal and civil law, juridical institutions, and the modern state's legal authority.

26. Is Greater Albania a Threat?

Paulin Kola

THE ALLEGATION

Granting independence to Kosovo and Metohija would de facto create two Albanian states in Europe, a dangerous precedent unknown to post-Cold War Europe. However ironclad the guarantees may be that such a scenario would not take place, once the right to self-determination was understood as the right to alter internationally recognised orders, what argument could be used against a Grater Albanian project?... to be precise, the Greater Albanian project could affect the territorial integrity of an already truncated Serbia (Presevo, Bujanovac, Medvedja) Albania itself, Macedonia (the north–western third, including the capital, Skopje), Greece (its northernmost part), and Montenegro (From Ulcinj all the way along the border with Albanian and the administrative boundary with Kosovo and Metohija).

(Vuk Jeremić, Senior Advisor to the president of Serbia).[1]

A very common allegation is that Kosova's independence is only the first step for the realisation of the old dream of Greater Albania, or the unification of all territories in the Balkan region where Albanians live.

The Answer

The creation of Greater Albania remains a much-hyped scenario that refuses to die out. Yet, as Kosova appears to be on a fast track

---

[1]'Past and Future Status of Kosovo', Testimony Before the House of Representatives International Relations Committee, 18 May 2005, www.house. gov/international_relations/109/jer051805.pdf [Last visited on 23 April 2006].

towards formal independence, however strange it may seem, this will remain an independent state on its own for a number of years and for a number of reasons.

The main proponents of Kosova's independence—the US, the UK and other Western nations—will be keen to see a curtailment of the period between formal statehood and the amalgamation of the newly-bestowed sovereignty into the European Union through membership of this body. This will help stave off any residual threats emanating from Belgrade, such as the oft-mooted possibility of declaring Kosova occupied territory[2] and thus hanging a Damocletian sword over its head by giving prospective nationalists an incentive to seek its return to Serbian sovereignty. EU membership will also guarantee in formal terms that no unilateral union with Albania take place.

In order to earn independence, Kosova Albanians have been called upon to make two main compromises: to cater for the 100,000 or so Serbs remaining in enclaves around Kosova through meaningful and sustainable devolution of power and to give assurances that they will not seek to unify their new independent state with neighbouring Albania or any other adjacent Albanian-inhabited areas. So far they consider the former a formidable request, a kind of Trojan horse that, mishandled, may invite Serbia back or lead to the partition of Kosova with Serbia—an apparently clear goal of Serbia contained in their remit for these talks. The latter possibility of creating a 'Greater Albania' is a prospect which sends a shiver down Western spines more than any-thing else. It is also one of the most widely misunderstood myths regarding Albanians and their nationalism. The reality is, however, that this is the easiest of compromises being asked of the Kosova Albanians, although they will be delighted to let it appear as their greatest sacrifice for the sake of regional peace and stability. Albanians themselves laugh the idea off privately, to the extent that a under 10 per cent of the Kosova Albanians support union with Albania.[3]

---

[2] The Serbian parliament has passed a resolution to this effect. Serbia entered final-status talks on Kosova apprehensive that it had lost the 'cradle of Serbdom'—its leaders vehement to avoid signing away what is an emotive polity that has histor-ically had the potential of making or breaking many a politician.

[3] A September 2005 poll found that an overwhelming majority of Albanian respondents—90.2 per cent—were in favour of independence for Kosova within the current borders, while 9.1 per cent were for the unification of

Albanians are the least nationalistic people in the Balkan peninsula, the only nation there that has always been divided and remained scattered in at least four different states at the beginning of the twenty-first century. Albanian leaders are unique in an attitude of parochialism that appears to even question the real foundation of the Albanian nation. So why are the Albanians, while endowed with all those attributes that constitute a nation as defined by Anthony D. Smith,[4] reluctant to create a state based on ethnic criterion—the overriding aim of most classical nationalists? An understanding of history may help to square the circle.

Having been at the receiving end of repeated invasions, the Albanians remained fragmented and unable to establish a unifying central authority that would command their collective allegiance. The lack of a central religious authority, which might have been instrumental in establishing the psycho-social prerequisites for a nation-state, may be part of the explanation. From their pagan days as Illyrians, Albanians became embroiled in the dispute between Catholicism and Orthodoxy, culminating in the separation of 1054. In the fifteenth century, under pressure from the occupying Ottomans, they embraced Islam. It was only when the dissolution of the Ottoman empire encouraged the newly emerged Balkan states to annex Albanian lands that some of the more prominent Albanian chiefs began to think in quasi-nationalist terms—proclaiming, in November 1912, an independent Albanian state over roughly half the territories inhabited by Albanians in the Balkans.

The subsequent Communist period—dominated by Enver Hoxha— also serves to belie the alleged nationalist credentials bestowed upon the paramount leader by most writers on Albanian affairs.[5] A cursory

---

Kosova with Albania; see *Early Warning Report, Kosovo*, Report No 11, UN Development Program.

[4]A human group sharing (usually by birth) an historical territory, common myths and historical memories, often a common language, a mass public common culture, a perception of threat and common legal rights and duties for all members, in Alfred Cobban, *National Self-Determination* (London: Oxford University Press, 1945), pp. 49–52.

[5]See, among others: Elez Biberaj, *Albania: A Socialist Maverick* (Boulder: Westview Press, 1990); William B. Bland, *Albania* (Oxford: Clio, 1988); Nicholas J. Costa, *Albania: A European Enigma*, East European Monographs (Boulder: distributed by Columbia University Press, 1995); Bernd J. Fischer, 'Albanian nationalism in the twentieth century' in Peter F. Sugar (ed.), *Eastern European Nationalism in the*

reading of the position of the Albanians in Yugoslavia, and a careful dissection of the Yugoslav Communist Party's modern experiment with the Yugoslav national question, would suggest that the destiny of that part of the Albanian nation was determined with little input from Tirana—and if there was any contribution, this was often in conflict with local Albanian demands. Officially, the reason given by Belgrade for having refused self-determination to Yugoslavia's Albanians, and for reducing them to a minority status, was the existence of a recognised state of Albania, but this was more a pretext that a valid argument. Firstly, Kosova was to be incorporated into Serbia to satisfy Serbian national sentiment and compensate the Serbs for the dispersal of the Serbian nation throughout the Federation. Secondly, far from contemplating the return of Kosova to Albania, Yugoslavia's Communist leader Josip Broz Tito was preparing to incorporate the whole of Albania into the Yugoslav Federation as a seventh republic— an apparent attempt to settle, in his own way, the centuries-old enmity between Serbs and Albanians and their rival claims on Kosova.

Enver Hoxha's memoirs on why the plan of incorporation did not materialise are generally unreliable, not least because they contradict the transcripts and manuscripts of Hoxha's own speeches at the time. Indeed, the memoirs appear to amount to a rewriting of history, since, despite Hoxha's subsequent denials, both he and the whole of the Albanian Communist leadership emerging from the war approved Tito's project and took concrete steps to make it a reality—encouraged also by the leader of the Communist camp, Stalin.[6] The apparent readiness of the Albanian Communist leaders to terminate the independent existence of a part of the Albanian nation must cast doubt on their presumed nationalist credentials.

Later, when Hoxha took his cue from Moscow to break up with his mentor in Belgrade, Albania became the most anti-Yugoslav country within the Socialist camp. But is there any evidence to equate Tirana's

---

Twentieth Century, (Washington, DC: American University Press, 1995); Gabriel Jandot, *L'Albanie d'Enver Hoxha* (Paris: L'Harmattan, 1994); Anton Logoreci, *The Albanians: Europe's Forgotten Survivors*, (London: Gollancz, 1977); Nicholas Pano, *The People's Republic of Albania*, (Baltimore: Johns Hopkins University Press, 1968); Peter Prifti, *Socialist Albania since 1944*, (Cambridge: MIT Press, 1978).
[6]Milovan Djilas, *Rise and Fall* (San Diego: Harcourt Brace Jovanovich, 1985), p. 152.

anti-Yugoslavism with nationalism, as Albania's Communist rulers claimed, now that the two main parts of the Albanian nation were fully separated? The truth is that despite the ideological rhetoric, Albania's Communist leaders never claimed Kosova, or even raised the issue at the UN or any other international forum until the final days of Communism.[7] Indeed, what Hoxha and his successor Ramiz Alia were focusing on all the time, (they professed being custodians of Marxism–Leninism[8]) was a relentless quest for personal political survival. There is no evidence to corroborate Albanian official statements that the breaks respectively with Yugoslavia in 1948, with the Soviet Union in 1960, and with China in 1978, were taken to 'preserve Albania's independence'—or of any consideration given to their impact on the rest of the Albanian nation. Furthermore, Albania's standing as Europe's least developed country, the limited rights enjoyed by its citizens and the country's isolation served to deny its people the wherewithal for developing and maintaining even a genuine patriotism, Socialist or otherwise, let alone the conditions in which nationalism could thrive.

It therefore follows that if an Albanian nationalism existed, it must have been resident outside the borders of the Albanian state—embodied in the changing fortunes of the Kosova Albanians within the frame work of repeated experimentation with the constitution in Yugoslavia that suggested that the Yugoslav national question, far from being settled, was in a state of flux.[9] Belgrade took several years to come to

---

[7]Elez Biberaj, *The Balkan Powder Keg*, Conflict Studies, no. 258, Research Institute for the Study of Conflict and Terrorism, London, 1993, p. 12: 'Hoxha's regime never claimed Kosova and indeed went to great pains to minimise the impact of recurring unrest in Kosova on Tirana–Belgrade relations'.

[8]Interview with Ramiz Alia, April 1998.

[9]Ivo Banac, *The National Question in Yugoslavia, Origins, History, Politics* (Ithaca: Cornell University Press, 1994), p. 415: '... despite occupations and wars, revolutions and social changes, after 1921 hardly any elements were introduced in the set pattern of South Slavic interactions. The game was open-ended, but pawns could proceed only one square at a time except on their first move, bishops always moved diagonally and were nearly always fianchettoed in Indian defences, knights were always least effective in the endgame, kings slowly advanced or retreated within their narrow square, and castling was permitted only if the king in question was not in check. And some kings fell ... The national question permeated every aspect of Yugoslavia's public life after 1918.

terms with the fact that it had to seek an accommodation with the third largest nation in the Federation, as its 1953 agreement with Turkey, paving the way for the deportation of thousands of Albanians, aptly illustrates.[10] The subsequent overhaul of policy, making Kosova one of eight equal federal partners in 1974, while suggestive of a final acceptance of the Albanian element in the Social Federal Republic of Yugoslavia (SFRY) nearly 30 years after the inception of Communist cohabitation in Tito's Yugoslavia, was primarily an exercise designed to curtail Serbia's powers. However, this apparent accommodation appears to have been neither comprehensive nor long-lasting as indicated by the violent suppression of the Kosova Albanian demonstrations of 1981, which demanded a 'republic' status for Kosova within the federation, and reunification with Albania. These events heralded the coming of age of Kosova Albanian nationalism, prompting Serbia to begin the process of constitutional change to impose its will and supremacy not only in Kosova but across Yugoslavia—a development which augured the beginning of the end of the SFRY.

Although direct evidence is lacking, the 1981 demonstrations mark the first instance of Communist Tirana's involvement in Kosova. Allegations have surfaced, suggesting that Tirana was, indeed, behind the riots. A senior official, who wished to remain anonymous, disclosed in 1997 that a senior circle of advisers to the regime, including several university professors, had come up with the idea of 'raising the people of Kosova' to demand more rights. The official would not be drawn on the motives behind the proposal or even on why Kosova was a subject of the meeting at all. However, the Albanian leadership appears to have appropriated the idea to incite trouble in Kosova in order to divert the attention of the people of Albania away from the acute economic crisis following the Chinese–Albanian rift. Amid growing signs of dissatisfaction with the Albanian destitution, trouble in Kosova would have given the Albanian authorities the excuse, and the

---

It was reflected in the internal, external, social, economic, and even cultural affairs.'

[10]Noel Malcolm, *Kosovo: A Short History* (London: Macmillan, 1998), p. 322; Hivzi Islami, *Kosova dhe Shqiptarët: çështje demografike* [Kosova and the Albanians, Demographic Issues], (Prishtina: Pena, 1990), p. 78; Zamir Shtylla, 'The deportation of Albanians in Yugoslavia after World War Two', in *The Truth on Kosova*, (Tirana: Encyclopaedia Publishing House, 1993), p. 235.

means, to clamp down on any form of dissent 'at a time when the nation risked being annihilated'. Allegations have been made that the Albanian secret service, *Sigurimi*, organised the Kosova revolts, mobilising the Albanian émigré community in Western Europe, mainly in Switzerland. Some leaders of the protests have acknowledged the assistance given by individual Albanians, though there has never been any recognition of official involvement from Albania. Nevertheless, these accounts dovetail not only with the overall course of events in 1981, but also with the developments in the 1990s, which brought into being the Kosova Liberation Army (KLA)—the armed group which began hostilities against the Serbs in 1998 in the quest for independence. The KLA, closely linked to Albania's former Communists, was founded by followers of the same group of people who were behind the 1981 riots in Kosova.

Albania's subsequent support for the rights of the Kosova Albanians remained in the domain of rhetoric, as its diplomats took years to raise the issue at the UN and even then advocated minority rights—similar to those offered by Belgrade.[11] But then, the stance of the Albanian Communist leaders on the national issue was not without precedent. Between the two world wars, King Zog also adopted an 'Albania-only' policy. And, more significantly, the first post-Communist government of Albania followed two tracks. It began in 1991 with a pledge to unite the nation,[12] and helped to internationalise the issue, having extended diplomatic recognition to a 'Republic of Kosova'. But as early as 1994, in the midst of the Bosnian atrocities—it also called for a resolution of the Kosova issue once democracy had been achieved throughout the

---

[11]'The Albanian government believes that minorities should be viewed as a bridge to unity and friendship among the peoples of the peninsula and not as a source of discord. Acceptance and recognition of their identities, cultures and national traditions and respect for their own languages and their spiritual bonds with their own nation would greatly contribute to strengthening an atmosphere of understanding and sincere co-operation.' Malile speech, 28 September 1987, at the forty-second session of the UN General Assembly, *UN, Official Records of the General Assembly.*

[12]Biberaj, *Kosova: The Balkan Powder Keg*, p. 11 (London: Research Institute for the Study of Conflict and Terrorism, 1993): '(Sali) Berisha stated that his party will struggle by peaceful means and within the contexts of the processes of integration in Europe to realise [the Albanians] rights for progress and national unity', from *Rilindja Demokratike*, 5 January 1991.

Balkans (including in Serbia), and the borders had been rendered irrelevant as a result of the virtual integration of the whole region into European structures.[13]

Shortly after the Socialists (the former Communists) returned to power in Albania in 1997, Kosova Albanians began their armed resistance to Serbia, which ultimately led to NATO's intervention and the establishment of an international protectorate. Although allegations that the Albanian Socialists actively participated in organising, sustaining and even leading the rebellion are difficult to corroborate convincingly, the kind of support they proffered had all the ingredients of nationalism.[14] It should not be forgotten, however, that, at that juncture, no other administration in Tirana could have conceivably withheld the kind of support offered to the KLA by the Albanian Socialists. Furthermore, Albania's own descent into chaos and anarchy in 1997, with the loss of institutional life and the ultimate corrosion of state attributes, often blamed on the same Socialists, has heavily compromised the cause of Albanian nationalism.

Where is the Albanian Nation Now?

It is, admittedly, an almost unique situation amongst members of a nation who are in a position to make informed choices about their future. But it is a fact that the creation of 'Greater Albania' is not in the plans of Kosova nor has never been official policy in Tirana. Albanian Communist governments have successfully inculcated in the people that sense of alienation from the rest of the nation through, among other things, progressive impoverishment, purging of text-books, and an information blackout on news surrounding Albanians beyond the borders of the country. Added to which there is the fact that, until late 1998, not a single individual, non-governmental organisation or government department in Albania had taken the trouble to produce a single draft of a memorandum or platform for the resolution of the Albanian national question. The challenge to the region therefore does not come from Tirana's claims or lack thereof, but from the strong

---

[13]Sali Berisha's speech, Vienna, June 1993, and speech to the Albanian North Atlantic Association, Tirana, 17 November 1995.
[14]Various interviews with KLA representatives, 1997–1999.

contradiction between the Balkan nations' desire for a new national assertion and Western demands for multi-ethnicity. They appear irreconcilable in the short term, but then the same was the case before European nations decided to set up a European Economic Community in the middle of the twentieth century after much recrimination and bloodshed.

27. Is it true that the independence of Kosova would destabilize the Balkans and endanger the possibility of stabilizing other areas of the world, for example, Chechnya or Nagorno Karabach?

Janusz Bugajski

THE ALLEGATION

The independence of Kosovo and Metohija would lead to a unilateral change of internationally recognized borders in the Balkans. This would politically destabilize the region, and would open the possibility of renewing past conflicts. (Statement by the President of the Republic of Serbia Boris Tadić at the UN Security Council Meeting, New York, 14 February 2006).[1]

An independent Kosovo would bring unrest and send a signal to Albanians in western Macedonia or Epirus in northern Greece, in the south of Serbia or east of Montenegro, to Serbs in Republika Srpska or Serbs in Croatia that they can get their own states. All separatist movements will be following the resolution of the Kosovo problem very closely and will see a chance for themselves in the Kosovo precedent. (Sanda Rasković-Ivić, Chief of the Coordination Center for Kosovo and Metohija).[2]

---

[1] 17 February 2006—English—ERPKIM Monthly Bulletin-Ticker Archive, http://www.kosovo.com/news/archive/2006/February_17/2.html [Last consulted on 13 March 2006].

[2] 'Serbian Arguments in Negotiations on Kosovo and Metohija', *Nova Srpska Politicka Misao*, Belgrade, 5 December 2005, in 14 December 2005—English—

The specter of weakening security in Serbia and the wider Balkan region is a common refrain of opponents of independence. Furthermore, as a precedent in international law and diplomacy, the independence of Kosova is seen as potentially explosive for the entire world.

If the UN charter is crushed, it will become a cancer that spreads quickly ... What will then happen with the Turkish part of Cyprus, with the Albanians in Macedonia? Would Bosnia be able to survive? What about the Basques, Northern Ireland, Ossetia? (Vuk Drašković, Foreign minister of Serbia and Montenegro).[3]

The most common argument made by linking the independence of Kosova to the spreading of secessionist rights is that it would destabilize the Caucuses, as Russian President Putin recently warned:

If someone believes that Kosovo should be granted full independence as a state, then why should we deny it to the Abkhaz and the South Ossetians? [Abkhazia and South Ossetia gained de facto independence from Georgia in the early 1990s and are now propped up by Russia]. *I am not talking about how Russia will act ... However, we know that Turkey, for instance, has recognized the Republic of Northern Cyprus. I don't want to say that Russia will immediately recognize Abkhazia or South Ossetia as independent, sovereign states, but such precedents do exist in international practice.* (Russian President Vladimir Putin).[4]

The Answer

There are three alternatives for the future of Kosova—the current status quo, re-incorporation into Serbia, and a period of supervised independence. Of the three options, supervised independence leading

---

ERPKIM Monthly Bulletin-Ticker Archive, http://www.kosovo.com/news/archive/2005/December_14/1.html [Last consulted on 13 March 2006].

[3]Speaking on the sidelines of an OSCE ministerial meeting in the Slovenian capital Ljubljana, quoted in Reuters, 'Kosovo Independence Would Fuel Separatism—Serbia', 6 December 2005, http://www.kosovareport.blogspot.com/2005/12/kosovo- independence-would-fuel.html [Last consulted on 13 March 2006].

[4]Vladimir Putin, speaking at his annual news conference in the Kremlin on 2 February 2006, http://www.rferl.org/features/features_Article.asp [Last consulted on 13 March 2006].

to full statehood is the least destabilizing alternative. Statehood, with the necessary development of a fully functional police and an adequate defense force, could deter and diminish threats, as well as contribute to the international struggle against organized crime and terrorism.

Maintaining the option of the current status quo, even with some modifications toward sovereignty under an EU mandate, would be counter-productive and ultimately destructive. It would reinforce the existing ambiguity and encourage both Serbian and Kosovar radicalism. Belgrade would see international indecision and prevarication as an invitation to further claims on the territory. And Serbia's major political parties would vie for power on the basis of who could most effectively regain Kosova. The Kosovar leadership would also remain preoccupied with gaining independence at the cost of the domestic reform program, which could come to a standstill. Without the visible prospect of independence, there would be no incentive to meet any standards for minority rights, the rule of law, and governmental accountability. A status quo instead of final status would also severely weaken the legitimacy of any elected government in Prishtina and simultaneously discredit the international presence. A frustrated and pauperized population would become increasingly susceptible to militancy and even armed resistance. Politics would rapidly become sidelined to a renewed movement for national liberation and armed attacks on the international presence could escalate.

Option two, Kosova's re-incorporation into Serbia or an international acknowledgement of Serbia's sovereignty over Kosova, would be even more destructive than the existing status quo. It would likely precipitate a new round of Albanian insurgency with fewer international tools available to handle the escalating crisis that could rapidly spiral out of control and even assume regional proportions. Any prospect of Serbia's institutional return to Kosova would be catastrophic. Moderate voices in Prishtina would be sidelined and international agencies would be discredited. Unable to leave the territory for better conditions in the West, a sizeable sector of Kosova's youth is likely to be attracted by insurgency and violent resistance. If Kosova was not recognized as an independent and self-contained state, borders would have little value and insurgents would have little respect for any Balkan frontiers.

Two additional proposals have been posited by Belgrade that could also provoke new instabilities: Kosova's 'entityfication' and territorial partition. These options are presented as the only solution to the problem of the Serb minority's security and rights, but could result in a serious weakening of the state-building process and may eventually undermine the integration of minorities. The creation of two entities in Kosova in imitation of the Bosnian model—a weak federal structure with strong entity government—is ultimately impractical and ineffective, if the goal is to build national institutions that implement the rule of law and foster reconciliation. The last thing international agencies desire is to create another dysfunctional and internally divided state in the Balkans.

Territorial partition without a bilateral agreement between Belgrade and Prishtina could also set a much more dangerous precedent in the region than maintaining the existing borders of Kosova. A unilateral or internationally-imposed partition would be a sure invitation for Albanian counter-claims to Serbian territory in the Preshevo Valley. Of course if an exchange of territory was mutually acceptable to the governments in Prishtina and Belgrade then this could also be internationally legitimized. But the likelihood of agreement remains slim and if it becomes a unilateral land grab sanctioned by some international actors, then numerous minority areas from Vojvodina to Sandjak would become fair game for secession.

A timetable for Kosova's independence supervised by international players, including the US, NATO, and the EU, coupled with a roadmap to EU entry for Serbia, as well as international guarantees for the Serbian minority, with a robust NATO presence, could minimize potential unrest and lead to the creation of stable and legitimate states. Nonetheless, one must not close ones eyes to the possibility that Kosova's road toward independence will be exploited by various neighbors to pursue their own territorial aspirations. Major crises could be averted by defusing the most probable trouble spots, beginning with the Albanian minorities.

Kosova's statehood must be accompanied by bilateral treaties with Serbia, Montenegro, and Macedonia on the unequivocal respect of the current borders. This would undercut the ambitions of guerrilla groups seeking the attachment of neighboring territories to Kosova and dispel the myth of a 'Greater Albania'. Kosova's legitimate statehood would thereby serve to remove the ambiguities and uncertainties that encourage insurgents to operate.

The only other significant and territorially compact national group in the Balkans that may seek advantage from Kosova's independence are the Bosnian Serbs. However, it would be difficult for their leaders to profit from the situation if there is sufficient international opposition and resolve. The case for the secession of Bosnia's Serb Republic is weak, primarily because this quasi-Republic was artificially created by massive ethnic cleansing in which the majority of the population who were Bosniak Muslims were forcibly expelled and many thousands murdered. Moreover, the Bosnian Serb leadership accepted the legitimacy of a single Bosnian state under the Dayton Accords in November 1995. Politically, the separation from Bosnia would require direct support from Serbia itself, the neutralization of the Bosniaks and Croats, and the acquiescence of key international players. While Kosova's status is being decided, the US and the EU need to declare a united and clear position underscoring that the solution to be achieved has no bearing on the Bosnian predicament.

All of Bosnia's neighbors must also declare their positions. With Croatia on track for the EU, there will be no appetite in Zagreb for reviving any latent claims to Bosnian territory in western Herzegovina. Montenegro will certainly not support an enlarged Serbia with the possible entry of the Bosnian Serb entity. Belgrade itself will need to receive a clear message that endangering Bosnian statehood will indefinitely delay Serbia's progress toward assistance, investment, and international integration. Moreover, Washington and Brussels are seeking to create a more functional Bosnia by implementing constitutional changes to strengthen the central government in Sarajevo. Any delays or even reversals in this process would lead to the isolation and exclusion of the Bosnian Serb leadership and the further pauperization and marginalization of the Bosnian Serb population. If Bosnia can be handled with all the diplomatic, political, economic, and military tools available to the EU, NATO, and the US, then Kosova's independence will not result in the unraveling of the region or a new phase of conflictive 'Balkanization'. But the onus will be on the major international players to make sure that regional threats do not become political realities.

The chances that Kosova's independence would set any precedent for separatism in the broader context of the European Union (EU) are very slim or none at all. The collapse of Yugoslavia, the Soviet Union, and Czechoslovakia, and the emergence of two-dozen countries in the early 1990s did not precipitate the breakup of Western Europe's democracies. Similarly, the possibility of the independence of three more territories (Serbia, Montenegro[5] and Kosova) is unlikely to give impetus to

---

[5]On May 21st 2006, Montenegro held a referendum and voted for independence. Serbia has recognized this decision and the union of Serbia and Montenegro is now dissolved.

separatist nationalisms in the EU for two valid reasons: democratic context and political record. Most of the sovereignty movements in the EU operate within a democratic framework. Several autonomy parties have won increasing local control for their territories within a federal or decentralized administrative structure. Obtaining full statehood has been and continues to be unlikely, as the majority of the public supports membership in a larger state because of the benefits that this brings.

This hardly applies to Kosova where, in stark contrast, there are no such loyalties among the vast majority of the population and there are few advantages to be gained within a semi-democratized Serbia. However, an independent Kosova could begin in earnest the process of European integration and profit from European stabilizing political and institutional assets. The lessons from most of Eastern Europe demonstrate that states must settle their minority disputes as an important component of their qualifications for NATO and EU membership. Similarly, Kosova will need to resolve the problem of the protection of the Serb minority's rights within this supranational framework. Undoubtedly, issues of political representation and administrative decentralization will surface over the coming years, as they have among older member states, and demand solutions, but without seriously threatening European security.

Kosova's independence does not establish any legal or political precedent for separatism in the broader international scene either. Nevertheless, it can be exploited as a pretext by expansionist states and their proxy radical movements in the pursuit of their political agendas. This is especially true in the case of Russia. Moscow will seek clear advantages from the Kosova status talks to further its regional aspirations in Moldova and the Caucasus. Russia's proxy secessionist movements in Moldova's Transnistria region and Georgia's Abkhaz region will use the opportunity to press for their own independence even though their situations are markedly different from Kosova. The separatist movements in Transnistria and Abkhazia have been directed by local power elites tied to Russian security forces and benefiting from cross-border criminal enterprises. Self-determination is not based on protection from a repressive state but on the cliquish objectives of a narrow group of power holders who promote the Kremlin's agenda by placing pressure on both Moldova and Georgia to remain within Moscow's orbit.

28. Is it true that decentralization is the key to security and stability in Kosova?

Isa Blumi and Anna Di Lellio

THE ALLEGATION

A sensible compromise would grant Kosovo independence ... create defined cantons and municipalities for Serbs (including key historical sites), and offer all Serbs who live in Kosovo a formalized 'special relationship' with Serbia (with compensation for refugees who cannot return to Kosovo ... Pristina will have to accept local Serb control over some Albanian villages and parts of towns as the price for its appalling record.
(Edward P. Joseph, former Macedonia Director for the International Crisis Group).[1]

Substantial decentralization as the sole guarantee for the protection of Serb minorities is presented by analysts of the region as the most realistic option to ensure security and stability. It is seen as the most realistic among diplomatic circles: UN Envoy Kai Eide's October 2005 Report on Kosova's readiness for the final status process assumes the need for substantive decentralization.[2] It is being discussed as the first and the most important point in the negotiation on Kosova's status, the required compromise to grant the former Yugoslav province some form of independence.

---

[1] 'Back to the Balkans', *Foreign Affairs*, January–February 2005, pp. 11–122, p. 119.
[2] 'A Comprehensive Review of the Situation in Kosovo' (S/2005/635, 7 October 2005).

The Answer

If democracy and security are the desired goal in the Balkans, decentralization is not a solution. On the contrary. Presented as a tool to protect—and substantially separate—Serb minorities, it takes for granted an understanding of Kosova's inhabitants and their interests in terms of ethnicity. As in the past, this approach continues to empower the 'representatives' of ethnic groups and creates new possibilities for conflict. Starting from the Congress of Berlin in 1878, and in each of the successive efforts to redraw the territories of previously heterogeneous Ottoman and Austrian–Hungarian empires, or to legalize the dramatic re-drawing of borders during the break-up of Yugoslavia, the ability of local societies to enjoy indigenous methods of cohabitation has been sacrificed in favor of a world vision resting on the identification of ethnic communities. Retracing the failures of the Great Powers of the nineteenth century to accommodate local objections to how events in the Balkans were being shaped by outside interests should be a prerequisite in today's debate.

In the course of the Ottoman Empire's 1878 military defeat in the Eastern districts of the Balkan Peninsula, signatory powers at Berlin (Greece, Bulgaria, France, Austria, Britain, Russia and the Ottomans), used statistical surveys about 'the people of European Turkey'— mostly categories of ethnicity and religion—to identify and single out 'alien' communities that could be justifiably forced to leave their homes, in order to assure 'order and stability' within re-drawn frontiers. The end result was that large 'minority' populations were to face years of violence as the newly created states of Montenegro, Serbia and Romania (and Greece) tried to homogenize their territories.[3] More instability, rather than order, ensued.

The people affected by creation of new states were naturally excluded from the negotiations. The story behind the frontiers dividing the Malësia e Madhe (the Alpine region that straddles modern-day Albania, Kosova and Montenegro, populated mostly by Albanian-speaking Catholics and Muslims) into Montenegrin and Ottoman

---

[3]For the sake of brevity, for sources drawn after extensive research on the period in the Ottoman, Italian, Austrian, Albanian, British and French archives, consult Isa Blumi, 'Contesting the Edges of the Ottoman Empire: Rethinking Ethnic and Sectarian Boundaries in the Malësore, 1878–1912.' *International Journal of Middle East Studies*, 35/2 (May 2003), pp. 237–56.

territories is a case in point. Russian and Serb geopolitical concern required the incorporation of Adriatic port cities that were populated mostly by Albanian-speakers, and demographic surveys were used in Berlin to manipulate an inconvenient reality. This initiated a process in Serbian circles to deny the existence of Albanian-speaking people altogether, by conflating their identity to that of 'Turks' or 'Albanized Serbs', a claim that recently has been repeated in the 2003 Memorandum of the Serbian Orthodox Church.[4] Belgrade intellectuals and Russian pan-Slavists initiated a public relations campaign in Western capitals that asserted Serbian historical claims to 'Southern Serbia' (Kosova and Northern Albania), of which Montenegro would be an extension. Signatory powers at Berlin were persuaded by ethno-cultural justifications noted throughout and awarded Montenegro parts of the Malësia e Madhe; the *vilayet* of Kosova and Işkodra were claimed by Serbia on 'historical' grounds that linked medieval Orthodox Christian sites with a modern ethno-national identity.

Once news of the formal plans for partition and annexation surfaced, local communities organized to resist implementation; they coalesced around a growing cluster of communal consuls that would soon become known as the Prizren League (*Lidhja e Prizrenit* in Albanian). Their pleas ignored in European capitals, local Albanian-speakers resorted to violence. When reports of isolated clashes between Ottoman troops and locals emerged, Istanbul panicked and sent a delegation led by none other than Mehmed Ali Paşa, a Hungarian-born convert and veteran Ottoman administrator who had opposed the plan. Ultimately, the task cost him his life when locals in Yakova (present-day Gjakova) killed him, his entourage and even his hosts, a prominent Albanian family. As resistance to the protocols of the Berlin Congress was taking the shape of a general uprising, Montenegro was eventually awarded the port of Ulqin (Dulcino) in place of the highland communities. Albanian-speaking communities straddling the newly established border were selectively expelled and settlers from Herzegovina and Serbia imported.[5] The Ottomans tried to settle refugees flooding

---

[4]http://www.Kosova.com/erpkim05sep03b.html.

[5]Reports from the field by a French consul suggest more than 100,000 Albanians were removed from the Morava region (located in present-day southern Serbia) alone. See French Foreign Ministry Archives, AMAE Mémoires et Documents, Turquie, vol. 95: de Ring Report, copy of an Albanian petition, dated 1879.

into the redrawn *vilayet* of Kosova, Işkodra and beyond, in the new under-populated frontier regions, ultimately destroying the inter-communal life in what would later be identified as the Macedonia crisis.

During the years 1897–1903 neighboring independent states started to expand their influence into the districts of the Ottoman Balkans identified in the documents as 'Macedonia', a region encompassing portions of the *vilayet* of Kosova, Salonika, and Manastir. Belgrade and Athens in particular succeeded in establishing 'national' agendas that aimed at eliminating Bulgars, Turks and Albanians from Macedonia. When Ottomans were pressured to initiate a series of 'reforms' designed to address what lobbies in Britain, Russia and France had framed as uncontrolled sectarian violence, they resorted to the use of force against key members of the local population, especially in Kosova, where local Albanians, both Christian and Muslim, rebelled against the state's centralizing efforts.[6] It is largely in response to this and other violent uprisings that the signatory powers at Berlin drew up a nine-point plan called the 'Mürzsteg Scheme'.[7] The goal then, like today in the discourse on Kosova decentralization, was to protect minority rights. The implementation of the plan caused further tension and violence.

According to the 'Mürzsteg Scheme', an international commission sent in 1903 by the Great Powers proposed the establishment of a regime that permitted 'ethnic communities' to be governed by 'their own' leaders within recognized, ethnically-homogeneous boundaries. The Russian delegation insisted that Serbian and Bulgarian residents be granted autonomously governed enclaves free of Ottoman (and Muslim) influence. Article 3 of the plan requested the Ottoman government 'to re-arrange the boundaries of the *vilayet* with a view to making regular groupings of different nationalities'. Article 4 ensured that Christians would have access to their own judicial and administrative institutions as well as a Gendarmerie that would be regionally based and divided along communal lines. Communities were to operate free of Ottoman

---

[6]What is called the Second League of Prizren or the League of Peja (*Lidhja të Pejës*) of 1899 is one of the best known cases of local outbreaks of violence.
[7]This is fully explored in Fikret Adanir, *Die Makedonische Frage* (Wien: Franz Steiner Verlag, 1979) and Steven W. Sowards, *Austria's Policy of Macedonian Reform, 1902–1908* (New York: East European Monographs, 1989).

state taxation, were allowed to administer their own government with the assistance of outside 'experts' and permitted to direct their educational and cultural lives free of Islamic cultural influence.[8]

Many self-styled community leaders enthusiastically embraced the plan, recognizing the immediate and possible long-term benefits to being identified a Serb, Greek, Bulgarian and Christian. Using the claim of Muslim [i.e., Albanian] persecution, many Serbian, Greek, Bulgarian and even Albanian Catholic (Latin) leaders won Europe's immediate attention and the financial and political support that accompanied it. In a matter of weeks previously stable villages began to splinter into factions. The implementation of the Mürzsteg reforms created dozens of incongruent autonomous enclaves, separating by March 1904 a total of 135 villages from their Albanian and Muslim neighbors throughout the Kosova *vilayet*. Protected by gendarmeries organized and led by participating powers like Italy, Russia and France, a number of reports suggest that Serb and Bulgarian 'communities' exploited their protected status and 'raided' Albanian lands. Any subsequent clash between Christians and Albanians was blamed on an Ottoman failure to curb its Muslim 'fanatics'. Such a reality, as noted by the French consul, created a sense of impunity among non-Albanians in the region, who then started to make new demands for the redrawing of land boundaries.[9]

By the time the Mürzsteg accords were declared dead, the heavy-handed approach to resolving local disputes ignited by the plan resulted in a new era of political consciousness in the Balkans, helping set the tone for the 'Young Turk' revolution of 1908 and 'nationalist' uprisings. Often with Serbian and Montenegrin support, Albanian communities in the Malësia e Madhe region and in Kosova revolted against the increasingly abusive and centralizing ambitions of the Young Turk regime. The instability caused by the massive counter-insurgency measures ordered by Istanbul basically mortally wounded the already weak empire.

---

[8]For a comprehensive report on the reform proposals and their translation into French and Ottoman that used these terms, see Haus- Hauf und Staatsarchiv, HHStA PA, XII/320, Calice an Goluchowski, dated Constantinople, 13 January 1904.

[9]Archives du Ministre des Affairs Etrangers, AMAE Paris, CP Turquie no. 47, Gauthier à Boppe, dated Monastir, 1 Novembr 1905.

In an attempt to resolve the successive wars that ostensibly were land-grabs by neighboring countries, the Treaty of London in May 1913, under heavy pressure from Italy and Austria, secured a truncated, ill-equipped independent Albania and assigned it a foreign sovereign, not unlike the Special Representative of the UN Secretary General in Kosova today. This decision did not resolve disputes over Russia's and Serbia's ambitions for greater control of lands populated by Albanians, Turks and other 'minorities' and for gaining access to the Adriatic Sea. Over the course of 1912 and 1913, the wide-scale use of violence to level Albanian villages throughout the *vilayet* of Kosova and Işkodra, as well as the immediate settlement of the Yanya and Salonika *vilayet* with Greek-speaking colonialists, stunned outside observers.[10]

The legacy of the decisions made in the past has consistently been ignored by policy-makers shaping Kosova's future. It was ignored at Versailles in 1919, for instance, when the principle of self-determination—today taboo in the debate on Kosova status—created the sovereign state of the South Slavs, which included a sizeable but unwanted Albanian population. As a consequence, the entire history of what eventually became Yugoslavia has been an exercise of systematic expulsion, persecution and impoverishment of the non-Slav population that periodically erupted in violent outbursts of rebellion.

The international conferences and peace plans designed to avoid the bloodshed in Yugoslavia from 1991 through to the 1995 Dayton Peace Accords are notable for following the same logic. Here the goal was to preserve national cohesion and multi-ethnicity, but ethnic categorizations were used to segment the territory, reflecting power relations established in the theatre of war. Kosova, where the overwhelming Albanian majority under Belgrade oppressive rule peacefully made national claims, remained completely absent from the negotiations. Sidelined and isolated, Kosovars started their first national uprising after a century of local rebellions that had mostly demanded only that local Albanians be left alone.

---

[10]Observers as diverse as American Consuls based in the area, Leon Trotsky, and the Carnegie Endowment of International Peace documented in 1914 and the Serb Social Democrat Dimitrije Tučević publicly denounced, Belgrade's and Montenegro's systematic campaign to rid the region of large numbers of the indigenous population.

A quick survey of this brief history is enlightening. The 1991 Brioni Declaration and the deferment of the Slovenia's and Croatia's declaration of independence only gave time to the warring parties to reorganize. The attempted arbitration of the Badinter Commission recognized the legal basis for the dissolution of Yugoslavia and by its silence on Kosova it implicitly affirmed, like Bismarck had done one hundred years earlier, that 'Albanians are not a nationality.' The Badinter Commission recognized that the constituent republics would stand on their own if they followed European democratic standards, but again forgot the abysmal condition of Albanians in Kosova under Belgrade rule.

The 1991 European Conference on Yugoslavia, with the Carrington Plan, addressed the special status of ethnic minorities but went nowhere. The end of 1991, with the Vance Plan, saw the emergence of the UN Protected Areas, where peacekeepers failed to guarantee security. When in 1994 the Zagreb-4 Plan (formalized by two ambassadors from the International Conference on the Former Yugoslavia and the American and Russian Ambassadors in Croatia) proposed that Krajina become a virtual state within Croatia, it did not find the favor of the Serb leadership and also failed. In 1992 the short-lived Lisbon initiative and the Cutilheiro Plan envisioned Bosnia as a state of three constituent nationalities, mimicking the aborted model of Yugoslavia. The following Vance–Owen Peace Plan, stemming from the London Conference, considered the link between ethnic nationality and territory as a basis—paradoxically—to preserve multi-ethnicity. It failed too in 1993, but was immediately succeeded by the Owen–Stoltenberg Plan and the Contact Group Plan, that accepted the de facto partition of Bosnia into national territories in 1994. While the leaders unsuccessfully discussed the Plan, the war raged on the ground; the credibility of the peace arbitrators, first of all the UN, finally died at Srebrenica. The Dayton Peace Accords of 1995 neglected Kosova again, thus leaving a free hand to Belgrade's repressive policies. Dayton did put an end to the conflict in Bosnia and Herzegovina, but created two distinct entities that are de facto separated although legally together, and could split if given the chance into three different nationalities.

The Kosova crisis exploded in 1998 with the disproportionately violent Serb state repression of the incipient Albanian guerrilla movement. International diplomacy tried to find a peaceful solution through several Security Council resolutions, Contact Group declarations, the 1998 October agreement brokered by US envoy Richard Holbrooke, and the Rambouillet Conference in February 1999. All these attempts failed in their stated goal to stop the violence on both sides and redress the human rights situation of the Albanian minority in the former Yugoslav state, even when they clearly refused to address the demand for independence of the Albanian majority in Kosova. After the 1999 NATO humanitarian intervention, Security Council resolution 1244 established a Kosova UN-led protectorate in the framework of Serbian sovereignty until self-government institutions could be created and a solution on status found.

Six years of protectorate have consolidated a de facto partition of Kosova along ethnic lines at the Ibar river: as NATO troops settled in the divided city of Mitrovica at the end of the war, they did not fulfill their mandate to secure the entire territory of Kosova and seem even more unable to do so now. Northern Kosova has always been alien to the international administration and security forces. It constitutes a physical and political magnet for Serb communities south of the river as the vital umbilical cord to an obstructionist Belgrade that maintains parallel structures of government and economy to the legitimate Kosovar ones, but nevertheless remains a privileged interlocutor on the status of Kosova. It has become the model for 'decentralization' as territorial independence of ethnic enclaves from Prishtina, and hardly a recipe for security and stability.

Afterword

By Ismail Kadare*

This is Kosova, the land that they wanted to empty of its people.

Twenty years ago, during a visit to Prishtina, I learned that in ancient times water flooded that vast plain. Then, as it drained, the Black Sea took part of the water through the Danube, the Aegean Sea took another part through the Vardar, and the Adriatic Sea took another part through the foaming Drin.

I have often imagined how fish, eels, snakes and water monsters left with the waves. Thus, in the pre-history of this land, the natural drama gave way to a wilder drama: the human drama.

When the time of the humans came, the hour of emptying Kosova of its Albanians, two of the above mentioned conduits—the one that led to Macedonia and the one to Albania—filled up again, in imitation of the ancient flow of water, this time with queues of displaced people. The third channel, that of the Danube, was replaced by a flow that was not possible for water, but possible for people: direction Montenegro.

They wanted to empty Kosova through three arteries. And we know what happened: within one season, Albanians lived an amazing miracle, they fell and rose again like Christ.

Kosova filled up again via the three channels by which it had emptied. In one of those counter movements that rarely happen in the world and that are called 'reversals of fortune', the death of a people was interrupted.

Centuries ago, at the dawn of this civilization, Homer's epic stories of war helped awaken the consciousness of antiquity. Three thousands years later, the Kosova conflict shook the whole of human society as no other modern war had done.

---

*This text is an adaptation of Ismail Kadare, 'Tiranë, Mesi i Tetorit 1999', pp. 144–45 in *Ra Ky Mort e u Pamë. Dita për Kosovën, Artikuj, Letra*, Tiranë: Onufri, 2003.